EXECUTIVE FUTURES:

A QUEST FOR QUANTUM

CURRICULUM

ENDORSEMENTS

I just love this book. With chapter titles such as "Dr Strange in the Multiverse of Madness," "Everything, Everywhere, all at once," and sections titled, "the new mutants", "the force awakens" and "leadership: everybody wants to rule the world" one cannot but be drawn into the future Mostert wishes for us to see. We understand the emerging future with new eyes: we see the changes he describes. As he concludes his book with detailing the Appreciative Disruption Framework - we change the world without becoming neurotic.

Prof Sohail Inayatullah, UNESCO Chair in Futures Studies

A game changer, providing practical strategies and visionary perspectives for those who are ready to seize creative and entrepreneurial opportunities. It's a must read for anyone dedicated to pioneering the future of executive development and innovation.

Val Jusufi, Chairperson: Leoron Professional Development Institute, Dubai

An ambitious quantum leap towards a new business school education in our world of complexity, in need of futures resilience. Executives can enhance their learning capacities and systems-oriented competitiveness through this inspirational call for business excellence.

Sirkka Heinonen, Professor in Futures Studies at Finland Futures Research Centre, University of Turku

The world is complex and interconnected. In response, Morne Mostert presents a theory of Systemic Leadership Learning for executive development. This innovative approach blends creative application with an in-depth understanding of multiple systems towards holistic leadership for the future.

Dr Jakkie Cilliers, Board Chairman: Institute for Security Studies

Mostert makes another great leap forward on the integration of Systems Thinking, Futures Thinking and Executive Education.

Prof John Pourdehnad, IESE Business School, Barcelona. Former associate director of the Ackoff Center for Advancement of Systems Approaches, University of Pennsylvania USA.

Mostert presents a bold challenge to the dominant paradigm governing executive leadership education globally. He reframes, in a metaphorical way, the highly complex systemic challenges facing leaders in our time without losing sight of foundational organisational and business imperatives. The book refocuses the role of education on developing the advanced human cognitive capabilities required to ethically supersede the 'artificiality' of technology.

Prof Luke van der Laan, Professor of Leadership and Foresight,
University of Southern Queensland, Australia.

Mostert brings his contrariness and irreverence, together with his profound insights with fistfuls of humour, to bear on how executives lead and learn. Be prepared to encounter Robert Frost as much as the Jedi and characters from Harry Potter while grappling with how humanity responded to Covid-19 and its aftermath, is coming to terms with AI, and the scenarios leaders need to grapple with to arrive at robust strategies.

His Excellency Dr Yacoob Abba Omar, former Ambassador to the UAE and Oman.
Mapungubwe Institute for Strategic Reflection.

First published in 2025.

ISBN: 978-1-991272-17-1
eISBN: 978-1-991272-18-8

Published by KR Publishing
Tel: (011) 706-6009
E-mail: orders@knowledgekr.co.za
Website: www.kr.co.za

Printed and bound: HartWood Digital Printing, 243 Alexandra Avenue, Halfway House, Midrand
Typesetting, layout and design: Cia Joubert, cia@knowledgekr.co.za
Cover design: Marlene De Lorme, marlene@knowledgekr.co.za
Editing & proofreading: KR Publishing
Project management: Cia Joubert, cia@knowledgekr.co.za

EXECUTIVE FUTURES:
A QUEST FOR QUANTUM
CURRICULUM

The mindsets, the methods and the madness
of becoming a 21st century executive

by

Morne Mostert Ph.D.

Foreword by Mamphela Ramphele

kr
publishing

2025

DEDICATION

To my son, Jonathan Hartman Mostert,

for helping me to learn

about new ways to live.

CONTENTS

FOREWORD

A TIMELY CONTRIBUTION TO
REIMAGINING BUSINESS EDUCATION

Our world is crying out for a reset of the education system that bears the burdens of successive industrial revolutions. The cries are muffled simply because many of us have yet to identify the sources of the multiple planetary emergencies upon us. Education is the least suspect. This is due to our inability to link our poly-crisis to the epistemological and ontological foundations of our education systems across the globe.

This book, in its appreciative disruptive critical analysis of current business education, and the propositions it offers to transforming the very pillars of high-end business schools, is inviting us to reimagine education and the process of learning. The 2023 UN Declaration of a Decade for Sciences for Sustainability offers a great opportunity for the appreciative disruptive ideas of this book to find space for enquiry and to challenge conventional business education and leadership development models.

Humanity has the opportunity to return to the essence of being human – interconnected and interdependent within the web of life. Our common African ancestors figured this out millennia ago by observing that everything is connected to *everything* else. They reasoned that the ebbs and flows of the Nile River were connected to the movements and placements of celestial bodies. They knew intuitively what baffled thinkers like Albert Einstein until quantum physics was accepted – that the entanglements between observer and that which is observed reflect the entanglements of life. This is the foundation of the African philosophy of *Ubuntu/Omenala*, which affirms the inextricable links between human beings, and the existential connections within nature of which we are a part. Indigenous cultures, being no more than 6% of the world's population, have remained true to this essence of life and have successfully continued to protect more than 85% of ecosystems and biodiversity essential to life itself.

I urged Morne Mostert to commit to challenging the huge industrial complex of business schools to come to terms with their complicity in propping up a business leadership model that perpetuates the status quo of our extractive, hyper consumerist, iniquitous economic system. The central idea of learning anchored on self-awareness and self-liberation from fear of the unknown and the unconventional, is critical to the transformative leadership our world so desperately needs.

This is a book for all those searching for a future defined by our return to the essence of who we are, living in harmony with ourselves within the web of life. Global equity for a healthy planet demands leaders who are learned about themselves and their place in the universe. This book is as good a starting place as you can find on the journey of lifelong learning.

Dr Mamphela Ramphele
Former Co-President: Club of Rome
Former Managing Director: World Bank

ABOUT THE AUTHOR

Dr Morne Mostert is an international advisor on strategic foresight and executive decision-making, having had assignments in Geneva, Paris, London, Rome, Barcelona, Madrid, Melbourne, Baku, Tokyo and several other economic hubs across Africa and the Middle East.

He was appointed by President Cyril Ramaphosa as Commissioner on the National Planning Commission, where he serves as an advisor on Economic futures, Internationalisation and Climate Change. He is a member of the renowned international think tank, the Club of Rome.

His multi-award-winning thought leadership has been published internationally and he is a regular contributor to the business media on longer-term policy and strategy.

Mostert was a member of the International Labour Organisation (ILO) international panel of experts on the Future of Work, was Director of the Institute for Futures Research and served on the board of the Bureau for Economic Research.

With a PhD in Technology and Innovation, Mostert is also the inventor of the Mindset Index, a world-first in the scientific assessment of strategic mindsets.

PREFACE: ARTIFICIALLY INTELLIGENT

Thus truth's established and borne out,
Though circumstanced with dark and doubt

Robert Frost, Beech

Most executives know more about how to use Chat GTP than they know about their own forms of intellectual processing. In the world of the machine, knowledge of humans is becoming more, not less important. And given the self-evident scale, pace and frequency of global mega-shifts, the competency for learning is moving up the priority list for executive excellence at an exponential rate. Yet, dedicated intellectual development is in desperately short supply in the global contestation for attention.

Despite these challenges, many executives hang on relentlessly to an outdated mechano-cognitive processing. It is entirely inappropriate for current levels of global systemic complexity. Paradoxically, some who have aimed to address this, have replaced it with quasi-cognitive EQ and mindfulness. This author contends that, while emotions are powerful drivers, the level of complexity facing executives cannot be dissolved by feeling. Managing emotions must now be treated as a minimum entry level requirement; a cognitive hygiene factor in order for higher order cognitive functioning to commence.

And what a difference a decade makes. In the 250-thousand-year arch of human learning, the decade since the first appearance of the concept of Systemic Leadership Learning has, presented the greatest era of risk for rendering the concept equally dated. Advancements in conceptions of intelligence and human systems have been exponential. The author, of course, is tempted to justify and defend erstwhile wisdoms, but the charge of time is relentless. It is, in the words of John Keats, a *Belle Dame sans Merci* (a beautiful lady without mercy).

Having doffed the hat to the exponential expansion in human knowledge, the futurist is also curious about variances in the pace of change and in the probable survivability of key constructs. Since SLL first appeared, I therefore argue, the need for further work on the understanding of human systems and their relationship to learning methodologies of those who lead those systems has now reached perilous levels of priority. It is at a stage of evolution where it now presents what might be described as a quantum conundrum.

In physics, the meaning of the concept of quantum is significant. By the start of the 20th century, scientific notions of classical mechanics were no longer able to explain the overwhelming number of emerging anomalies from the study of nature at a scale below the atom. It is within the canon of knowledge catalysed by this epoch-defining shift in the scientific paradigm which this book aims to investigate the nature of executive learning. The notions herein contained have been inspired by the imagination of the courageously curious scientific minds who have grappled with the complexity of a new frontier. The emerging knowledge of the mind, I argue, now represents another such liminal moment.

The concept of quantum inspires its own provocations for search. It represents firstly a discrete quantity of energy. The notion of energy is an essential part in the investigation of systems. Fascinatingly, like the system operating at a sub-atomic level, social systems appear to be possessed of energy, generating energy and in constant need for new energy. Learning offers one opportunity for creatively energising the system of the executive, organisation and broader containing systems, such as sectors, national and global economies as well as natural ecosystems.

Furthermore, the energy described by the notion of quantum is proportional (in various respects) to the frequency of radiation it represents. Therefore, it also describes potential energy. I have been delighted to learn from global work for over two decades that human potential is as undeniable a force as gravitational, electromagnetic, strong or weak nuclear forces are in nature. This is not to suggest that such potential is always wisely applied. Quite to the contrary, the need for a book of this nature is exactly due to the glaring competence deficits among many executives in times of hyper-flux and the countless opportunities it presents. If ever there was a time when the world needed the wise, talented, sensitive and circumspect to emerge as leaders, it must surely be in the hyper-complexity of the current epoch.

Intriguingly, in the study of Physiology, the concept of quantum describes the unit quantity of acetylcholine released at a neuromuscular junction. It is the intention of creative, generative, meaningful learning that it should be released at strategic junctions in the trajectory of the life cycle of the executive, the organisation and the ecosystem. Acetylcholine, for completeness, is a neurotransmitter, which is a chemical substance released by the arrival of a nerve impulse. The systems of the executive, the organisation and their containing ecosystems are now bombarded more frequently, aggressively and, paradoxically, insidiously than at any other time in human history, with the obvious exception of full-scale global wars. Neurotransmitters diffuse across the junction to affect the transfer of the impulse to another nerve fibre, a muscle fibre, or some other structure. They are, therefore, systemic communicators which facilitate interconnectedness in the overall containing system of the organism, in the same way that creative ideas may be transferred during the learning journey for executives. Executive insights offer signals of possibility. The synaptic leaps born from the learning journey present enormous and essential opportunities for the dissolution of the complex conundrums confronting organisations today.

The concept of quantum entanglement (coined by Schrödinger in 1935) produces further inspiration for learning. In ways yet to reach full consensus in science, particles in groups (as sub-system) present the property whereby the measurement of one particle in an entangled pair cannot be done independently from another. They have a definitive reciprocal impact on one another, even at a great distance. Such nonclassical interrelatedness reminds us of the irrefutable interconnectedness of phenomena. The notion of quantum entanglement challenged Einstein's perspective of local realism. It introduced a distal quality to relationships which may significantly educate us on the nature of relatedness, while scientific care must be taken not to generalise quantum reality to general physical reality. And while correlation of distance must not be equated with causality, it is nevertheless of interest to investigate the holon nature of the universe, that is the extent to which insights at different scales and containing system levels of reality inform each other.

> *For executives to study without the consciousness of interrelatedness is to deprive yet another generation of leaders of the opportunity to contribute more meaningfully to the world.*

It is for this reason that this book borrows its title, even if metaphorically, from the quantum world.

My extensive work around the globe for more than two decades has led to the disturbing belief that working for large organisations is inherently an unnatural activity. This philosophical view is based on the notion that human beings are simply more creative, more self-organising and more divergent in their thinking than most organisations can absorb. It is seldom the ideal containing system for human endeavour.

The juxtaposition of these two complex entities, i.e. organisations and humans, poses a complex integration challenge. Recent evolutions in the psychological contract between employer and employee have aimed at achieving so-called shared value, but employee behaviour after the Covid pandemic has revealed significant fissures in the relationship.

It is the predominant intention of this book to make a contribution to the executive development industry that helps executives to lead with advanced consciousness of the impactful role they play in the multiple complex systems of which they are a part; to create the conceptual framework, structure and catalytic processes that will enhance the learning experience to the degree that it generates creative insights for a more harmoniously flourishing co-existence between executives and their organisational, financial, economic, social and planetary systems.

The value of such an aim is further accentuated if one appreciates the large number of people impacted by each leader. Despite attempts at flattening hierarchies, such as holocracy, participative management, neuro-based and human-centric approaches, the power differential remains an intractable organisational dilemma. This continues to mean that, as leaders advance in the hierarchy to aspirational nose-bleeding, dizzying heights of authority, the scope and impact of their decision-making expands exponentially. Indeed, it is in the very nature of strategic decision-making (still predominantly the preserve of senior leaders, despite bottom-up theories in the domain of Strategy) that internal organisational tactics are integrated with external dynamics. Therefore, every contribution to the leader's learning has an exponential impact on organisational systems, borne out by the benefit to staff as well as through the wider reach that leaders have in organisations with regards to the utilisation of resources, such as financial, human, capital, natural and others. It is imperative, therefore, to argue for the exploration of not only what leaders learn from their organisations, but also what the organisation may learn from its leaders.

This work is inspired by a relentless curiosity in the boundless possibility of the human mind. It examines the development of that mind as it relates to executives in the pursuit of knowledge about themselves, their organisations and the worlds in which those organisations aim to thrive. It is an exploration of the interaction between the divergence of human ingenuity as a ubiquitous characteristic of the learning process and the convergence of organisational realities that attempt to channel and direct human effort.

In the process of exploration, I have engaged with numerous organisations worldwide that have aimed to enhance the abilities of their leaders to articulate direction and capture the hearts and minds of those within their influence.

One of the critical multiple partial views in the ecosystem of any book is the reader. The reader is a system in its own right, with its own dynamic energy and complex interactive sub-systems, including the reader's own paradigms, cultural perspectives, education, philosophies and purpose. To this unsuspecting system of the reader, I therefore, once again, propose a journey of inquiry, with the immutable conviction in the self-organising powers of the minds who will read it and in the emergence of their creativity.

My own curiosity journey as futurist, advisor and author has guided me to a deep investigation of paradigms. In particular, I have become fascinated by the meaning and movement of Mindset. I must recognise that my own recent scholarly ventures have informed and guided my approach to this book.

> *Notes: I have extended my liberal use of the work of the poet Robert Frost, by quoting his poetry where relevant. The reason for this is that I find in Frost a philosophical ally – one who is concerned with the achievement of work and great endeavours, but simultaneously wishes to explore the human condition and the reality of the individual in a complex world.*
>
> *The terms "leader" and "executive" are used interchangeably. I have not laboured on the distinction but use both to illustrate the realities of leaders who must facilitate execution, and executives who must seek alternative, more preferable futures.*
>
> *I have made use of the female pronoun on occasion. Pronouns have become significant indicators of identity for many. I use the female as a proxy for identifications of gender.*
>
> *I have also chosen movie titles to support the titles and subtitles of the book. The rationale here is that the power of a visual inter-text energises the reader.*

DR STRANGE IN THE MULTIVERSE OF MADNESS

The chance is the remotest
Of its going much longer unnoticed
That I'm not keeping pace
With the headlong human race.

Robert Frost, Some Science Fiction

One of the most significant mistakes our species made during the first and second industrial revolutions, is the adoption of the notion that the machine is the paramount model. With its enticing characteristics of standardisation, predictability and repeatability, the machine became the ideal. So severe is this conviction, that someone with determination and perseverance is often complimented by being called a machine, e.g. *"That guy is a machine"*. As though it is really a compliment. Simultaneously, competencies of creative intellectual processing, despite admiration from a distance, have often been denigrated. The extent of the later is also evident in our language. Consider, e.g. *"That is your imagination"*. As though it is an insult.

Now, in the tumult of the 21st century, we bemoan, on reflection, our affinity for the machine and our disdain for, and dissipation of, what makes us truly human. Paradoxically, in the age of the machine, we must revisit with urgency the nature of being human. As the borders between ourselves and our artificial creations appear to wane, many organisations appear to know more about Artificial Intelligence (AI) than they do about the way in which leaders think, learn and make decisions.

We must now investigate how machine learning is distinct from leadership learning. The presence of emotion is no longer a satisfactory answer. How can organisations learn more about the way in which leaders really learn? This book represents the articulation of a theory of learning that has emerged as the result of engagement with clients who have requested the acceleration of the growth of their leaders. It represents the integrated and synthesised findings of one observer who has aimed to create meaning from chaos; and order in the place of control.

What has made it quite so challenging to navigate? One answer may be found in the exponential degree of complexity leaders have to navigate. Such complexity is proliferated by six dominant drivers:

1.   The sheer number of elements in the system, grown through expansion and, paradoxically, reductionism

2. The interconnectedness between elements. For interest, the formula for demonstrating the exponential number of connections in the system with the addition of elements is: $n(n-1)/2$

3. The expansion of choices, often referred to as purposiveness in Systems Thinking, in order to demonstrate the purpose-driven nature of systems

4. The publication of rules, particularly in a counter intuitive attempt at control, including, tacit, implicit and meta-rules. The counterintuitiveness arises, in part, from the reality that adding rules to the system implies the addition of elements.

5. Speed – inversely proportional to predictability in human endeavours

6. Dematerialisation – a key differentiator from the First Industrial Revolution (1IR) paradigm dominated by positivism, meant here to suggest the philosophical view that knowledge can only be deemed valid if it yields to the senses and reductionist logic.

Judged by the six criteria above, it is indisputable that, while some complexity has always existed, the 21st century confronts leaders with intellectual challenges at levels never faced in human history. Therefore, one may be justified in examining whether a 1IR paradigm of cognition, decision-making and learning is still appropriate for a world in which its tenets have all but disappeared.

The book presents a theory of leadership learning referred to as Systemic Leadership Learning. This theory describes the application of Systems Thinking to the field of Learning within the specific application of Executive development. In this context it proposes an alternative approach to the linear processes often used in executive development. It presents learning as an integration of systems that require profound understanding. But it moves beyond analysis to avoid the pervading reductionist mindset that is such a tremendous barrier to the identification of meaningful application opportunities from the learning process for leaders. Simple cause-and-effect relationships between systems present during learning are avoided and, in their stead, systemic frameworks are proposed.

In making observations about an entire industry, there is a risk of gross generalisation. I recognise that not all organisations experience executive development challenges to the same degree. Indeed, given the global market-leading positions of some of the clients engaged in the fieldwork for this book, there is obvious evidence of global best practice. I have had the tremendous privilege, for over 25 years, to work across the globe, in both developed and developing economies. From Geneva, Paris, London and Rome, to Kigali, Jordan and Azerbaijan, to name but a few. In all these regions, great companies have demonstrated the unusual courage and humility to learn, based on the immutable belief that there must be a better way of finding a better way.

Chapter 1

EVERYTHING EVERYWHERE ALL AT ONCE

Fantasy island: Learning in turmoil

> *"...The sureness of the soul is loosely bound*
> *By everything on earth the compass round*
> *And only by one's going slightly taut*
> *In the capriciousness of summer air*
> *Is of the slightest bondage made aware."*
>
> **Robert Frost, The Silken Tent**

Mega-shifts appear to have rendered leadership in a constant state of crisis. And the learning competence of leaders seems to be lagging. One may go as far as to suggest that leaders are not demonstrating the ability to learn in the hyper-flux of their contexts. Learning, at least among the top echelon of leaders, seems to be broken. Yet billions of dollars are spent globally on the development of leaders in organisations on an annual basis. Research suggests that the return on this investment is limited, or at best, difficult to observe.

We have moved even beyond a world characterised by VUCA (Volatility, Uncertainty, Complexity and Ambiguity), already described in 1985 by Bennis and Nanus in their book, "Leaders. The Strategies for Taking Charge". Authors create ideas, which trigger a non-linear lineage. Following Bennis and Nanus in that spirit, one might argue that the world has evolved to VUCASSU, with the addition of at least three dimensions:

1. Simultaneity, that is the synchronous, but unsynchronised, occurrence of multiple events which exacerbate complexity. Not only is internal simultaneity greater, but in the broader context, concurrent shifts are happening at the level of contextual redefinition.

2. Self-interest. Whether driven by a culture of participation prizes, the dominance of Instagram since 2010, or the need for bravado in the face of apparently insurmountable complexity, self-regard, and even hubris, appears to typify the corporate and political leader in many spheres. Acquisitive and opportunistic leadership behaviour has increased inequality and alienated voters and employees alike.

3.   Utilitarianism. Despite the apparent search for meaning among millennials and Gen Z, functional decisions, devoid of higher-order purpose, appear rife. All systems display a rebound effect, and here the counter-reaction has been significant. Examples may arguably include, Occupy Wall Street in 2011, Black Lives Matter in 2013 and the MeeToo Movement in 2017 (although the phrase was already coined in 2006 by activist Tarana Burke.)

Yet the demand for leaders with high-level competence required by the 21st century is growing exponentially, and, while organisations are attempting to close these competency deficits, they are simultaneously confronted by increasing competitor activity and ever-more educated consumers demanding up-to-the-minute information and service benchmarked against that of the tech giants. Simultaneously, technology is evolving at a higher pace than ever, leaders are more globally mobile than ever and the search for talent is becoming increasingly competitive.

Despite this global phenomenon, many organisations still make use of executive development processes that employ models of education created in ancient Greece and consolidated in Europe in the Middle Ages. Such educational models are characterised by content-driven processes in which respected subject matter experts, employed by educational institutions, 'enforce' (cynics might say 'inflict') their wisdom on students, whose attention spans appear to wane with every duetting split-screen nano-vlog on TikTok (released in 2016). These students are often deemed competent based on their ability to 'comply' with the learning content. More recent evolutions in this basic model demand from students to internalise learning content and demonstrate such content in the performance of their duties for the benefit of their institutional sponsors through methods such as Action-Based Learning, first made popular by Reg Revans in the 1940's. Despite this incremental improvement, the same basic model still applies: leaders as students are subordinated to the demands of their sponsors through learning content and guided to compliance to the learning process by teachers, now called facilitators or educators, who hold subject matter expertise. So entrenched has the model become (as indeed is the nature of paradigms) that the very mention of alternative models may appear un-educational.

The research process was one in which I immersed myself as an active observer in the daily praxis of the consultant's craft. The theory that has emerged from this research is known as *Systemic Leadership Learning. It proposes an integrated approach to executive development in which the systems of the leader, organisation, learning content and facilitator are integrated into a systemic whole.* This is done against the background of the integration of three fields of study as reviewed in a wide range of literature, namely Leadership, Systems Thinking and Learning, supported by the use of Story.

Following peer reviews and numerous engagements with a wide range of organisations, the suggestion emerged that the leader holds a self-perception of being the supra-system during the learning process. This means that the leader assumes, actively or passively, that he is the main containing system of the learning process and content. All content and method need to serve his needs. This insight has significant implications for the way in which organisations conceptualise, design, develop, facilitate, assess and evaluate executive development processes. Most notably, the learning process needs to start with the leader. The learning needs of the leader, as highlighted by a personal and unique story, form the foundation of the learning process. All other systems involved in the learning process are required to understand the reality of the leader as a means of optimising the return on investment from the non-linear learning journey.

For those new to systems thinking, it is worth noting at this point that a system, for the purposes of this book, is defined as a set of at least two elements or parts, which are in some form of interactive relationship. Every system (such as an organisation) exists within multiple containing systems and is itself a containing system for other sub-systems, i.e. every organisation is viewed as a holon. Every part of every system is thus contained, but not limited, by systems beyond the system in focus. Each system increases in complexity as the purposive elements and their interactions increase in number and become less predictable, despite the proliferation of rules produced to control the system. Failure to see, exploit or design the type and quality of connections will lead to a failure of understanding and will result in misguided engagement with the system. Systems have purpose. Such purpose may or may not be the stated, explicit intent as expressed by organisational leaders. Stafford Beer suggested the heuristic of POSIWID, that is the Purpose of a System Is What It Does. Although Beer recognised the interconnectedness of parts to form new systems, I fear he may have over-emphasised the loudness of the voice of the system and undervalued the nature of purpose as an emerging property of the system. Purpose emerges as the result of the interaction of elements and sub-systems, both internal and external to the system. All boundaries, and therefore all relationships, are viewed as temporary, both because of natural system evolution and due to purposive connection and disconnection of the multiple parts which constitute the system under investigation.

Due to the centrality of the leader as system in the learning process, a multi-dimensional orientation framework is developed that provides a means for both the leader as well as the other systems in the learning process to analyse, interpret, understand and co-synthesise the system of the leader. Within this framework, the organisation is viewed as part of the system of the leader. The organisation becomes a focus area during periods of professional development for the leader, but does not subordinate the leader as a *tabula rasa* (blank slate) recipient of education. Learning and its results are probabilistic, rather than deterministic. This means that the design of learning as a (containing) system cannot claim to 'produce' graduates. It can only invite leaders, inspire learning and allow learning to emerge as leaders and systems engage with other elements of the learning system, such as the content. The learning content is viewed as both a system in its own right, and as a tool for enhancing the performance of the leader, while the facilitator is a guide at the service of the leader in order to increase the probability of personal, professional and organisational success, however defined.

Systemic Leadership Learning (SLL) integrates the systems in the learning process which appear hitherto to have been left disjointed and fragmented. Since it is the executive - and not the facilitator, learning content or nebulously defined system of the organisation - who is ultimately required to deliver improved performance as a result of learning, SLL presupposes integrity on the part of the leader and allows the leader the requisite supra-system status to improve the probability of purposive learning.

The executive development industry comprises a wide range of entities that deliver and govern executive development services. A number of key challenges are present in the delivery and governance of entities in the industry, as described below.

1.1 Silver linings playbook: Quality Assurance STILL lacks Return on Learning (ROL) metrics

Key entities that deliver executive development services include:

- Public universities, most with their own business schools,
- Private universities,
- Non-Governmental Organisations (NGO's),
- Government agencies,
- Private training companies and institutes,
- Private individuals,
- And others.

Quality assurance of these entities appears problematic since, despite the increasing bombardment of regulation, ROI remains lacking. Quality criteria tend to describe processes and procedures, rather than qualitative experiences of leaders. In particular, thought processes, such as decision-making capabilities based on emerging insights, appear severely lacking. Furthermore, there appears to be very limited evidence of criteria relating to the impact of learning on organisations in any of the criteria for higher education institutions. It is not difficult to understand the absence of such criteria, as enforcing them would be a practical impossibility. But the result is that providers of executive development services can offer these services for years without any proven impact on the organisations footing the bill for the education of their leaders.

1.2 Now you see me: Boxes and borders and boards in disorder

Positivism is not optimism. It is a paradigm, again, with deep roots in the 1IR, which deems as valid only that which yields to the senses and can be argued through deductive reasoning. The prevailing mindset of 'seeing is believing' no longer serves executive decision-making. It fails to acknowledge the 21st century reality of dematerialised value creation. Not only has value been digitised, but it has furthermore been conceptualised. Consider, e.g., how the 1IR convinced humanity that only machines and their tangible products are worthy of consideration. Increasingly, financial capital as a form of value became the dominant pursuit. The latter part of 20th century saw movements towards 'human capital' and other forms followed shortly afterwards. The traditional accounting system has failed to 'account' for the multiple intangible realities shaping organisations today. Consider, as just a few examples, the incorporeal forms of perceived value below:

- Commitment, such as from suppliers, which is critical for systemic competitive advantage
- Loyalty, a key dimension of predictable value if displayed by key stakeholders like customers
- Patriotism, particularly as it relates to the realities of war, however misguided
- Profitability, especially beyond financial metrics
- Leadership, notably its powers of other impalpable qualities, such as inspiration
- Values, central to the challenges related to globalisation
- Thinking, the central input to decision-making
- Creativity, a 21st century business imperative
- Gravitas, a leadership quality in short supply
- Social cohesion, a driver of nation-building
- Well-being, finally recognised as essential in all its various forms, including mental, physical, financial and others
- Intent, a determinant of strategic decision-making
- Ambition, drive and grit as vital competencies for talent

- Engagement, the elusive quality of talent that delivers results
- Motivation, markedly of the essence in a world of turbulence
- Inspiration, an input to creativity and a driver of higher-order thinking
- Brand, including brand equity, brand values, brand promise and other corollaries which shape the psychological contract with stakeholders
- Trust, the bedrock in times of investment and employment uncertainty
- Recognition, the universal need for acknowledgement of effort and achievement
- And so many others.

Yet boards and executive teams often appear to believe that "boxed is better", in other words, their behaviour suggests that the only elements worthy of investment and even exploration are those that are easily measured, predicted and controlled. It is not difficult to understand the motivation for such leadership conservatism – businesses have to make commitments to shareholders and deliberate risk may create untenable levels of caution for current and potential shareholders. The conservatism may even, paradoxically, be based on the insight that human beings are naturally creative and should therefore be controlled.

This clearly displays an inherent contradiction. It may be explained by the fact that, while most top executives in organisations recognise the need for innovation, they are incapable of managing the divergence of thought that would emanate from true innovative thinking. What they can manage with some degree of predictability are those processes that have already proven themselves to work.

The cycle of positivism is thus reinforced, characterised further by linearity and the relentless analytical narrowing of the boundaries of the potential of human pursuit. It poses a great threat to Systems Thinking as a discipline in organisations and serves only to perpetuate a one-dimensional approach to management thinking and learning. The immediate threat for learning is that it prevents leaders from learning optimally, as the boxes for the results of learning have been predefined. If one accepts that learning is inherently a divergent process of exploration, then such premature convergence of thought, possibility and solutions poses a significant hazard to the identification of innovative application opportunities arising from insights in the learning experience.

If one then considers that leaders impact their staff and others in their sphere of influence, the potential value of learning is infinite, and the opportunity cost of lost innovation application opportunities appears a cost seldom considered.

1.3   The new mutants: Leaders who follow

One of the main reasons for the opportunity cost incurred from loss of innovation is the paradox that many leaders are expected to *lead as followers*. This means that many senior managers are referred to as leaders, but the expectations upon them prevent them from exercising any real leadership. Although consultation is often espoused, what they are frequently expected to do is to achieve the objectives predetermined on their behalf, and to execute their tasks in a manner similarly dictated. Thus, they are told what to do as well as how to do it, and they are reprimanded on deviations from both these determinants. The question can therefore be reasonably asked, "Are they really leaders?" The implications seem to suggest a response in the negative. The deviant alternative can also be observed: top managers who lack granular insight into the realities facing those reporting to them, often ask staff to create objectives themselves, and then frame their abdication of responsibility as empowerment.

Such paradoxes demand further investigation into why organisations would refer to senior managers as leaders, while limiting their creative flair so dramatically. One possible motivation for the apparent contradiction is that being referred to as a leader has become a popular aspiration, and, while organisations can call their senior staff leaders, they are unable to manage the true implications of every senior manager being exactly that – the divergence of approaches and thinking simply seems overwhelming to executives and boards. Thus, admittedly somewhat conspiratorially, the title of leader appears to be awarded as a soothing anaesthetic to those with ambition, but who often lack real power. It strokes the egos of those without any real influence and creates the illusion that everyone can be a leader in their organisation and thereby acquire more authority – the model for advancement in a capitalist system.

Again, it is not the intention here to change the capitalist system. It is simply the intention to highlight flagrant contradictions in the system and examine the implications for the way in which leaders learn in organisations.

1.4   You can't take it with you: Blank slates

The learning process in organisations is further complicated by the principles that underlie the selection of leaders who join the organisation. It has become a truism that organisations aim to attract and retain the most talented people in the market. They employ rigorous selection processes to ensure that only the top available talent enter the organisation. Given the great investment made in selecting the right leaders – the best and brightest talent in the market - learning programmes such as executive development programmes are then paradoxically delivered as pre-digested principles and theories. While it is true that business schools and training providers often consult top management, the typical process is that there is almost no consultation with the leaders who will attend the programme before they enter the learning space (still typically a classroom). This approach to executive development appears to deny the very criteria identified in selection processes, such as initiative, creativity, innovation, change management and others.

Such a *tabula rasa* (empty vessel) approach to learning prevents leaders and their organisations from benefiting optimally from learning, as the reality of the leader is not examined as part of the conceptualisation of the learning design process. Talented leaders, who often already have a developed set of competencies, require a different approach to learning that respects their context and previous development, and more directly supports the dissolution of challenges they face both personally and in the workplace.

1.5   One thing leads to another: Blind to connections

A preliminary scan of programme designs at leading executive education institutions shows a glaring absence of systemic design.

Programme designs appear to be presented in boxes, i.e. each field of expertise is shown as a separate arm of study, almost without exception.

This while the reality of the leader is hyper-simultaneity: no leader has an HR problem from 9-10, a strategy problem from 10-11, a finance problem from 11-12, and so on. Leaders face their complex challenges all at once. This requires forms of intellectual processing which may enable leaders to navigate such interwovenness.

1.6   The imitation game: Haven't we learnt this before?

The design process for executive development programmes often follows the following sequential steps:

i.   The organisation's top leadership has an idea for the development of their executives.

ii. A representative from the leadership team briefs the head of the Human Resources Department, if this person is not represented in the executive team.

iii. The head of the Human Resources Department briefs the head of Training or Learning.

iv.   This person briefs the person responsible for executive development in the training team.

v.   The responsible person briefs three providers, often a sales representative from the providing company.

vi.   A provider is selected using predefined criteria of quality. Occasionally learning philosophy is considered.

vii. The provider is appointed and the provider's representative briefs the responsible trainer's manager.

viii. The trainer is then appointed internally, or, very frequently, the provider subcontracts the work to a sub-contracting trainer.

ix.   This trainer then, in the ideal scenario, refines existing, standard training material and delivers the training to the client's leaders, who then return to their staff and other stakeholders.

The result of such processes is that the executive arrives at the training venue (not learning) and has very little insight of the intended purpose and value of the learning journey, with the occasional exception of an email or letter welcoming them to the programme, coupled by a few general aims. The trainer/professor is armed with a deck of slides, but often has little appreciation for the challenges facing the executives.

The accreditation process is such that all learning content must be covered, despite possible attempts from executives to discuss their own insights and creativity.

The overall result is an over-emphasis on the learning content and a high risk of disengagement from the leaders in the learning process.

If business leaders had to make mega-project decisions with such levels of risk, they might often abandon the project. The fact that learning goes ahead, is an indication either of the lack of insight into the learning process, or the token status with which learning is often implicitly viewed.

Given the inextricable link between learning and innovation, and the indelible need for innovation in an increasingly competitive systemic landscape, the missed opportunity to innovate during learning not only represents an opportunity cost, but also implies a *de facto* retardation of organisational growth and development relative to competitor activity, especially if the latter follows a more systemic approach.

The risks of poor investment in executive development extend far beyond the actual financial cost of the programme and the implications for organisations are significant. Given the risks highlighted below, this book also serves as mitigation of operational risk, including:

- Disillusionment for leaders as a result of learning causes a lack of motivation and drive.
- Broken promises destroy the implicit trust relationship between the executive and the organisation.
- The investment made in terms of financial expenditure on executive development paid to service providers can be enormous. The lack of ability to exploit the value of executive development prevents a meaningful return on the investment.
- Investment is also made in terms of the time the leader spends on the learning process, during which salaries are paid by the organisation. Stopping short of leveraging the value of the time spent incurs an opportunity cost that can create a great burden.
- Operational time and resources expended by internal learning coordination processes are also squandered without return.

Furthermore, competitive advantage is also sacrificed if learning is not harnessed and insights about the organisation are not integrated into product design, process innovation, strategic insight or improved customer and other stakeholder insights and engagement.

The main focus of this work is that executive development must lead to creative application opportunities from insights gained during learning through the convergence of the various systems at work in the learning process.

Chapter 2

OPPENHEIMER:

METHOD IN THE MADNESS

How to train your dragon

To make sure what star I missed
I should have to check on my list
Every star in sight.
It may take me all night.

Robert Frost, On Making Certain Anything Has Happened

Executives make decisions. The intellectual process by which they arrive at those decisions may be opaque, even to themselves. It is noteworthy that the etymology of the word decide is from the Latin *decidere*, meaning 'to cut off'. Any decision, therefore, is not simply an addition to the status quo; it is a sculpting thereof. Just as the sculptor must remove marble to reveal the beauty of the art piece, the executive must constantly consider the severing impact of decisions while noting the emerging connections. No problem, therefore, can be solved without creating another. The challenge, then, is merely to create a better set of problems. With the multiple dimensions present in the learning situation, it is often challenging to evaluate what is valid. Certainly, the complexity of learning dynamics calls for a new approach to understanding, and traditional research, based on a hypothesis and reduced to the smallest components, appears to have significant limitations for study that attempts to explore the dynamics of larger, complex systems in continuous interaction.

2.1　The perfect storm: Seeking validity chaos

Let chaos storm!
Let cloud shapes swarm!
I wait for form.

Robert Frost, Pertinax

The questions for investigating validity in the dematerialised world of learning, especially in hyper-complex environments, reveal intractable circularity. Is the test of validity a valid question when examining chaos? Will a search for the smallest indivisible parts (classic reductionism) lead to any insight in such complexity? Can self-referencing (insight deemed to be true because it is based on what I deem to

11

be true) replace validity as a test of acceptability? Can analysis (often viewed as the enemy of systems thinking) help us to understand a systemic approach? Can systems thinking be applied to Systems Thinking?

As this book falls broadly within the Social Sciences, it is also characterised by a philosophical underpinning. I must assert that it is based upon the belief that all leaders have the capacity to improve their ability to lead. All leaders can learn to lead better.

I have been cautiously aware of multiple dimensions that influence the success of a learning programme. In fact, it is one of the fundamental principles of the theory of Systemic Leadership Learning proposed in this book that an in-depth understanding of the multiple systems at work in the learning process is essential for the optimal advancement of creative learning application opportunities. The number of variables in the learning process is almost limitless. It may even be argued that the learning process is so complex due to the number of variables and the infinite number of possible responses from leaders, that the isolation of one element may be virtually impossible. Some of the most obvious variables include:

- Size of the group
- Industry of the client
- Leader receptiveness to learning prior to the programme
- Communication and change management of the learning process
- Venue, including air conditioning, lighting, meals, levels of luxury and comfort, etcetera
- Operational pressures of the leaders on the programme
- Programme duration
- Pace of facilitation
- Level of complexity of learning content
- The personalities of leaders on the programme
- Intelligence of leaders on the programme
- Motivation of leaders on the programme
- And many more

With such a staggering array of variables, a multi-method approach is essential as a risk mitigation measure.

It is a truism in the decision sciences that the nature of question formulation, including its content and type, determines the content and type of responses. Structured methods of inquiry are distinguished, therefore, by the nature of the questions they pose. For that reason, it is essential to become conscious of the methods of inquiry in use to evaluate the suitability of the method employed.

A multitude of methodologies and methods of inquiry may be identified. In general terms, one may think of methods as the behaviours, tools, techniques and procedures employed in the process of collecting and analysing data, while methodology is a description of the system of methods; the overall, complete rationale, approach and strategy which aids understanding of the problem. Simply put, the guiding methodology question is this:

> **Do the methods of inquiry elicit the type of responses which increase the probability of resolving the problems, mitigating the risks and accessing the opportunities defined in the social consensus of interpreting the problem?**

In support of the goals and aims of the work of the National Planning Commission, this author posits a selection of methodologies below. A brief description is provided for each.

> *Note:* These descriptions are NOT intended to offer the final definition of the methodology. Descriptions are offered simply as first-level descriptors. It should also be noted that, while each methodology possesses distinctive characteristics, various schools of thought exist within each methodology, and that there are several areas of overlap between them.

Analytical Thinking

In classical analysis, problems are divided into parts. This is based on the assumption that an improved understanding of the parts will lead to the identification of a sub-optimal part which, if improved, will improve the whole.

Strategic Thinking

Typically, a strategic approach extends the time horizon beyond the timeframe of operational goals to achieve longer-term intent. It emphasises the role of competing forces as well as the shifting needs of beneficiaries by considering the connections between internal and external dynamics. It transcends operational and tactical investigation by allowing for a permeable organisational boundary which enables institutional vibrance. Within the competitive landscape, it establishes its identity through differentiation.

In advisory work on Strategy around the globe, five principles for strategic awareness have been identified which may elevate the thoughts of the leader beyond the realm of operational and tactical thinking towards more strategic levels. These principles highlight the nature of strategic work:

i.   Strategy is a cogent and coherent set of choices

ii.   Made in a game of your choosing

iii. In a competitive landscape

iv.   For the longer term

v.   In order to increase the probability of winning.

These principles highlight the incontrovertible truth of strategy, whatever the philosophical orientation, that Strategy is the process whereby internal tactics is connected to external systemic consciousness. Strategy is not possible without external awareness. A typical example of strategic failure is the absence of competitor consciousness in senior leaders, with several companies running the impending risk that their senior leaders believe they have few competitors, or even worse, that they are so differentiated in the market, that they have none. This is a dangerous fallacy. Despite the calls for collaboration, business competition can be brutal. A competitor should therefore be defined as any entity which takes any resources your organisation should be taking. This is not limited to revenue, but extends to customers, attention, status, security, predictability, risk mitigation, opportunity provision or any other form of value.

As no entity can dominate all aspects of the market, and since perfect market equilibrium is a now-debunked myth, strategic thinking must ask: *how is the market asymmetrically structured in our favour?*

Creative Thinking

This methodology deliberately generates alternative, novel options. It is often used to escape a sense of 'stuckness' from current solutions. Far from being a case of 'anything goes', it is a disciplined approach which explores both new methods and new solutions. It is a deliberate departure from conventional solutions towards imaginative, inventive and artistic alternatives.

Design Thinking

Born from the parents of idealised design in systems thinking and the science of industrial design, design thinking employs empathy through immersion into the realities of beneficiaries and systems in order to identify new insights and generate new solutions. It is often characterised by Human-Centric Design (HCD).

Computational Thinking

The fundamental principle of this approach is to solve problems in a way that a computer could solve the problem. Typically, that means reducing the problem to a series of simple processes. Such processes are akin to Analytical Thinking in that they attempt to reduce a problem to its fundamental components. Following analysis in this methodology is the dimension of abstraction, in which parts are categorised and classified to produce a model, framework, principle or even purpose. Processes are characterised by decision-trees, which may include typical if-then steps as well as more expansive decision trees, which may include a degree of linear circularity (i.e. returning to the same line of a process to repeat a step in the same process). With more advanced computer analytics, thinking may draw on increasingly large data sets and generate very large quantities of decision options as new connections are made with every new data point. The principle, however, remains the use of a programmatic, repeatable, unemotional, deterministic mapping of decision and execution processes. The aim is typically to achieve automation.

Effectual Thinking (vs Causal Thinking)

Effectual Thinking (also Effectuation) is an approach to problem solving which is often associated with entrepreneurship and innovation. It is distinguished from causal (or traditional managerial) thinking in two main ways:

1. It is resource-based rather than goal-based. This means the process commences with a thorough understanding of the self and the entity and its multiple forms of capital, including its networks.

2. It is emergent and explorative, rather than deterministic about a pre-defined outcome. Through high levels of awareness and agility, it allows for fluid learning and heuristic approaches to discovery of opportunity and risk.

Systems Thinking

In a certain sense, systems thinking is the opposite of Analysis. It investigates the multiple containing systems of a problem in order to facilitate change through established and new areas of connectedness. It is holistic rather than reductionist in its approach.

A guide to systems thinking is included in the addendum in the form of the SODCAST Framework.

The day after tomorrow: Futures Thinking

In this approach, horizons are further extended, and multiple possible futures are identified as the foundation for decision-making. The key differentiation between traditional Strategic Thinking and Futures Thinking, is that the former considers only a single future, namely the future it wants, typically only for itself. Futures Thinking necessitates the investigation of multiple futures. Among several such futures, heed is paid to:

- The current or projected future: a future state as the result of the perpetuation of current patterns.
- Explorative futures: what could happen.
- Normative futures: what should happen.

Attitudes towards multiple futures may vary. For that reason, a simple Futures Appreciation Levels Framework with four levels was developed:

i. **Futures Resistant**

   Experience around the globe has demonstrated that many executives have little appetite for the exploration of undesirable futures, irrespective of their probability. Executives at this level simply do not want to know. Their wilful ignorance places the organisation at severe risk.

ii. **Futures Tolerant**

   At this level, executives permit discussions on multiple futures, but conduct the exercise begrudgingly. They endure and abide by it but absorb little to none of the insights it may offer.

iii. **Futures Oriented**

   Adjustments are made for future-preparedness at this level. Executives are able to locate their strategy within the constellation of possible futures evident from a futures investigation.

iv. **Futures Based**

   Multiple futures form the starting point of strategic dialogue at this level. Not only does the future inform strategy, it sculpts the very nature thereof. The strategy is created only by what the future would, could and should hold in its various forms of possibility, preferability and probability.

Futures Thinking recognises the past, has a trans-disciplinary reading of the present and invites a mental rehearsal of multiple futures. Essential to the appreciation of Futures Thinking is the strategic implication that the current model can only ever produce the current future. When that future has become undesirable, alternative futures are no longer optional; they are a matter of survival.

The theory of nothing: Back-to-basics

In times of economic unease, in which many businesses are showing lower returns, pressured by sedate growth and tenuous trading conditions, uncertainty increases exponentially. The paradox for senior executives is that, at the very moment where creativity and innovation are required, the default intellectual mode for the mind under duress is to lock down, batten down the creative hatches, narrow the imaginative parameters and do a cerebral run for business shelter. The most clearly observable safe house appears to be the realm of what is already easy to prove: the past. The logic-under-pressure argument then suggests a return to the apparent fundamentals of a time gone by. Perhaps (so the delusion goes) it is time to return to the rudiments of business practice. The basics. They seem secure. Tangible. Seductive in their clarity. It is only a few small, slippery steps to the launch of the apparently inevitable appellation of the turnaround or rescue initiative: the *back-to-basics programme*.

The theory is based on a return to the 'essentials', with the intent to create stability. But the ubiquitous back-to-basics programme theory is riddled with a number of intractable intellectual conundrums. The first is that it is simply not possible to 'go back', whether to basics or any other option. Chronological time simply does not allow for this preference. Very few have ever suggested a back-to-complexity programme. Why should basics be easier to revert to than any other option? The view seems to be that the simplicity from a time gone by holds the answer to the current malaise. But the past, while lingering in its effect and footprint, simply cannot be revisited. When Trump wants to make America great 'again', the futurist would ask, 'Like when?'

The second dilemma for a back-to-basics programme is the identification of the so-called basics. Clients often answer this by assuming that 'everyone knows the basics'. This assumption is easily refuted through scientific experimentation: simply ask the executive team and their staff to write down what they perceive as the basics and measure the level of consensus. It is easy to cheat with the usual suspects of 'profitability', 'people are our greatest asset' and 'customer centricity', but in the achievement of these objectives a long list of often contradicting 'basics' will inevitably emerge from the group. The leader will often then (ignoring the level of potential ridicule) be tempted to point out the 'real' basics. Thus, the basics are wickedly difficult to define and require elusive levels of honesty and consensus.

The third difficulty with 'back-to-basics' is the inherent contradiction that it was exactly the so-called basics of the past that now necessitate a 'back-to-basics' programme. This is supported by the fact that the so-called basics have already proven un-resilient. Were they as tenacious and timelessly universal as their supporters suggest, surely the basics would still be in place. Put another way, if the basics from the past worked so well, why are we now in trouble?

The fourth and perhaps most disturbing and compelling intellectual conundrum of a back-to-basics programme becomes evident when the temporal argument is more thoroughly understood: a decision is always made in the present. Even if a plan exists to make the decision at a future time, by the time that decision is made, it will be the present. The basics have already succumbed to the pressures of the emerging realities. The decision, though made *during* the present, with all the concomitant noise and urgency of the moment, is *based on* the past – a time which is purported to contain the requisite basics, but which can never be visited again. And that decision is made in the interest of the future (presumably all decisions are), with the assumption that the basics from a time which can never be revisited, and which have proven not to have survived into the present, are the exact same basics that will be the solution for the future - a time that has never been visited before. In the words of LP Hartley in her opening line of The Go-Between, "The past is a foreign country: they do things differently there".

Therefore, if past-orientation is as nonsensical as the argument above suggests, and present-obsession is a deception of the headlines, the logical conclusion is to explore the only remaining temporal option: futurity. And the most viable option is to do so with the creativity, imagination and inventiveness required by the sheer rapidity of the industrial and social revolution. Although many charlatan leaders derive their authority from a romanticisation or redemption of the past, the time yet to come is the sole residual option worthy of further exploration for the robust intellect wishing to advance business and society. It is exclusively in the future that business may navigate emerging risk and where opportunity may be accessed.

A guide to Futures Thinking is included in the addendum.

Theory of Constraints

This is a methodology characterised by the identification and elimination of the most significant limiting factors which prevent or curb the achievement of success. It is a way of distinguishing activity from that which limits impact. It is a paradigm which holds that restrictions (rather than goals or actions) determine performance.

Theory of Change

This is the plausible narrative of HOW intent is realised in the link between action and result. It describes the content of a belief in a model of the method by which a transformation is facilitated and secured.

Naturally, several other methodologies exist. The selection included here is made on the experience of this author in the facilitation of strategic dialogue in various international environments. It is not essential that each methodology be employed separately before strategic decisions are made – the reality of the scale and pace of problems simply will not allow for such luxury. What may indeed be useful is to remain conscious of which methodologies dominate, and which combination of mixed methods should be explored to add richness to the quality of strategic dialogue – especially if the default method has already failed.

In practice, a multi-method mindset adds richness to the dialogue and enables new avenues of thinking and learning.

2.2   **Under my umbrella**

> *A scent of ripeness from over a wall.*
> *And come to leave the routine road*
> *And look for what had made me stall.*
>
> **Robert Frost, Unharvested**

To exacerbate the lack of focus by external providers on the actual learning needs of the organisation as informed by the systemic strategic landscape, they typically involve themselves in what I have come to describe as "the fight for the umbrella", i.e. they all argue that their specific offering presents the panacea of learning needs; that all learning requirements would be covered by what their content offers (and therefore everything fits under their umbrella). Emotional Intelligence (EQ) is perhaps the most prevalent in this regard. The argument is: "Humans are at the heart of everything. Humans have emotions. Therefore, EQ will solve this problem." Others make themselves guilty of similar 'umbrellafication'. Change Management specialists, for example, would argue, "Everything changes. Therefore, all learning is change". Performance Management consultants would suggest, "All business activity is about performance. Therefore, our content is what you need". Financial gurus would propose, "The purpose of business is to make money. Without our services nothing else matters". More formal institutions such as universities would say, "The most important aspect, irrespective of the need, is accreditation. Without that you can never be sure of the quality of learning". And quality experts would suggest, "Without quality management processes you would compromise delivery standards, and then there would be no business". Operational efficiency experts had similar fights for the umbrella, as they would contend, "The aim is to be better at what you do. We help to streamline your processes. This will improve productivity and save costs. What else matters?" And so-called 'leadership consultants' (far too often disillusioned middle to senior managers who have grown disillusioned by the realities of large corporates) have taken up permanent residency under the fallacious argument that their work alone offers the answer to whatever the question might be. Of the abundance of 'coaches', visibly in in need of coaching themselves, I would rather not speak.

We should note that clients often buy these services in the same way as vendors sell them to organisations as mentioned above, that is, they would ask about a product list, rather than discuss their own systemic needs. Ironically, buyers of development services may make it very difficult to support the learning needs of their own organisations if they shopped for learning as if in a supermarket. They often appear to show little insight into the real needs of their own organisations, and demonstrate more concern with the credentials and content offering of the service provider than the strategic risks and opportunities in the organisational context.

It thus emerges that not only vendors, but also clients, have become accustomed to buying learning services such as training programmes as product packages, rather than as strategic change experiences that would advance their organisations. The behaviour is therefore not limited to vendors but extends to clients themselves.

A theory of learning began to show itself that now forms the basis of this book. It became clear that learning providers and often clients too, were either unaware or disinterested in the multiple intersecting containing systems they are attempting to serve. Content is mistakenly positioned as a kind of supra-system, which alienates leaders and makes the learning outcomes highly limited beyond knowledge of the concepts presented. The result, counterintuitive as is often the case in misread systems, is that while smiley faces on feedback forms abound, there is a dire implication for learning sustainability.

2.2.1 The force awakens: Catalysing learning

Two roads diverged in a wood, and I –
I took the one less travelled by,
And that has made all the difference.

Robert Frost, The Road Not taken

The observation that learning content often dominates the learning process for leaders, has developed into a fundamental tenet of the theory on Systemic Leadership Learning (SLL). A principle of SLL is that the leader is a system in her own right, as is the organisation – the leader is not subordinated to the organisation. Nor is the leader made servant of the learning content. Such content is merely applied as a catalyst to serve the system of the leader. The humility of the facilitator, coupled with a profound respect for the system of the leader and organisation, allows the system of the leader in the learning situation to serve as supra-system, incorporating the learning content, expectations from the organisation and experience and knowledge of the facilitator.

The humility of a learning design team to recognise the leaders as their own supra-systems during the learning process, allows for infinitely greater creative possibility.

A critical identifier of all systems is that they produce emerging properties. These are incipient qualities of the system which only make their presence known once the elements have interacted. Such qualities do not belong to parts of the system prior to synthesis and may not survive the disintegration of the system. But they thrive in the particular artistic interwovenness of the elements of the system, which sustains them as it produces new emerging properties, which may ultimately replace a selection of early properties as the system evolves. Mechanistic system designers often claim foresight after the fact, but system behaviour is never entirely predictable.

In the system of learning, it is noteworthy to observe the emergence of a new system as a result: together the facilitator and the client form a new, evolved relationship which constitutes a new entity that promotes a dynamic approach to learning design – the entities of the facilitator, leader, content and client evolve to form an entirely new system in itself.

As a complex set of interrelated subsystems, learning thus has the potential of being self-organising (autopoietic), at both an individual and group level. One example of this is self-driven learning. Self-driven learning is defined in this context as learning processes based on specific and agreed learning needs that are unique to every individual; and are initiated, driven, administered and monitored by every individual for their own development. It is often informed by self-perception and personal paradigms. This means that an executive would discover a learning need for themselves, articulate the exact need after refinement through consultation, and then co-design behaviour that would embark upon learning for that development need.

While such a process requires a great deal of consideration, it does allow the leader to drive personal learning, and to do so at any time. Compare this approach with a leader facing a decision-making challenge but having to wait for a training session on decision-making to be scheduled at some time in the curriculum delivery plan by an external provider.

A description of how the emerging theory was tested with industry peers is shown belowf (Chapter 3).

Chapter 3

THE BIG SHORT

Emerging Thoughts

Was something brushed across my mind
That no one on earth will ever find?
Heaven gives its glimpses only to those
Not in a position to look too close.

Robert Frost, A Passing Glimpse

Based on the research and extensive field work in both developed and developing countries across the world, a theory has emerged that has shaped the architecture of this book: Systemic Leadership Learning (SLL).

It proposes that leaders learn more impactfully, specifically with regards to the identification of creative application opportunities from learning, if the learning occurs in a systemic way, that is, with key systems in the learning process possessing an understanding of the role and nature of every other system involved in the learning process. The systems involved reach far beyond the immediate boundary of the executive.

SLL prioritises a number of systems in the learning process itself, and posits that the primary systems are the following:

- The leader,
- The organisation in which the leader works,
- The learning content, and
- The facilitator.

The diagram below shows the four systems that form the major emphasis of SLL.

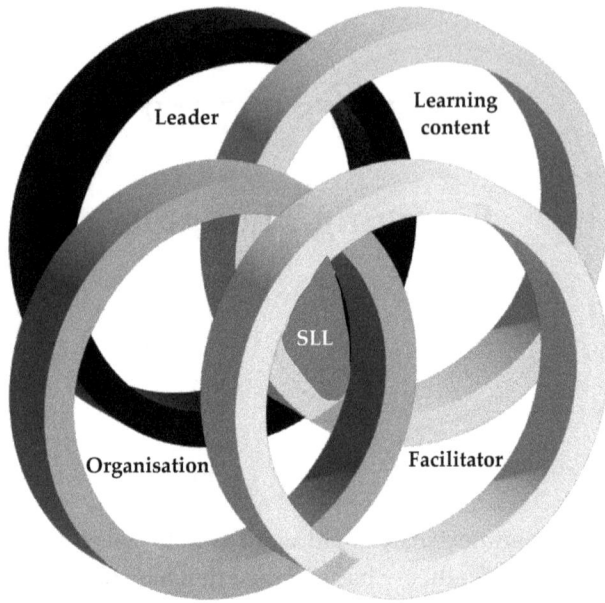

Figure 1: Integrating four primary systems

All the above systems are viewed as systems in their own right, that is, they are capable of prevailing without the existence of the other systems. While they exist in mutual impact, they are nevertheless discreetly identifiable as systems. This approach differs from traditional executive development practices in that it does not subjugate the leader as a sub-system of the organisation as so much practice and literature on the subject appears to do.

3.1 Better to light a candle

3.1.1 Into the woods: In search of definitions

The quest for defining qualities is often referred to by academic researchers as "ontology". In this pursuit, the implication of paradigms emerges at the very onset. One of the definitional challenges in creating a new concept such as SLL, is that it often merges previously existing concepts to constitute the new. For this reason, it is critical to have a set of working definitions that enables the navigation of the emerging idea. While a myriad of definitions exists for the terms below, I offer conceptualised definitions to facilitate the use of the terms specifically within the framework of Systemic Leadership Learning.

3.1.1.1 Systemic: It is all connected

Everything its parts can do
Has been thought out and accounted for.
Your least touch sets it going round,
And when to stop it rests with you.

Robert Frost, A Trial Run

In the recent explosion of complexity theory, some critique has been registered on the notion of 'systemic' approaches. The main contestation appears to be that the complete mapping of systems is unattainable. The implication is that not all cause-and-effect relationships can be chartered, due to the constant evolution and fluid nature of all reality. While the infinite complexity of hyper-wicked problems is patently true, I humbly contend that leaders in the real world of organisations, i.e. real humans with limited time, attention and other resources, do not have access to the academic indulgence of inexplicability. They are compelled to make decisions, despite the glaringly obvious insufficiency of data and other resources. The term "systemic" in the context of SLL therefore does not claim perfect or complete knowledge – such an assertion would simply deny the extreme complexity of reality. The term relates, in this context, to the use of a systems-mindset during the learning process. For greater completeness, it should be acknowledged that the 'learning process' has no real beginning or end. A fruitful life as leader, if definable at all, must surely be characterised by incessant curiosity. The needs of a myriad stakeholders in the dynamic context simply demand it.

Texting: Takers and makers of sense

In an attempt to define the notion of a process as 'systemic', the concept of 'context' has an unavoidable connotation. Because leaders have to make decisions in complex environments, it is essential that they develop the art and science of interpretation and sense-making – what is often described as hermeneutics for leaders. Because leaders operate in the complex learning system described, other key actors in the learning system, such as designers, facilitators and content creators, are equally compelled to develop the art and science of hermeneutics. In the first instance, leaders must make a critical decision about their roles in the systems of both learning and work. They are confronted by a critical personal decision: are they to be takers of sense or makers of sense? In order to accept the mantle of leadership in any form, the leader simply cannot be a passive 'taker of sense'. The pre-digested sense-making presented by the world of the organisation in its dynamic context will render the leader a mere participant; a boat at sea without rudder or compass; utterly at the mercy of the violent vicissitudes of the context. Leadership requires activism. That is not to suggest that leaders should lack sensitivity. Quite the contrary is the real demand. Leaders, in addition to being indefatigable students driven by insatiable curiosity, cannot pretend to lead while hiding behind the 'way of the world'. Stakeholders in the 21st century are demanding that leaders move beyond describing the world as it is. Leaders, if they are to serve the journey towards more preferable futures, are obliged to contribute towards the redesign of the world as it should be, while their curiosity guides an investigation of the world as it could be. To that end, they can no longer be mere 'takers of sense' as presented to them. Leaders in the hyper-complexity of the 21st century must be 'makers of sense', recognising the interwovenness of their context. *Leaders must sculpt original meaning from the noise and delusions in the organisational ambience.*

It is noteworthy that the etymology of the word 'context' reveals much of its challenge. From the Latin *con*, meaning together, the text is derived from *texere*, meaning to weave. Context, therefore, is that which is woven together with the text. In this sense, text refers to the world as it presents itself to the leader, i.e. the sense the world is presenting as reality. Text also connotes implications of the glaringly obvious, the apparent and the tangible. It is the visible reality and propaganda observable in a superficial reading of the world. Text in this sense is hermeneutics based only on positivism, i.e. text is simply the shallow observability of words, devoid of meaning and divorced from any deeper sense. Context, therefore, is that which the leader must grasp 'with the text' in order to create sense from the apparent chaos.

Of particular interest is a related etymology, namely that of 'complexity' (already in use from the 1650s). The etymology is almost an overlap: from the Latin *com* meaning together, and *plektere* meaning to plait, patently related to *plexere*, meaning also to entangle. The quantum reference is self-evident.

Both notions of *context* and *complex* therefore illustrate the hermeneutic (interpretational) imperative to 'read together' the various elements in the system in the effort of making new sense.

With text and context, leaders must also develop the interpretational competence of reading subtext. From the Latin *sub* meaning under, subtext is essential as leaders must search for veiled, less obvious risk and opportunities in their decision-making. Implicit meaning in the behaviour of key stakeholders and other actors in the context is a critical input to the 'weaving together' of new meaning. Beyond the explicit reality, subtext offers leaders a deeper sense of understanding, which they are compelled to use to the benefit of stakeholders.

Beyond text, context and subtext, leaders are further challenged to observe the increasing pervasiveness of pretext. This dimension of the sense-making process alerts leaders to the deliberate subversion of interpretation. It is closely related to the understanding of motivation. Pretext is often applied to obfuscate the real reason for behaviour, by offering noble intent as explanation when more insidious rationale is the reality. It is the ability to look beyond the ostensible meaning of the propaganda in the pretext which allows leaders to read the true text and construct meaning without misdirection.

As a precursor to the definition of the term "systemic", a more foundational definition is proposed for the term "system". A system may be defined as a clustering of at least two entities that act or are required to act in a relationship of engagement, within a temporary boundary. It is clear from this definition that a system is not only comprised of multiple groups of entities in engagement, but also single entities in engagement. This implies that any two entities in such a relationship form a system, even if those entities form part of a larger system, and notwithstanding the fact that any entity may itself comprise several other entities. The main rationale for this definition is an attempt to remove all hierarchy, value judgement or bias from the basic definition. This allows for greater flexibility in the use of the term.

The term "systemic" in the context of SLL may therefore be defined as "with an understanding of the interdependencies of the multiple dimensions present within a real or conceptual entity". By "real entity", reference is made to corporeal constructs, such as teams, organisations, business units as well as people, structures and bodies of knowledge for learning purposes.

By "conceptual entities", reference is made to theoretical constructs, such as concepts, theories, ideas and paradigms.

3.1.1.2 Leadership: Everybody wants to rule the world

One looks out last from the darkened room
At the shiny desert with spots of gloom
That might be people and are but cedar.
Have no purpose, have no leader.

Robert Frost, On the Heart's Beginning to Cloud the Mind

The vast majority of literature of the concept of 'leadership' aim to identify characteristics of effective leadership, without offering much insight into the process. Very few explore leadership as a curiosity-driven journey.

The term "leadership" may be defined as the people-driven process of migrating a system from the current to the intended or preferred state of that system. It is defined as a people-driven process on the assumption that, unless people are moved to action, no leadership has occurred. This definition underscores the reality of dynamic movement by emphasising the notion of migration, as the construct invokes natural, complex, adaptive systems in flow. Such systems are not adrift. Not aimlessly afloat. The journey is directional and intentional, albeit not entirely linear.

The migration of the system is critical, as simple execution of existing rules or system stagnation does not constitute the leadership thereof. As an example, consider an executive attending a development programme without any attempt to induce any change or worse, imagine the leader's response as simply defending whatever is currently happening at work. This deprives the learning investment of any possible return and suggests that learning itself requires greater leadership.

It may be argued with some validity that the character of the "intended state" of the system is a subjective view. While this argument is conceded, it does not eliminate the existence of leadership purely because subjective measures are used to define the intended state. This implies that leadership of one system is not the same as that of another, as the requirements for the "intended state" of that system may be different.

Note that no value judgement is made on the quality of the "intended state" in the definition. Such a target state is imply preferred over the status quo. The only measure is whether migration towards the intended state is made – not whether the intended state meets the expectations of all concerned. Herein lies a paradox of leadership: it has to propose and articulate the intended state while asking constituents for their proposal for that state. The circularity of the sense-making process is unavoidable in any form of meaningful leadership learning.

3.1.1.3 Learning: Eternal sunshine of the spotless mind

What comes over a man, is it soul or mind –
That to no limits and bounds he can stay confined?

Robert Frost, There Are Roughly Zones

The cognitive realities of learning remain almost mysterious, not least due to the traditional focus on training, with greater emphasis on the role of the trainer than on the experience, learning process and benefit to the executive and systemic stakeholders.

The term "learning" is defined here as the process of transforming information into creatively applicable knowledge, that is, internalising information into a personal system of understanding of the current and anticipated interconnectedness of multiple systems on their migratory journey. One may dispute whether to create applicability or pertinence of knowledge should narrow such a definition. One may wonder whether learning may not occur irrespective of relatedness. For clarity, application in the definition does not aim to mechanise learning. In fact, SLL is diametrically opposed to outdated mechano-cognitive forms of learning.

It is in the transformative engagement with information that the crux of the definition lies. Access to information patently does not constitute learning. Nor does learning occur with the mere exposure to information. The learner must engage with information in a personal relationship with learning content until the content is known, that is familiar, and until the learner has transformed information into knowledge with the potential of modifying personal, stakeholder and system behaviour.

One may further argue that this definition presents a utilitarian approach to learning, and that learning according to this definition is not encouraged for its own sake. Again, this argument is conceded, as learning is defined here within the context of organisational and personal evolution. Organisations invest in the learning process and expect a return on the investment. This places a distinct obligation upon the learner to engage meaningfully with learning content and process, and to translate emerging insights into creative application opportunities and outcomes for the benefit of the organisation and its containing systems. Benefit to the organisation may indeed be derived in an oblique manner through the personal growth of the learner, but ultimately the organisational benefit is a requirement for learning in this context.

It is noteworthy that the learner as leader only leads by the grace of the organisation as containing system that allows the leadership role to exist. The return on learning investment is therefore a requirement of the organisation as investor – another reason for the requirement of applicable knowledge in the definition.

At the same time, the definition calls for a "personal system of understanding". This is based upon the belief that the work of a leader, while executed in conjunction with others, is also possessed of an individual dimension. The leader must ultimately lead in a personal capacity. Only a personal system of understanding can allow for the fulfilment of the individual requirements of the work of the leader, albeit in an interconnected system.

It is clear from the definition of learning above, that it allows for both formal and informal learning.

3.1.1.3.1 The way we were: Knowledge Transience Map

Following from observations made of the observable behaviour of executives in the learning process, a tool has emerged as an instrument for mapping the levels of learning receptiveness and openness towards learning.

Table 1: Knowledge Transience Map

	Known	Not yet known
Will know	Q1: Remains certain	Q2: Becomes certain
Will not know	Q3: Becomes uncertain	Q4: Remains uncertain

The Knowledge Transience Map shows four variations of the movement to and from knowledge and ignorance. It should be noted that this model explains what leaders believe about their own knowledge transience.

The horizontal axis refers to the leader's current knowledge and suggests that there are things that are both known and unknown.

The vertical axis introduces a temporal, anticipatory dimension. It refers to the leader's future knowledge as well as knowledge to which the leader is yet to be exposed.

In **Quadrant 1**, the leader believes that the learning content is already known and that it has and will remain at a suitable level of consciousness. This quadrant explores that domain of knowledge in which the leader's current knowledge will either remain the same or will simply be confirmed by future learning. The value of this quadrant is for the facilitator of learning to know what the leader already knows about matters that are unlikely to change. The risk of this quadrant is that the leader is unreceptive to learning as the leader already assumes sufficient knowledge. The facilitator's responsibility is then not to train leaders on more of the same content, but to examine the level at which content is known and the possible creative application opportunities that may lead from this knowledge.

Quadrant 2 is the typical assumed mode of most learning programmes: the leader does not yet know the content about to be engaged and intends (with varying degrees of motivation and sincerity) to become familiar with it. This mode is described as "assumed" because it is very seldom tested. In this quadrant the facilitator is challenged to facilitate learning content with as much insight of the system of the leader as possible. The risk in this quadrant is that the facilitator enforces the content in a one-directional way based on the belief that the content is worth knowing and that it has relevance to the leader's present. The opportunity is the novelty of the content for the leaders, which could create great enthusiasm and open new avenues for dialogue and exploration.

Quadrant 3 expresses an example of organisations going through change. Leaders learning in this quadrant believe that they know the intended content, but they are sufficiently self-aware to know that their current levels of knowledge are insufficient. The risk here for the facilitator is, similarly, to repeat content already known. This could alienate leaders as they will be unable to see the value of the content to the challenge of the systemic evolution they are experiencing. The opportunity in the quadrant is the emphasis that 'change requires change', that is if change is inevitable, something else in the organisational system will also be required to change, which demands a commensurate change in the levels of knowledge and action of the leader.

Quadrant 4 is every facilitator's greatest challenge. Leaders in this quadrant are aware of their lack of knowledge in an area, but simultaneously believe that the content is simply not worth knowing for the purposes of dissolution of current personal, organisational or contextual challenges. This situation often arises when learning content is being enforced without any prior consultation with leaders about their learning needs and how these needs interact with the system as experienced by the leader. Leaders operating in this quadrant have become disillusioned with the possible value of new content or new, creative application opportunities from content. They may also be so overwhelmed by the challenges they face at work that learning could seem like a meaningless activity that is unlikely to add value, while absorbing valuable time. The risk for the facilitator is enforcing irrelevant learning content (however recent it may be) without recognising the emotional state and learning receptiveness of leaders. The opportunity is an appreciative, in-depth exploration of the systems of the leaders until a learning need is revealed. Should such an opportunity be identified, it will present a powerful incidental learning prospect, which may lead to breakthrough levels of insight and growth.

The Knowledge Transience Map expounded upon above could serve as a catalytic tool for facilitators to determine the level of exploration required of the leader's system, thus increasing the likelihood of impactful learning and creative application opportunities, irrespective of the initial receptiveness levels of leaders to the learning programme.

3.1.1.3.2 The mother of invention: Learning and Innovation

> *So people and things don't pair anymore*
> *With what they used to pair before.*

Robert Frost, The Door in the Dark

While the focus of this book is not to examine the opportunities and processes underpinning the advancement of new products and services in organisations, it is proposed here that the field of innovation is inextricable from the field of learning. The main underpinning for this assumption is that learning is by definition an investigation of the new. A review of only that which is already known may be essential for ensuring continuation, but cannot adhere to the criteria of innovation, which must by definition involve a degree of divergence from the known.

Herein lies yet another paradox of a traditional approach to executive development: it exposes leaders to new concepts in a paradoxical attempt to confirm and emphasise what is already 'known' by them and their organisation. While it is conceded that some programmes aim to inspire innovation, it is not the emphasis of most leadership programmes. This traditional approach not only actively inhibits organisational benefit from potential innovation by leaders who have been exposed to new concepts, but also creates frustration in the minds of talented leaders who had become enthused by the potential and energy of new knowledge.

For organisations to facilitate and advance innovation as business driver and competitive advantage, it is therefore essential that they actively invite and allow for the innovation that emanates from learning. It is proposed here, as an echo of the philosophy underpinning this work discussed above, that talented leaders are inherently divergent in their thinking. This means that they have a developed ability and inclination to explore beyond the realms of their responsibility and control. In fact, these competencies of leaders are often actively sought at the selection phase, only to be frustrated in the limitation of innovation and creative application opportunities resulting from a linear and narrow learning experience.

The model of innovation below shows how innovation requires integration into the very fabric of the organisation. I am certainly not proposing that organisations should allow for random innovation and fund all conceivable ideas (although a brief interlude of such freedom could contribute greatly to a culture of innovation). Rather, due to the reality of financial constraints, SLL necessitates an alignment between the needs of the customer, the innovation culture and the processes that govern innovation in the organisation, together with the needs present and emergent in the institutional context. Such alignment is ideal as content worthy of exploration along the learning journey.

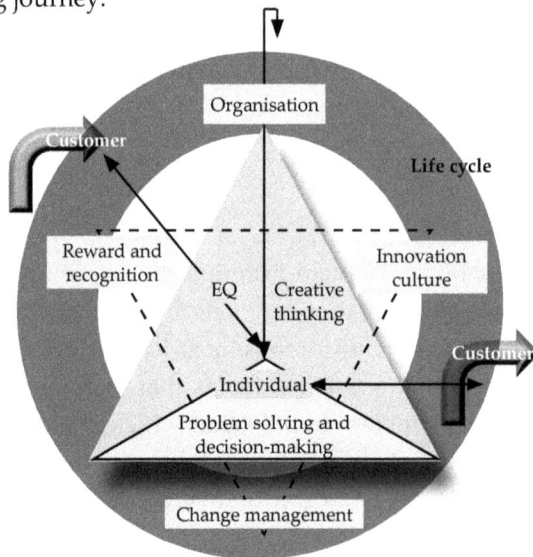

Figure 2: Innovation

It is clear that innovation can be both reactive and proactive, that is reactive to meet the need of customers based on customised designs, and proactive to create and inspire new markets and needs.

The simple model implies that, whether reactive or proactive, innovation should begin and end with the customer – without meaningful engagement of the customer, there is no sustainability of innovative ideas. Note again that a dynamic interpretation is encouraged. In this sense, customer refers not only to current buyers, but also to potential current and future customers.

It further shows that due consideration should be given to the phase of the organisational life cycle the organisation is in and that innovation cannot be limited to random behaviour: a culture of innovation is required. This means that innovative organisations make innovation part of the organisational fibre and dialogue. Innovation in these organisations is not an activity; it is an active business driver. A working definition of culture is suggested: simply that it is the dominant patterns of behaviour, including the rituals of providing or withdrawing recognition, reward and attention.

The model shows the individual at its very core. This is because all organisational action is ultimately taken by individuals, even when those individuals operate in social groups. As the model shows, the organisation needs to develop three critical competencies in individuals:

i.   EQ (Emotional Quotient), that is emotional intelligence, brought to popular dialogue in organisations with the work by Daniel Goleman.[1] This is essential because of the stress, uncertainty and resilience required from the innovation process.

ii.   Creative thinking, that is, the ability to design something new. Without the new, there is simply no innovation.

iii. Problem-solving and decision-making, that is the addressing of a particular organisational challenge, whether in the present or anticipated in the future, and the mental fortitude and intellectual wherewithal to decide on a meaningful course of action.

It is clear from the outline above that an individual or group of individuals exposed to learning, that is knowledge new to those individuals, recruited for their independent-mindedness and advanced problem-solving capabilities, require intellectual room to manoeuvre and the cognitive space to navigate the divergence that will result from their learning.

Attack of the clones: Four clients at the intersection of decision-making

Decision-making is both art and science. Since all decisions are made for the future and most intentions for growth will be realised by a client at some point in the value chain, a deep appreciation of how the clients make decisions may offer new insights for innovation.

Portfolio managers and investment entrepreneurs are known for their ability to design new products and services to meet client demand. But today the interpretation of those demands is more complex than simply responding to a client request. With organisational structures becoming ever more complex, even what is meant by 'client' needs to be revisited if we aspire to the wide-scale adoption of innovative ideas and designs. To maximise client understanding and capitalise on innovation opportunities, investment entrepreneurs (and intrapreneurs) may consider four distinct 'clients' for every intended transaction, based on the multiple client vantage points.

The first and most obvious client is the **buyer**. This is the party who fulfils the transaction of requesting and ensuring that goods or services are transferred. It is often the party who decides which product to procure from which provider. From a personal example as advisor, if a company sells high-technology medical devices to private hospitals, the buyer is the procurement department in the hospital. While the buyer is important, expanding the design orientation to a broader view of the client presents additional avenues for product and service innovation.

A second client is the **payer**. This is the party responsible for disbursing the fee to the provider. Of course, payment may be made in various ways, and because of this, as will be seen below, all four clients are payers. That is because payment is done not only in financial terms, but also in the form of time and anxiety, the latter exacerbated by an era of increasing uncertainty. In the example of a company selling high-tech medical devices, the financial payers are the shareholders of the hospital. It may further be argued that patients of the hospital also pay in the form of their contributions to medical aid funds, and medical aid companies (HMO's in North American parlance) also act as indirect payers.

A more complete understanding of the 'client' is achieved by considering the **user**. This is the entity that will control the deployment of the product or service in order to fulfil a practical or emotional need. In the high-tech example above, the user is the medical doctor who uses the device as part of conducting surgery. The user is crucial as the value of the product or service is practically experienced at the point of application. It is the experience of the user that innovators study with methods like immersion, that is, they immerse themselves into the reality of the user in order to understand the real need and to sense further opportunities for yet further innovation.

The final critical client is the eventual **beneficiary** once the user has applied the product or service. The beneficiary is the party that enjoys the real benefit of the innovation and its full applicability. In the current example, the beneficiary is the patient. Beneficiaries are crucial to the entire intra- and entrepreneurial process, since they often constitute the very party for whom the product or service was required in the first instance: in this example, without the patients, the products would have no value whatsoever.

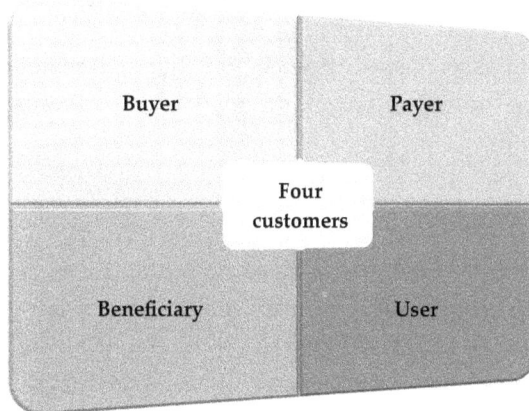

Figure 3: The Four Client Framework

The true complexity becomes exponential with the realisation that multiple parties play multiple roles. Consider, for example, the multiple buyers in a complex value chain at various phases of that chain. Or in the case of the high-tech business above, consider that surgeons are also beneficiaries, as indeed are other contextual role players, such as the families, employers of patients and even the professors who trained the doctors.

In a certain sense, all decisions for growth are meta-decisions, that is they are made based on the most likely decisions of others (in this case clients). As investment entrepreneurs consider alternative product and service designs, the fact that they are correct and clever seems a necessary but certainly not sufficient condition. Multiple clients converge at every transaction, and this presents exciting opportunities for enhanced client insight as foundation for enhanced decision-making and innovation.

3.1.1.3.3   I see your point: Idea Appreciation Continuum

> *The fault must partly have been in me.*
> *The bird was not to blame for its key.*
> *And of course there must be something wrong*
> *In wanting to silence any song.*

Robert Frost, A Minor Bird

Not all ideas are valued at the same level. Nor is quality always the only predictor of adoption. Paradigms generate filters for leaders, which lead to selective curiosity and idea espousal. In engagement with senior leaders in large organisations across the globe, a continuum of idea appreciation on the part of leaders has emerged.

The continuum describes six levels of appreciation, that is, the extent to which leaders internalise the learning content and examine creative application opportunities. The levels are described below.

Level 1: Aesthetic elegance

At this level, leaders appreciate emergent or presented ideas as though they are observing an inanimate object, such as a work of art. Leaders can see the innovation and creativity the ideas represent and give recognition to the insight of the idea, but at this level, there is no systemic resonance with the idea; it is simply the object of description.

Level 2: Schematic resonance

Schema in this sense refers to the total volume of experiences which have shaped the leader's perspective. Similar to paradigms, schemas represent the sum of exposure which creates the filters for engagement with the world. Therefore, at the level of schematic resonance, leaders not only appreciate the quality of the idea, but also find conceptual agreement with it as it achieves touch points within the shared and separate schema. There is a philosophical match between the fundamentals of the idea and the filtering taxonomy of leaders.

Level 3: Contextual relevance

Leaders who appreciate an idea at this level can identify explicit examples of the phenomenon of the idea in their own world experience. Leaders who are sufficiently engaged with the concepts at this level, believe that the ideas accurately reflect or describe some dimension of their experience, which lends credence to the validity of the ideas in their view. The ideas are therefore relevant to the leader's experience, while at previous levels the ideas may be valid, but lack relevance.

Level 4: Creative Opportunity Sensing

At this level of appreciation leaders show a clear sense of an opportunity for potential personal and/or organisational growth. The idea is not only relevant; it presents a realistic chance of adding value. Creative opportunity sensing further generates intellectual excitement about the implications of the idea.

Level 5: Personal Responsibility

At this level leaders experience a personal sense of responsibility for the further exploration, expansion and potential execution of the ideas. These leaders have an emotional drive for and attachment to the emerging ideas.

Responsibility criteria for creative ideas

For leaders to migrate from conceptual blindness to personal responsibility is an intensive journey. Conscious and unconscious drivers wreak havoc with the complex decision to adopt and connect meaningfully with an idea. Especially with more creative ideas, particularly the ideas of others, leaders often test ideas, explicitly or implicitly, on a ladder of hierarchy which has emerged from innovation and creativity consulting:

i.   Viability, that is, can the idea come to life? Can it be born? Is it a viable foetus? Unlike more purist artists, leaders can be so pushed for time, that if the very possibility of existence of the idea in the real world seems unlikely, they seldom indulge in any further exploration. Naturally, the leader's own paradigm, and indeed the collective institutional paradigm, will generate the filters for appraising likely viability.

ii. Feasibility, that is, if we accept that the idea can be born, can it survive infancy? Could it show early promise? Can we imagine that it could learn to walk on its own?

iii. Operability, that is, could it function within the institutional, cultural, legal and technological architecture? Is execution at least possible?

iv. Profitability, that is, could it create and contribute to what we perceive as value, whether financial, reputational, combinational (i.e. yielding synthesis), emotional (especially avoiding angst), temporal (i.e. time-positive), executional or other notions of profit?

Level 6: Enactment

Admittedly a rarity, at this level leaders start taking action even while on the programme. They develop a rudimentary plan and start to identify contingencies to some of the barriers anticipated. This level is more than a personal sense of responsibility; it is the first steps towards implementation. While the previous level stops with an emotional obligation, this level sees leaders designing and even taking the first steps towards accomplishment.

Programmes are often falsely deemed "successful" when few executives have moved beyond Level 1. The fact that there was little criticism and most leaders appreciated the ideas, is almost no indication that any creative application is likely to follow as a result of the learning experience.

3.1.1.4   Ghost protocol: Systemic Leadership Learning (SLL)

Within the context of the definitional properties offered above, the intangible but essential overarching approach to a learning methodology deserves equal attention. As the methodology has evolved, so has its definition deepened in richness. In its evolved form, Systemic Leadership Learning (SLL) may therefore be defined as reciprocal cognitive catalysing in the sense-making migration of systems to a preferred state.

It is reciprocal due to the multi-directional impact of the myriad catalysts in the system. Cognition is explicit because, even if learning is on the subject of emotion, it remains a process of sense-making. Insight into the nature of the system in migration is essential as it underlines the dynamic nature of the multitudinous system present during learning.

Chapter 4

GUARDIANS OF THE GALAXY

Four weddings and a funeral

It couldn't be called ungentle.
But how thoroughly departmental.

Robert Frost, Departmental

At the core of Systemic Leadership Learning is an in-depth understanding of the various systems in an active interplay in the learning process. Each system is in a dynamic marriage with each of the others, and as a result, the prominence of learning content finds its suitable modest place in the evolving ecosystem of learning.

A traditional model of executive development places the organisation in the status of the supra-system, that is, the overarching system into which all other systems should fit - if not naturally, then by force. It implies that the leader's business unit is a sub-system of the organisation, and that the leader is an entity within that sub-system. The leader as learner, then, is traditionally viewed as a kind of subordinated sub-system.

This traditional approach views learning content as a tool that helps the leader to fit into the organisation as supra-system. It supports the implementation of organisational operations by further subordinating the leader to the learning content, with a view to ensure that the leader follows and implements procedures predefined (somewhere) as optimal.

Such a traditional approach further views the facilitator/trainer as the guardian of the learning content. In this model the facilitator/trainer is responsible for the enforcement of the learning content. The job is to ensure that the leaders present understand and accept the content proposed. As one client put it to me: "We will teach them until they like it." This role is often dysfunctionally comfortable for facilitators/trainers as the learning content is their area of academic mastery, and they therefore find the defence of the learning content an easy obligation to fulfil.

The leader is paradoxically perceived to be at the very bottom of the systems hierarchy during the traditional learning process, despite being the main supposed beneficiary. This poses a great challenge to the creative opportunities identified by leaders during learning. It is almost ironic if one considers that the main espoused (yet seldom enacted) aim of the learning process is the very growth of the leader as a driver of organisational performance.

SLL proposes a more harmonious galaxy of the relative status of the systems involved in the learning process. It elevates the status of the leader and proposes that such elevation presents an increase in the likelihood of creative opportunities from learning.

The exposition below shows the respective roles of four key leverage systems as interactive nodes in the learning process, namely:

- The leader,
- The organisation,
- The learning content, and
- The facilitator.

It shows that these systems are in a dynamic interplay in the learning process – and suggests that an in-depth understanding of this interplay presents great opportunity for enhancing learning effectiveness and the resulting identification of creative application opportunities. It shows further the surprising emergence of a learning system, that is, a system that has as its main purpose, the promotion of optimal learning through the exploration of the ideal relationship between the various entities in the system. The learning system thus examined places creative application opportunities at the forefront of such a system.

A review of each major system in the dynamic exchange is done below, which results in a synthesis characterised by creative application opportunities as emerging fractals.

4.1 The last Jedi: The Leader as System

May my application so close
To so endless a repetition
Not make me tired and morose
And resentful of man's condition.

Robert Frost, In Time of Cloudburst

It has already been explained above that the leader is often viewed as a passive recipient in an antiquated *tabula rasa*-type approach to learning that still pervades many development programmes, that is the leader is expected, despite superficial calls by facilitators to "challenge everything", to accept the learning content and theories presented and then to leave the programme in the hope of finding ways of applying the content learnt. Such a traditional system places the leader as a low-status participant in which the organisation is paramount and the facilitator is the guardian of knowledge, charged with the responsibility of ensuring that leaders absorb the content.

In SLL, such a traditional system is criticised for its inherent contradictions: the leader is asserted as the main beneficiary, appointed to the organisation for high levels of talent, intellect and independence, but is then plunged into a largely passive role in the learning context.

More recent approaches have encouraged after-lunch sessions in which leaders stand around tables with flipchart paper and board pens. Learning is assumed to occur partly due to the theatre of the liveliness in the room. Cynically, this is the ideal time for an observer, like a learning project sponsor, to pop in to inspect the learning. It is unclear what such observers are hoping to observe. Learning, after all, is an invisible intellectual process. Suppose that leaders were reflecting in silence during the observer's visit, would that suggest higher or lower levels of learning effectiveness in the mind of the observer?

The theatre - group activity, flipcharts, visiting observers and walls plastered by scribbles – often ignores the fundamental shifts both required and occurring during the learning journey.

SLL proposes that, in the learning situation, the leader is the supra-system, that is, while the leader learns, she engages critically with the content and measures the organisation and context against the content proposed. The leader filters content to find insight into unique challenges with the aim of creating order within the systemic realities of the organisation and its multiple containing systems. This is because every leader is unique and represents one of the multiple partial views of the organisation and greater system. This fact is widely recognised by organisations at the interview and selection stage, where panels debate at length the unique differences between candidates in the matching of candidate leaders to the needs of the organisation and for the justification of their final selection decisions.

But insight into the unique potential contributions of leaders does not appear to enter the learning situation quite as frequently, where predesigned content is force-fed to the very talented leaders that were the subject of rigorous assessment and debate.

The leader joins the organisation with a unique combination of knowledge, skills and attributes, shaped by a unique accumulation of experience and learning. Some of the most salient variables that influence the learning experience include that each executive is characterised by:

- A cognitive style,
- An ethnic culture,
- A mother-tongue language,
- Religious beliefs,
- A family background,
- An educational background, coloured by the type of school and university and the levels of academic achievement attained,
- A unique self-perception,
- A unique level of intellect and problem-solving ability,
- A unique philosophical view of the world, including a philosophy of the world of work and education,
- A distinct personality, determining several factors of engagement with those she will lead,
- A unique professional background, shaped by different organisations, with different leaders and challenges,
- A unique combination of (often multiple) talents,
- A unique view of the working environment and the challenges it faces,
- A unique level and kind of emotional intelligence,
- And, perhaps most significantly, the leader has a unique (and often secret) ambition for the possibilities of change and improvement of the self, organisation and context.

Naturally, the list of variables that differentiate individual leaders is almost endless, but even those listed above make it clear that an off-the-shelf, one-size-fits-all approach to learning content, which is then held up by the facilitator as "the solution" poses enormous difficulty to inspire creative application opportunities for the executive as a result of the learning process.

Naturally, it is not proposed that a unique programme be designed for each executive – the practical realities of operational demands would render such an approach impossible. What is proposed is that leaders are shown a new way of engaging with, I daresay *dancing* with, learning content, colleagues and facilitators, and that facilitators guide the learning process with greater sensitivity and insight into the systemic realities of the learning dynamic. If one considers the multi-dimensional nature of just one leader, and then appreciates that many executive development programmes have several delegates in attendance, the complexity of the systems involved becomes obvious. Such complexity may be further exacerbated by the fact that, in public programmes, such as those at business schools, and learning institutes, leaders often come from different client organisations.

The leader as system is thus placed in a learning situation characterised by a multitude of other systems in constant interaction. This leaves the leader with no alternative but to behave cognitively as though she is her own supra-system, that is all other systems, including the learning content as system, the facilitator as system and the other leaders as systems, are subordinated to the reality of each leader on the programme – the multitude of variables and systems present in the learning situation is so complex that the leader assumes supra-system status during learning in the interest of survival.

This subordination by the leader of all other systems into a unique supra-system is simply the reality, and this reality should be noted by all the other systems participating in the learning process. This is not to suggest that the leader wishes to control the learning process, nor is it implied that the leader makes any value-judgement of the other systems – there is no implied malicious intent by the leader. It is also not implied here that the leader is in any way selfish in the subordination of other systems, or that it is arrogance that is the root cause. Leaders still consider the needs of the organisation; they simply do so with a unique vantage point, understanding, purpose and need. The leader is simply attempting to derive and create sense, meaning and value from the learning process.

4.1.1 Fatal attraction: The Entrenchment Curve

His mood rejecting all his mind suggests.
He paces back and forth and never rests.

Robert Frost, The Bear

It is clear from the discourse above that SLL views the leader as a sovereign system in the learning situation.

Part of the understanding of the leader as system is the personal advancement of that leader within the organisation and in the arch of a career.

Leadership in typical hierarchical organisations is inextricably linked to financial autonomy – the higher the degree of leadership authority (that is legitimate positional power granted by the organisation), the higher the financial reward to the executive.

Therefore, the only way for leaders to become more liberated financially, is to become more entrenched philosophically, behaviourally and structurally, achieved through serving the organisation as system, moving up in the hierarchy of that system and promoting the character of the system; thus, perpetuating the organisation as containing supra-system.

In the process, senior executives are entrenching themselves in an ever-narrowing environment and limiting scope of behaviour, while they are increasingly rewarded for doing so.

Their authority appears to increase, but this is an illusion, since their authority increases only as the scope of decision-making on their identity as their own supra-systems decreases. In the process, the self surrenders its supra-system status to:

- the organisation
- wealth
- status
- fame
- physical comfort and luxury
- positional power
- career advancement (again as defined by the organisation and the economic system).

However, executives do not always recognise this due to some of the following reasons:

- They are financially rewarded.
- They acquire status based upon their positional power in the organisation.
- Their worlds become limited to that of their organisations, that is the boundaries of their systems begin to narrow, even as their apparent authority is expanding. Thus, because they have high levels of authority at work, they may assume that this extends to their entire world and being.

This demonstrates the continuous and ever-increasing entrenchment of leaders into the organisation as supra-system. The experience of such embeddedness presents a barrier to a true systemic understanding of the learning process and it is referred to here as the phenomenon of the *Entrenchment Curve*.

Financial freedom
and authority

Supra-system freedom and authority

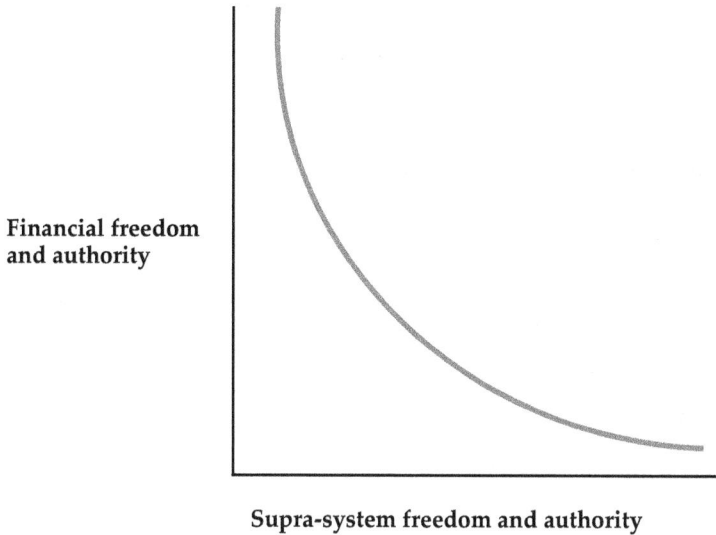

Figure 4: Entrenchment Curve

The entrenchment curve stands in strong contrast to the supra-systemic perspective attributed to leaders in the learning situation through SLL. This is another reason for the lack of creative application opportunities from learning in traditional programmes – leaders can see the glaring organisational and personal gaps in their assessment of their organisations against the learning content proposed, but their level of entrenchment in their organisations is so great that they believe they would have to disengage from the organisation to make a contribution. This is one reason why external consultants often make greater contributions to organisations in terms of thinking – they are rewarded for new thinking, while leaders are rewarded for implementing current thinking.

4.1.1.1 Losing my religion: The Authority Paradox

> *The world has room to make a bear feel free;*
> *The universe seems cramped to you and me.*
> *Man acts more like the poor bear in a cage,*
> *That all day fights a nervous inward rage.*

Robert Frost, The Bear

Related to the entrenchment curve, but with a different emphasis, is the phenomenon of the *Authority Paradox*.

This phenomenon shows that the leader as a system evolves as the level of authority provided to the leader by the organisation increases – a continuous dance of mutually impacting engagement, but with more observable impact on leaders due to their surrender of their supra-system status. It demonstrates that leaders are rewarded for the investment of their physical, emotional and intellectual effort into the organisation by the provision of ever-increasing authority in that organisation. Such increasing authority is evidenced by:

- Larger budgets,
- Bigger teams,
- Greater decision-making authority,
- Longer-term projects,
- Work done on a larger scale,
- Greater apparent independence,
- Cross-functional work,
- Work with potentially greater impact,
- Control over more physical or capital resources,
- Access to others who work at higher levels of authority

One of the anomalies of the increase in authority is the relationship between increased authority and the degree of client contact. There does not appear to be a direct correlation, and in some cases, such as in some retail environments, there even appears to be an inverse proportionality: the higher the level of authority of the leader, the smaller the degree of direct customer contact and the greater the distance between the leader and the customer. This inverse proportionality appears to contradict a commitment by many organisations that the customer is their first priority, since those talented members of staff who perform best appear to be rewarded for their brilliance through reduced contact with the customer, leaving the customer to engage only with those who have remained at the lowest rungs of the organisation, and are sometimes awarded the lowest forms of remuneration.

Whatever the characteristic of the higher levels of authority awarded to the leader, that authority brings with it an interesting paradox for the self-actualisation of the leader: as the leader's authority in the organisation increases, so also do the levels of responsibility increase. An increase in responsibility means a commensurate increase in the focus and energy required to meet the responsibilities. As a result, the leader calls upon the reserves of free time and personal goals to fulfil these responsibilities. What happens as one of the ripple effects in the system is that the leader spends less time and effort on personal goals and ambitions, and more time on organisational goals and ambitions. In some cases, the organisation even has a code of behaviour for executives that dictates required behaviours.

The authority paradox therefore lies in this: as the leader increases in authority inside the organisation, so the leader decreases in authority in terms of the fulfilment of personal goals and ambitions. Some senior leaders have even commented that they lead two lives: one in which they behave like the model of leadership in their organisations, and one in which they try to redeem their own identities in their private lives.

Millennials have been the most vocal and expressive on the traps of the entrenchment curve and authority paradox. They have espoused alternative models and perspectives of careers, including:

i.   Multiple careers

ii. Non-linear careers

iii. Career breaks

iv. Side hustles

v.   Job-hopping

vi. Digital nomadism, especially as the result of the Covid pandemic.

These new models have begun to challenge traditional outlooks on the psychological contract between the leader and the organisation.

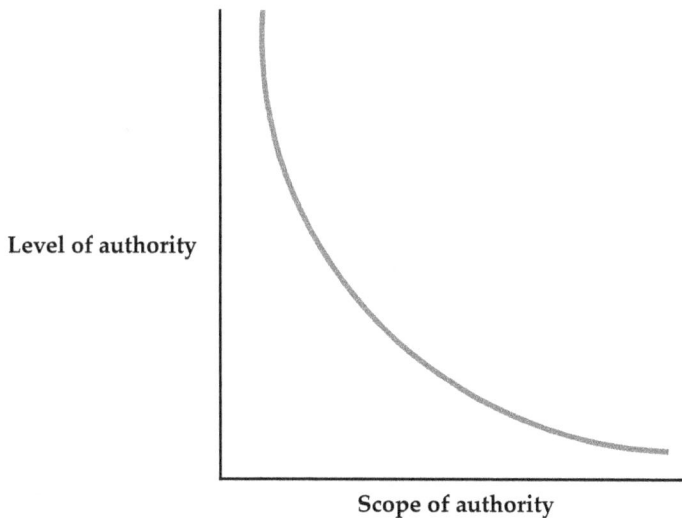

Figure 5: Authority Paradox

The reality of the authority paradox contributes to the insight of the leader as system and encourages the designers and facilitators of learning to appreciate the systemic challenges and pressures facing leaders.

4.1.1.2   Insurgent: The Responsibility of the Executive in SLL

The lowly pen is yet a hold
Against the dark and wind and cold
To give a prospect to a plan
And warrant prudence in a man.

Robert Frost, A Blue Ribbon at Amesbury

There is a clear implication in the discourse above that various systems are engaged in the learning process and that the learning situation poses a number of paradoxical realities for the leader. Despite these realities, the leader is still accountable for the identification of creative application opportunities from the learning experience.

The traditional view of the role of the leader in the learning situation appears to be one that requires memory and participation. Memory is required for recall of theory and participation is required (under good traditional conditions) for a discussion about the extent of the problems in the leader's organisation and how this (for whatever reason) relates to the content.

In SLL leaders are therefore encouraged to move beyond the insight of the facilitator and use their own system as the vantage point for learning. This is not to suggest that leaders should reject the input of the facilitator (unless it is patent nonsense), but that they should continuously scan the dance of their own minds with the learning content for emerging creative application opportunities. Such continuous scanning should occur instantaneously, that is while the content is being engaged – the theory that leaders will digest content and apply it later seems one that remains largely unproven.

Approaches such as Action Learning do promote higher levels of application from learning content. This is certainly the case as leaders are actively encouraged to discover creative application opportunities from learning content. But one criticism that may be lodged against Action Learning, is that it claims to use the reality of the leader as the vantage point for learning, while in practice it is the organisational challenges that form this foundation, which are reinterpreted to fit within the containing system of the expertise of the expert faculty facilitating the programme. In traditional educational Action Learning, learning content is still the dominant system, into which the leader must organise personal and organisational challenges. More recent developments in action learning have started with an organisational challenge and built content around the perceived business *problematique*. Even this evolution of Action Learning places the organisation, rather than the leader at the centre of the learning process, while it is ironically the leader who is required to interpret the often-predefined problem as well as the learning content proposed as solution.

In SLL it is proposed that the leader be viewed as the supra-system, that is, the leader selects and articulates the challenges to be addressed within a learning system that respects the leader as system. It is the responsibility of leaders to identify challenges as well as opportunities and, significant in this approach, to define their own role for the dissolution of the challenge as an active leverage point within the complexity of multiple containing and interwoven systems. This last requirement is critical, as several leaders comment that, while they appreciate the learning content proposed, they simply lack the authority to take any significant action on the challenges identified, beyond the possibility of proposing a solution to those who do have such power. Even leaders who may appear to have the power to change things, such as members of executive committees and boards, often comment that their authority is limited to the box represented by their portfolio – a thoroughly fragmented and un-systemic reality that further limits the potential value from traditional development programmes.

Take heed that the call is not for the direct translation of content into application. The leader first has to internalise the learning content into meaningful insight about the systemic realities of the challenges faced in the systems of the leader and self, before progressing to the identification, design and/or selection of a creative application opportunity.

The leader is further charged in SLL with the responsibility of provoking the facilitator and other participants to explore the unique challenges of the organisation. The practical reality is that detailed learning needs analysis is not always possible, but there is a clear opportunity for the leader to continue the needs analysis while attending the course and to communicate the results to the facilitator in order to guide the facilitation of the process. In such a learning dynamic, the supra-system of leader leads the facilitator in SLL. In fact, every leader in the learning space becomes a co-facilitator, continuously making sense of insights gained while learning and co-creating the learning outcomes with colleagues.

The leader then has to go beyond the content proposed and examine the systems implications of the learning content for that leader as well as for the organisation. Such emerging implications should also be continuously communicated as part of the creation of a more realistic insight for the facilitator, who acts as occasional node within the system.

Beyond influence on the facilitator and continuous scanning of the learning content implications for creative application opportunities, the leader is further required to explore personal transformation and individualised meaning formation. One of the ways that this may be done is by using story. According to the principle of story, the leader is encouraged to share personal experiences of the reality of the challenges faced, the opportunities identified and the application and systemic implications of these opportunities. The leader must explore, in a highly personal way, those creative learning application opportunities not only for the organisation, but also for the self. This is critical for the simple reality that, as the organisation evolves and morphs its structures, and as people and strategies change, the leader will remain her only unique constant, that is for the leader with high levels of self-awareness, the entity most knowable as the containing and related systems evolve continuously, is the depth and character of the self.

Artificial intelligence is set to have a significant impact on the energy for self-knowledge. Already, as argued above, most leaders know more about how to use ChatGPT than they know about their own forms of intellectual processing.

4.1.1.3   Casino Royale: Return on Learning

While leaders may understand the concepts proposed in the learning content, and even see the possibilities for creative application, they stop short of actual creative application on the grounds that they are likely to face some opposition from others in the organisational ecosystem. Other barriers leaders often observe in the learning situation is that there is a good reason *not* to apply the content, which is typically defended by some degree of complexity in the organisation, or by the observation that some risk will be incurred should they attempt application. On the dark underbelly of organisational culture, leaders are even motivated by the prospects of reward for making the status quo work rather than changing it. Performance management systems are often designed based on the assumption that targets set a year ago simply require an above inflation increase to become the targets for the next year. This means that there is often significant delay in reviews of the systemic implications of performance targets. Such perspectives naturally limit the possibility of responsive creative application opportunities emerging from learning and have a direct impact on return on learning investment from the learning experience.

It is a bizarre contradiction continuously encountered in international executive development that leaders are well-informed on the pervasive realities of change, but that they judge change as being the responsibility of others or of the context. They know things are changing, but often push for 'just one more year' of this kind of growth. In a dreadful mix of metaphors, one senior executive told me "I know we have to face the music, but for now I just want to kick the can down the road."

A simple yet impactful model has emerged that challenges such scepticism about the likelihood of successful creative application and encourages leaders to explore in more detail the implications of the opportunities available to them. Named the

Learning Outcome Parameters Assessment (LOPA), the model explores the best- and worst-case scenarios of application of the learning content.

The diagram below shows that the LOPA examines four scenarios, based upon the best and worst results of success and failure.

Table 2: Learning Outcome Parameters Assessment

	SUCCESS	FAILURE
BEST RESULT	Q1	Q2
WORST RESULT	Q3	Q4

The scenarios presented by the LOPA are as follows:

Quadrant 1 explores the best result of successful application of the learning application opportunity identified. The articulation of the content of this quadrant alerts leaders to the full scope of the opportunity that presents itself with successful application. It is an interesting observation that, once leaders have examined in detail the possible benefit of application for them and their organisations, they are less likely to accept minor barriers as legitimate reasons to prevent application.

A reason why leaders may fail to explore the best result from successful application, may simply be due to the novelty of the idea with which learning confronts the leaders. Consider, for example, the role of team ethos for leaders. Many leaders simply leave ethos to the domain of emergence or chance. Once leaders become aware of their potential role in designing the ideal ethos, the opportunities represented by a conducive ethos become clear.

Quadrant 2 explores the best results that may emerge from failure or from the unsuccessful application of creative opportunities identified. Executives often find it challenging to populate this quadrant, and are tempted to confuse it with Quadrant 4. The quadrant asks this question: Are there benefits to be derived even from a failed application? May we not benefit even if we are unsuccessful? In rigidly hierarchical organisations where failure is simply not tolerated, the question is often met with dazed confusion. In such organisations, however, innovation is typically not actively encouraged. Such low tolerance for failure are often found in organisations, that it remains a surprise to many that benefits are often derived even from imperfect projects. Not least of these benefits is the enormous wealth of learning, especially if done rapidly. Leading innovative organisations have the capacity to leverage failure and respond with alacrity to emerging insights and opportunities.

Quadrant 3 explores the worst result of success. At first glance, this appears negative - it may highlight elements that may detract from motivation and create detrimental attitudes. While this possibility exists, the main value of the exploration of this quadrant is to remain rational about the value of possible success. Quadrant 3 thus introduces a degree of sobriety into the excitement that may be created by the identification of creative application opportunities and makes leaders more conscious of possible risks. This does not suggest that creative application should not proceed; it simply argues for a more circumspect evaluation of the risks and systemic implications involved.

Consider, for example, the fallout from a restructure. Often the new organogram is so appealing in its leanness that leaders are seduced by the apparent simplicity. Exploring some of the systemic implications and ripple effects on the downside often leads to insight which would have remained in the blind-spot of gung-ho over-optimism.

Quadrant 4 is to some degree an intensification of Quadrant 3. It does not attempt to balance risk with benefit, but asks brutally honest questions about the possible damage that may be caused in the case of failure. While at first glance this may again appear to introduce a negative slant, leaders naturally migrate to this quadrant. It appears that the psychological power of the negative is difficult to avoid. It may therefore be raised as recognition of their concerns, as a means of ensuring integrity in the evaluation of learning parameters. Once they observe this quadrant in the context of the other three, leaders will have developed a more comprehensive assessment of the value and weighting of Quadrant 4.

An example of this is the classical forms of risk assessment. The likelihood of a negative result is juxtaposed with the resultant impact to give a clearer (albeit nonetheless opaque) insight of the scale of the potential risk.

In the study of Strategic Foresight, a contradictory insight emerges from Quadrants 3 and 4. The aphorism appears to be this: the more the overshoot scenario is explored, the less likely it is to occur. In this sense, the futurist (who dares not make predictions in classical Futures Studies) often wishes to be wrong. And the results are counterintuitive. By positing a possible collapse scenario, actors are alerted to its probability, and take preventative action, thus reducing its probability. This principle is akin to the Expectation Theory of John F. Muth in Economics in the 1960's.

Another interesting dynamic observed in terms of the leader as system, is that leaders who converge in a room for the purposes of learning form a new emerging system. The collection of various leaders creates a system with its own rules (mostly tacit) and structures (mostly fluid). This new system continuously evolves in its own structure and rules and resembles a transient, at times elusive system that will significantly influence the key outcomes of the learning process.

Dimensions of considering this bounded and temporary system include the hierarchical levels of various delegates. In an attempt to examine this dynamic, two rudimentary questions at the start of learning programmes show the relationships of those in the new learning system, namely,

i.   Who here has a manager that is also here?

ii. Who here has a member of staff who is also here?

These questions are usually met with laughter, alluding to the implicit power differential between hierarchical levels that undoubtedly have an impact on the free flow of open and honest dialogue and the emergence of learning insights and consequential creative application opportunities.

Worthy of consideration in the group composition constituting the newly created system is whether the parties responsible for implementation of creative learning application opportunities are present in the room. This provides great elucidation for the probability of creative application opportunities from the learning experience.

Gender, race, age, disability, personalities and overriding philosophies may also play a role, and they are at very least worthy of noting.

Whatever the composition of the group as new system, each leader remains a discreet system, held in supra-system honour in the mind of each leader. Leaders in the learning process should take the responsibility for exploring the best and worst results from success and failure of the creative application opportunities that become apparent as a result of learning. This will allow leaders to move away from an emotional response to learning content towards a realistic assessment of the risks and benefits to be derived from an attempt to apply their emerging insights.

4.2   The Empire Strikes Back: The Organisation as System

The focus of this book is on the relationship between the organisation as system and the leader as system, for the purposes of imaginative learning.

A critical perspective offered by SLL is that the organisation is not without qualification assumed to be the supra-system during learning. As stated above, the traditional model of executive development views the organisation as the system into which all actors must fit. It is the all-encompassing, all-embracing unit, with parameters of behaviour for all who wish to benefit from its systemic impact.

In SLL it is proposed that, during the learning situation, the leader is a discreet and sovereign supra-system. This poses interesting questions about the role of the organisation in the process where leaders learn. Leaders are appointed for their acquired experience and skills, but also for their learning potential, responsiveness to change and proactive dissolution of anticipated problems. Similarly, organisations are appraised by investors based on their past performance, but with a clear expectation of their ability to grow, respond to markets and proactively create innovative value. The intersection between the systems of the leader and the organisation is somewhat predictable when the only requirement is for the implementation of predefined processes, but where they intersect at the point of growth for both systems, the movement and evolution in each system redefines the rules of engagement between them. Such rules are equally emergent in nature, and therefore not yet codified by the time learning is expected to occur.

The organisation as a system has its own rules and architecture. It has predefined objectives and processes and aims to predict a minimum system output in terms of revenue, driven by a predefined conception of its market, customers, talent, technology and contextual dynamics. Consider, for example, the phenomenon of "the company way". This is a phrase used by organisations to explain the intentionally mythical quality of their organisational culture, which they believe to be one differentiator in the competitive landscape.

While some organisations take great pains to define their "company way", others simply refer to it in the belief that all employees know intuitively what it might mean.

The reason this is significant to the process of learning for leaders is that it is assumed to underwrite the tacit, implicit rules of the organisation as system. Unwritten as these rules of the system may be, they sculpt and perpetuate a culture that governs the behaviour of leaders and consequently the behaviour of their staff and stakeholders in their broader ecosystem. Another significance of the "company way" for executive development is that those business owners and senior executives who invite their company leaders to learn, often believe that the implicit rules that govern the organisation are clearly understood, while in fact they may be proven during learning to be ill-defined, disjointed pieces of random dialogue that do little to guide leaders on their learning journey. This phenomenon of uncertainty regarding "the company way", coupled with the earlier observation that talent is inherently divergent, together with the innovation sparked by exposure to new knowledge for the leader, create a learning situation in which an almost infinite number of creative learning application opportunities may emerge. I conclude from this analysis that every time a learning situation occurs, it is an opportunity for the organisation to evolve with meaningful input from its talented, creative leaders. The degree to which this opportunity is seized, will depend on the organisation's ability to allow for the divergence of the executive's thinking as new knowledge enters the leader's system and integrates with a myriad schemas of learning gained from years of divergent and occasionally random experience.

4.2.1. Great Expectations and the Power of Purpose

Having examined the system of the leader in the learning process and having concluded that the leader holds a self-perception of being the supra-system during learning, and further having examined the system of the organisation and concluded that every learning situation invites an evolution of that system, it is imperative to explore further the nature of expectations held by both systems.

All systems are possessed of a purpose. This purpose, in 21st century organisational behaviour, is typically encapsulated in a statement such as the vision. More ambitious organisations, such as those referred to as 'exponential', embrace a purse which is grand in scale and noble in intent, referred to by Silicon Valley as a Massive Transformative Purpose.

But even systems without an explicit purpose possess a sense of purpose. One might distinguish between the intentional purpose and the consequential purpose. The former is the institutional intent socialised and percolated in organisational discourse. It is akin to what the futurist Sohail Inayatullah describes as the litany, and which the Harvard organisational theorist Chris Argyris denotes as the Espoused Theory. It is a recitation and supplication of the institutional temple. By contrast, the consequential purpose is that which results from the de facto behaviour of actors in the system. By this definition all systems achieve their purpose at all times. This is because purpose is an emerging quality of the system. It does not belong to any of the parts, but is nevertheless produced by the interaction of a specific set of parts behaving in very particular ways. Systems, then, always deserve their results, beneficial or disadvantageous, because the results are produced by the system itself. For this reason, executive development must conscientise its participants to the course correction required to migrate towards the assumed preferable purpose of the system.

It appears, from experience across the globe, that leaders expect to learn relevant content, but more importantly expect to be allowed to navigate their own systems in relation to that of the organisation.

It is also clear that organisations have certain expectations from leaders who participate in a learning process that the organisation has sponsored. Such organisational expectations are often limited in scope to the current challenges facing the organisation. While discussions are often expansive, results are typically incremental, if discernible. Only on rare occasions, when innovation is specifically pursued, are opportunities explored alongside burning challenges. This organisational tendency to respond to current challenges and ignore opportunities during the learning process creates a mundane learning experience for the talented executive. This means essentially that leaders are expected to become more comfortable with the "as is", rather than being invited to navigate their way to the preferred state of the system.

The nature of successful programmes lies in the ability of the leader to think creatively, solve problems and access opportunities, current and anticipated. This directly addresses the kind of competencies for which the leader was first appointed. The talented executive therefore relishes the opportunity to exercise those competencies.

In the logic of SLL, leaders should be permitted, and even encouraged, to redesign the organisation whenever they learn. What is proposed is that there is a possibility to do so in response to challenges as well as opportunities. This further requires that organisations are honest with leaders about the expectations they have from the learning situation. Such honesty will prevent the frequent occurrence of disillusionment with the learning process and the resultant inhibition leaders experience due to the organisational expectation for the incremental improvement of current processes.

The essential nature of the explicit articulation of mutual expectations is further driven by the current point at which organisations find themselves in the evolution towards a balance of power – the current power differential favours organisations and leaders that habitually respond based on tacit personal expectations, both of themselves and of the psychological contract with the organisation.

4.2.2 Double indemnity: Value, Values and Valuations

Organisations as social systems are burdened with a host of interrelated obligations in the 21st century. They must, still, deliver shareholder value. This requirement, present since the dawn of business, has been exacerbated by investors' need for so-called 'sustainable' growth. The Club of Rome, in its first report in 1972, Limits to Growth[2], has suggested that growth, at least in its classical form, is not sustainable by definition. Such definition is founded upon two key premises: 1. The finite nature of natural resources, and 2. the increasing probability of systemic planetary collapse, from which recovery will be unlikely, should certain systemic tipping points be breached.

Executives of the future will have to grapple with the reality of how value is perceived and generated. As an example, I argued in a recent paper for the Club of Rome that alternative conceptions of value may be applied to so-called debt-for-nature swaps, a financial mechanism in the global financial industrial complex in which countries with the simultaneous curse and blessing of disproportionate levels of debt and vast ecological assets, may trade one for the other. In that paper, which inspires the title of this section, Value, Values and Valuations, I suggested examples of an axiological taxonomy of value for such 21st century transactions, including:

1. **co-existence value** - the mere human experience of knowing that biodiversity continues to exist has a psychological and socio-environmental value

2. **political value** - political parties who seek to acquire power on the 'green ticket' value the opportunity to demonstrate their policy proposals

3. **bequest value** - the knowledge that future generations may inherit ecological assets

4. **option value** - a type of call option which may allow the creditor access to the future use of natural resources even if that potential use is currently unclear

5. **hygiene value** - wealthy nations benefit from the maintenance and mitigation effects of the remaining ecological assets as compensation for the ecological damage produced by those nations.

In addition, 21st century organisations must serve society. They are encouraged to combat inequality and contribute to the eradication of global poverty. And, thus argues the activist, they must do so in ways other than mass employment to produce profits. Furthermore, they must act as caretakers of the emotional and physical well-being of their staff and associated actors in their ecosystem. The dramatic escalation in environmental, social, and governance (ESG) investment is but one indicator of this institutional imperative.

One dilemma is that classical for-profit organisations are masters at managing the systemic flow of value and cost. Such organisations optimise the internalisation of all value, whether in the form of revenue, reputation, security or another form. Simultaneously, they externalise all cost and potential damage to the social and planetary context, where such damage may be diffused, and the burden averaged out to the society as a whole. This is one reason for increasing inequality: value is directed to flow inward, while cost is directed to flow outward. In this way, value is centralised, and the cost of damage distributed. Because actors in the system are already differently resourced, the averaging out of the shared burden effects those with limited resources in the most significant way. The low resource base of the majority also renders them less resilient, which further reinforces the circularity of vulnerability.

The alternatives are not clear. Despite the rise in ESG investment, companies have gamified the process. Measurement instruments remain unclear. Greenwashing is the order of the day.

One key responsibility of the organisation is to develop a systemic understanding of the learning process. This means that the organisation requires insight into the implications for learning if indeed the leader possesses a self-perception of supra-system status during the learning process. The most significant implication here is that the organisation should clarify expectations from learning and enquire from the leader the opportunities that the learning process has revealed. Executives in influential organisations are therefore frequently burdened by the cognitive dissonance of creating value for themselves, their organisations, their communities and the planet. Scenarios are emerging for alternative conceptions of how value is created. This is most notable in so-called developing economic regions, such as Africa, where the context is significantly swayed by the suitability of policy to traditional business value creation. One may question a priori the very nomenclature of economies as 'developing'. The dominant paradigm appears to be that so-called 'developed' economies have set the standard for all others; as if those economies should be the ideal model of a normative future for those that are still 'developing'. It is patently and painfully obvious that all economies are developing, including those referred to as 'developed'. In fact, there may be sound argument to be made that, while it is recognised that 'developed' economies have contributed the vast majority of carbon for the acceleration of climate change, they are in desperate need of developing levels of meaningful interconnectedness with society and the ecosystem.

The Lost Kingdom: Alternative Scenarios for the SEA-EV Valuation Model

For the wealth of Africa to emerge from its dormancy, the way in which systems of finance and economics apply their methods of valuation must be reinvented. In a misguided attempt to be exact, traditional valuation methods have been characterised by paralysing positivism in which only the observable and numerically calculable have qualified for status worthy of valuation. Such reductionist mindsets have further exacerbated the pervasive separation of sciences and the drive towards hyper-specialisation. Matters of finance have become disjointed from economics. This is contrary to the view that economics has been financialised. The basis for the segregation argument posited here is that the field of finance used to fit neatly into that of economics. If the latter is viewed as both the product of and residing within the domain of the Social Sciences, then finance has divorced itself entirely from either measuring or contributing to the science of being human. Both these fields have formed even greater chasms between themselves and the human experience, with the concomitant alienation of appreciation of the impact on natural ecosystems. While the contribution has been the vast expansion of epistemological content, it has come at the expense of holistic understanding, often characteristic of ancient African wisdom. As the role of Africa within the complex reality of global dynamics has unfolded, more systemic approaches have become essential for grasping the limitations to the proffered wisdom of spreadsheets.

In a recent paper to the Club of Rome, this author underscored the importance of integrating the erstwhile disjointed concepts of value, values and valuations into perspectives on Africa. Financial conceptions of value must assimilate deeply human notions of values, and the implications for methods of valuation are significant.

Lost in translation: Towards workable definitions

The nomenclature of the financial system and the economic system are not simply interchangeable. In one sense, **Finance** may be conceived of generally as the flow of capital, including the acquisition and overall management thereof. The acquisitional dimension is typically characterised by attempts to secure and direct such flows towards centralised, personalised control, while the management dimension is mainly concerned with the achievement of focused capital growth within a system of governance. By contrast, **Economics**, in an attempt to describe behavioural dimensions included in the pursuit of the fulfilment of needs within conditions of constraints, provides the social atmosphere within which such capital is distributed. In this sense, then, (to use a metaphor central to Africa), finance is the river system in the water cycle of economics. This distinction is critical because of the financial risks of practices in global financial markets akin to exploitative arbitrage, often enabled by the evaluative ineptitude of economics.

If **risk** is treated as the probability of realising expected returns, and the harmful consequences of failure, then financial risk constitutes the likelihood of misdirected capital flows. To detect such misdirection, an initial intention is a prerequisite for identification of deviations. One key risk for Africa, therefore, may be found in the degree of clarity of intent. While Agenda2063 presents an inspirational expression of intent, the commensurate dissolution for capital flows in support of that intent remains opaque.

In order to counter such vagueness, a system of rigorous **governance** is typically introduced. But a critical conceptual conundrum is found in the very nature of governance: in an attempt to introduce controls to ensure compliance to legal and ethical standards for longer-term advancement, a system of governance, however intricate, often has the counterintuitive consequence of enforcing and perpetuating little more than the status quo. Therefore, even the most stringent forms of transparency-driven systems of governance often discourage deviation from the known. As a result, governance, well-intentioned and principled, should not be regarded as the crucible for innovation. For when the present and future are thus juxtaposed, the implicit and patently fallacious assumption is that an enforcement of the status quo (typically derived from the past) is the most effective way of achieving an alternative desired future. When the outcomes of such a financial system are then expressed in the economic system through outdated measures of rudimentary averages like GDP or income per capita, the undesirable status quo is consolidated and advanced rather than reinvented.

What's in a name?

The nomenclature of 'emerging' economies is akin to that of 'developing' ones. The terms are often used interchangeably. As illustrated above, both 'developing' and emerging' economies arrear, typically, to be defined negatively, that is they are described as those which are not developed, or not yet as developed as their 'developed' counterparts. This is particularly problematic when 'developing' and 'emerging' economies are automatically characterised in the biased taxonomy as belonging to the 'third world', as if a universal ranking truth places the 'developed' economies as belonging to a primary group known as the 'first' world. The *problematique* of the naming conventions is glaringly uncomfortable and holds overtones of superiority and undertones of derision. The taxonomy is clearly the product of so-called Western minds. This is evident from the traditional absence of a group described as 'emerged' economies. The logic appears to be that 'emerging' economies are only named thus as they represent the extent to which a sovereign is starting to present the qualities associated with the silently emerged. For that reason, it may be argued that 'emerging' refers to those economies which are starting to demonstrate investment prospects for Western investors and global influence through their rising levels of democracy, literacy, innovation, political influence and other traits deemed desirable by those of global influence.

The taxonomy is exacerbated by the use of the term 'global south', which appears to be experiencing something of a revival. This term gained popularity after the second world war as an alternative to the use of 'Third World'. It is typically used to denote countries with shared characteristics, typically associated with the so-called emerging economies described above, particularly those viewed as economically disadvantaged. It is often erroneously equated with geographical location, particularly south of the equator. The latter implication is that countries to the south of the equator are therefore automatically somehow economically inferior to those of the north. In recent times it has been applied in scholarship to refer to political and ideological alignment in a network of the formerly colonised. The latent implication is often that mere location in the northern hemisphere implies a kind of economic flourishing. Les than subtly implied in the general discourse, especially in developmental studies of the Western paradigm, is the implication that GDP per capita is rendered low in the 'global south' by the unsustainable growth in population.

Many are therefore surprised to discover that such simple classification adds more confusion than clarity. Consider, for example, that Africa, boxed firmly in the global south, has the majority of its countries (33 of 54 according to the UN or 55 according to the AU) residing in the northern hemisphere. Furthermore, the smallest Valeriepieris circle, created in 2015 by Singaporean professor Danny Quah, is centred on Mong Khet in Myanmar - clearly in the northern hemisphere. More people on earth live inside this 2050-mile circle than outside it – a staggering concentration of population.

Planning development and development planning

For many of these so-called emerging economies, then, it may even be of significance to revisit the very notion of **development planning**. In this endeavour, a meta-planning perspective is essential, that is a developed view on the philosophy and methodology which will guide developmental planning. Consciousness of the meta-planning dimensions may act as early-warning system, since many politicians in developing economies have abused the notion of development planning to serve their personal nefarious objectives. Populism is the most obvious technique for such subversion: by appealing to the largest segment of the population and blaming their woes on a contiguous but different group, insidious politicians have misdirected development planning for personal gain. They present messiah-like messages of salvation and blame any currant malaise on a phantom dominant ideology. One example from personal experience is the ideological contention that, although unemployment is rife, government cannot be more business friendly since it might cause jobless growth – as if the inverse of growthless jobs might be more preferable! The claims of the saviour politician are as absurd up close as they are from a distance.

One test of the bona fides of such opportunistic political leaders is to ask about the extent to which planning is futures-oriented or whether the patters of the proposed so-called development plans reflect reactiveness coupled with outrage. Another technique for insight is whether planning is teleological or oppositional. The former encourages a future state, while the latter reacts to the status quo ante, and involves a romanticised version of past prior to a time where the presumed antagonists on the border of the populist group commenced their regime. Both state capacity and government intentionality are therefore essential in development planning.

As a form of planning, development planning is concerned with accelerating the perceived remedial requirements of an economy in order to create a self-organising, thriving economic dispensation.

No Way Home: Towards alternative futures

Both finance and economics have flourished, in part, due to the mindset of traditional strategy. In this mindset, the status quo is measured, after which a so-called 'to be' state is articulated. From the perspective of the futurist, strategy has made itself guilty of the same reductionism as finance and economics, by reducing the complexity of interrogating the future to the identification of a single future: the ideal. For the futurist, longer-term strategy starts with the recognition and imagination of multiple explorative futures. One methodology for the articulation of multiple futures is found in scenario processes. Far from being predictions, scenarios attempt to sketch manifold futures in an attempt to conduct a mental rehearsal within a range of possibility. Such an approach has significant implications for **risk** as it often casts a light on the variability of potential risks. It also aids the identification of **opportunity**, which arises as an emerging property of interacting drivers of possibility.

In exploring African futures, scenarios offer an integrated perspective on the critical drivers of Africa's key assets: its people and natural ecology, within the context of imperatives for wealth creation (as one possible inverse of poverty alleviation). These drivers of African futures each operate on a range of possibility, which may be articulated in various ways. Drivers will be examined for their **potential impact** on the future of the continent.

The sociological dimension

People dynamics in Africa may be described as the sociological dimension. Due to the incontestable African demographic profile, the range of possible impact may be regarded to exist on a continuum from high to extreme.

The ecological dimension

This reflects the future health of Africa's natural assets, both green and mineral, and the way these are both leveraged and protected for the future of the continent. Africa's dominant share of earth's remaining mineral and ecological resources is well documented. On a range of significance, it is therefore reasonable to anticipate a similarly high to extreme impact on Africa's future.

The economic dimension

In broad terms, this dimension is meant here to refer to the financial well-being of the citizens and nations of Africa. It holds connotations of empowerment, choice, freedom and confidence. The latter, that is sure-footedness and self-assuredness, is expressed in myriad ways by the classical triad of the economy.

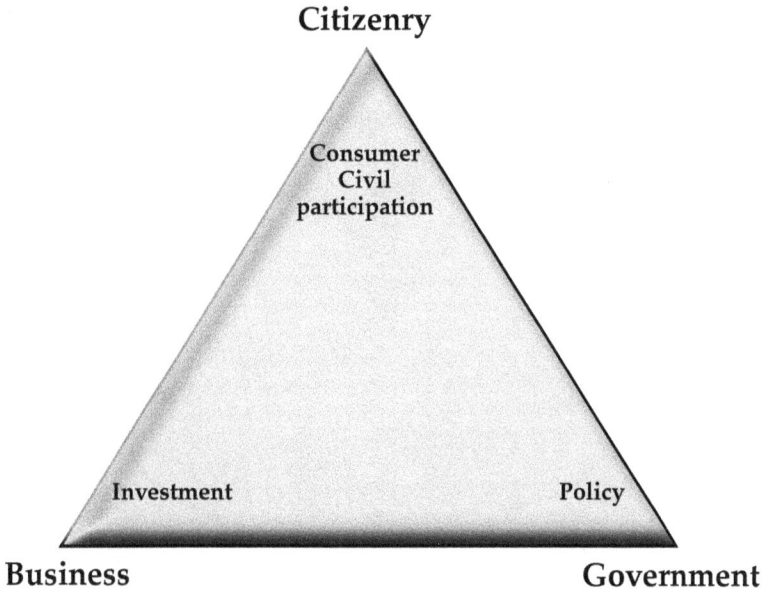

Figure 6: The confidence triad

i.   Citizenry: citizens are patently more than mere 'consumers'. They are human in the fullest sense of the word, and are defined as 'citizens' only by the randomness of their birth or their geographical choices. But all citizens are also consumers. The imagination will be stretched by the notion of a citizen who does not somehow acquire and consume goods and services. In this narrow identity as consumer, citizens express confidence in three main ways. Firstly, confident citizens participate in civil society on the belief that change remains possible. The second expression is active participation in the economy through consumption and production. Of late, the latter behaviour has invited criticism from those with a greater planetary and egalitarian consciousness, but a degree of consumer spending continues to suggest confidence. The third is that the better resourced citizenry retain and even increase their investments in local bourses.

ii. Business: this sector expresses confidence through investment, which presents in the form of employment, procurement (particularly through capital expenditure) and, in a global environment, the strategic retention of assets within the sovereign in which it was generated.

iii. Government: Governments express confidence through non-partisan state capacity and a high degree of policy certainty.

The inverse of the Confidence Triad is unbearable: limited consumer spending, inadequate creative productivity, withdrawal from local bourses, declining investment with capital flight, and policy uncertainty.

In order to produce meaningful explorative futures, high quality scenarios demand referential simultaneity. Simply put, this means the concurrent acknowledgement of drivers of such futures. Such intellectual honesty ensures that bias is minimised when painting possible futures. For that reason, scenarios are often visually illustrated by intersecting drivers. Figure 7 below illustrates the complexity of such interconnectedness.

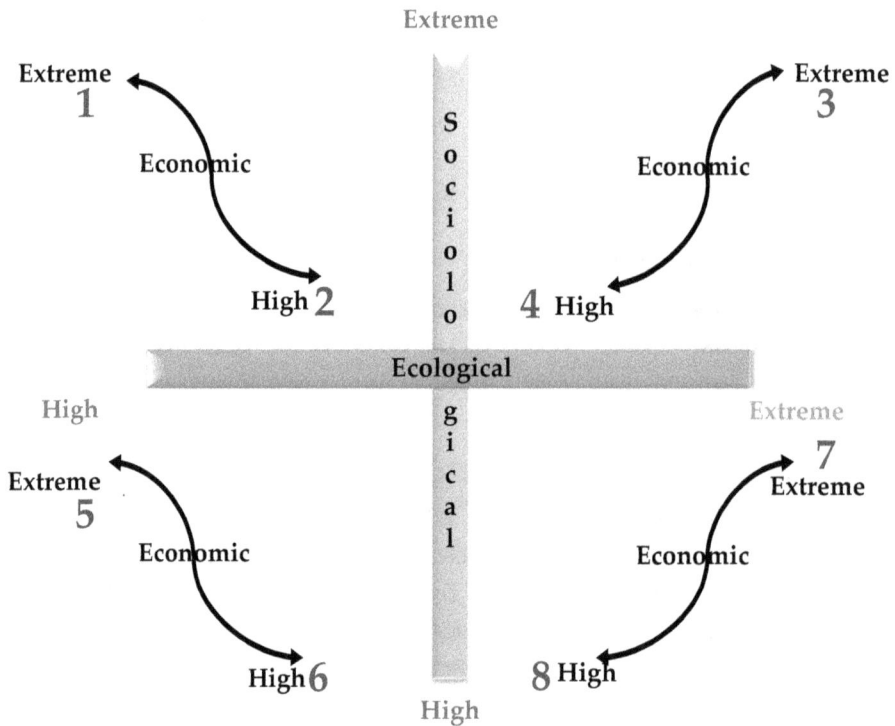

Figure 7: Socio-Ecological Impact Scenarios for Africa

The diagram elucidates the scenarios which emerge at the intersection of drivers on their assumed ranges. Each scenario represents a possible future. With this methodology, it is clear why Futures Science holds that more than one future is always possible. For ease of reference, scenarios are numbered in the diagram, in no order of hierarchy. Note that the ranges have been illustrated as high to extreme for all three stated drivers. The assumption is therefore that nothing less than a highly significant impact on Africa's future can be expected from all three. With consensus on the extent or range of the relative impacts, scenarios emerge which are already within the realm of possibility. As scenarios are sketched to produce multiple explorative futures, one key consideration for policy makers is whether there are commonalities in the scenarios. If indeed there are, then policy may be created with greater confidence, having had the benefit of foresight from scenarios. A brief description of each scenario appears below.

Scenario 1: The demographic dividend has not yet materialised as social needs persist at extreme levels of urgency and economic well-being remains elusive. Ecological consequences are high, but not yet extreme.

Scenario 2: Economic needs are slightly moderated, possibly due to more intelligent, longer-term international deal-making by cabinets and an amelioration of sovereign credit ratings. But the impact of the ecology remains critically high and social needs remain intractable, conceivably due to the failure of distributing economic benefits to those most in need.

Scenario 3: The impact of all three drivers is extreme. Socially, the African demographic profile has shown its implications. Ecologically, the run on African ecological resources has increased, while the need for economic well-being has reached critical levels. This shows a dystopian scenario in which African policy makers have neglected to design impactful policy to ensure alternative pathways for Africa.

Scenario 4: The ecological impact has moved to extreme levels, to the point where climate migration has become the norm. Citizenship itself is under threat as the sheer numbers of migrants have rendered identity administration virtually powerless. As a result, social needs have shifted beyond the grasp of political leaders. Economic implications are high, but not yet extreme, due in part to the sale of natural assets for short-term gain by unscrupulous leaders who have remained immune to policy or have evaded policy through political power.

Scenario 5: Ecological well-being has maintained some semblance of normalcy, which has aided social well-being. But the economy has deteriorated dramatically. The persistence of vapid economic metrics, such as GDP and other crude averages such as income per capita have masked the slow crawl to the fiscal cliff. Governments are finally realising that economic measurement techniques are outdated and that circular and well-being economic metrics are urgently needed to reflect the reality of social and ecological health.

Scenario 6: All three drivers are high, but not quite yet life-threatening. Economic systems have had pedestrian progress, poverty has stabilised at low levels and the natural ecosystem has demonstrated mild resilience. The sobering realisation is dawning that, within the scope of possible futures identified, this is the best-case scenario, despite its obvious undesirability.

Scenario 7: The ecological impact now takes the lead as the most critical determinant of well-being in Africa. Deforestation has accelerated desertification; ecological assets have been sold on the international markets to invisible global polluters who keep a clean ecological record in their countries of origin while externalising the ecological costs of their carbon-intensive production practices to Africa. Social well-being is not yet extreme, but will soon worsen as a lag effect of an unbalanced ecology. The economy has already tipped into extreme vulnerability.

Scenario 8: The ecological system has all but collapsed, and is about to have severe consequences for social and economic well-being. Destructive production practices have remained unregulated, most likely in exchange for foreign direct investment that appeared lucrative in the short term. Anxious governments have reneged on debt-for-nature swaps due to weakening economies, thus exacerbating already-critical debt levels. Desperate governments, sensing the imminent economic decline, have raised Eurobonds which offer attractive but unsustainable returns, given the limited government capacity to deliver timeously on large-scale infrastructure projects. Such projects were offered as despairing salves to intractably high levels of poverty and unemployment. Water resources are showing the full extent of pollutants from decades of weak maintenance and poor governance of foreign industrial development. So-called Western governments are blamed for the continuing malaise of the African continent.

It is clear that the scenarios have significant commonality. That is partially due to the narrow ranges of possibility: all identified drivers will have momentous impact, rated on the diagram from high to extreme. This thought experiment shows the power of scenarios, if well-developed, for the drafting of policy, as it diverts attention from ideology and makes patent the most likely futures. For policy makers, the implications are substantial: once probable futures have been observed, they can never be unseen. Policy must therefore respond to what has been learnt from explorative futures.

Don't start now: Conundrums of strategy and innovation

With explorative futures thus revealed to be within the realm of possibility, one key conceptual conundrum for policy makers is to identify normative futures, i.e.

the desired set of futures. The drafting of such normative futures requires social consensus and longer-term strategic consciousness of how society may unfold. This is a notable departure from the more traditional approach, in which policy makers simply note a selection of difficulties of the current day and decide upon a path of repairing current ills.

These scenarios further reveal the risks inherent in the current future: perpetuate outdated habits of ecologically insensitive FDI deals, bonds and governance, and a deplorable future becomes painfully clear and highly probable. It shows the undeniable systemic impact of ecological well-being and the indisputable interconnectedness of the ecology, society and economy as systems.

Strategic redirection has proven enormously challenging in high income countries. A dramatic course correction may appear undesirable. But scenarios illustrate the relative desirability and the balance of lesser evils. With the current future highly unfavourable, and with even the best-case scenario less than appealing, innovation matures from a fad or mere option to an incontrovertible compulsion. Innovation is now a matter of survival, almost irrespective of the challenges of implementation.

While various avenues for innovation exist, perhaps the most impactful of those may lie within the systems of finance and economics. This is due to the dominant supra-system status that these systems have enjoyed above that of society and ecology. The epistemological fractures between social and financial systems mentioned above have led to severe consequences, with humans in many societies who remain disenfranchised - mere observers rather than active participants in the financial system. Etymologically, however, there are interesting connections to be discovered between these apparently disparate systems. One such example may be found in the notions of value, values and valuations. Value as a construct operates within the financial systems with equal ease as it does in the human system. Societies value certain norms, and financial systems value certain forms of financial performance. Both systems have values (a concept with the same etymology). Social values describe standards and norms of social behaviour, while financial systems have norms of regulation and practice that govern its own behaviour. Astonishingly, while the financial system was created by and operates within the social system, its own values have evolved on notions of capital growth, while social and ecological standards have favoured homeostasis, distribution and evolution rather than linear increases and centralised beneficiation. The result has been that fractures have expanded beyond epistemology to the point of unrecognisability: the system of finance, created by the social system, appears to have developed many norms that no longer serve its creators. This has reached a point of veritable competition between the two systems – a combat in which, in many cases, society and ecology appear to be losing. Growing inequality and intractable poverty serve as notable examples, together with the (deliberate or inadvertent) damage to the natural ecosystem in which the human system resides. To shelter itself from the same fate, the world of finance has both globalised and virtualised – an option not available to many who find themselves ensnared by a system which they no longer influence in any meaningful way.

The matrix reloaded: New values for new valuations

But what of the longer-term outlook? Which system, human or financial, will dominate in the foreseeable future? There is a growing realisation that the system of finance requires reintegration into the social system if it is to survive. Limitless growth, with **social and ecological moral hazard**, appears to have reached an impasse with the concomitant growth in poverty. It was the German poet Bertolt Brecht[3] who opined that, "Because things are the way they are, things will not stay the way they are". Thus because of the scenarios outlined above, it seems unlikely that things will stay as they are. Rejecting this premise is a type of status quo bias, in which policy makers either favour their own benefit from the present to the point of future self-destruction or simply fail to notice the inevitable. The scenarios indicate the irrefutable need for a dramatic course correction. In the domain of value, it may therefore be explored with some degree of confidence whether the financial system will be allowed by the social system to produce its valuation of assets at a higher level than the social system itself values that asset. Increasingly, societies are recognising their interdependence with the ecological system which contains them, while the financial system, feasibly due to its escapist manoeuvres illustrated above, appears to ride the momentum of a time preceding **ecological intelligence**. It is therefore not inconceivable that methodologies of valuation in the financial system will be drawn towards approaches used by societies to evaluate themselves and their ecological assets. It is posited, therefore, that the valuation of corporate assets may well evolve beyond traditional corporate valuation approaches, such as P/E Ratio, Enterprise Valuation or EBITDA Multiple. An example of such a scenario is one in which the valuation of corporations in the future of Africa will be done on a **Socio-Ecologically Adjusted Enterprise Valuation (SEA-EV)** basis. This possibility, made ever more probable by the scenarios above, transcends current early moves in corporate responsibility such as ESG and fines for ecological damage. ESG is rife with inconsistent metrics and greenwashing, while court-imposed fines are reactive by definition and respond linearly to environmental impact assessments, often after the fact. SEA-EV posits a direct relationship between corporate valuation and socio-ecological well-being. As a method for valuation, SEA-EV recognises the inextricable relationships between the social, financial and economic systems and addresses the dilemma at the direct level of valuation.

Such an approach to valuation will have significant implications for all relevant systems. Most notably, it will combat the spiralling African debt book by revaluing African ecological assets. It will redefine the notion of growth and help to reimagine prospects for prosperity. Such revaluation will offer essential collateral for the economic advancement of Africa. For investors and rentiers, investment target assets and asset classes will be reclassified. In pension funds, for example, blind investment, in which pension contributors have little to no line of sight of their investments beyond the risk levels defined by the paradigm of the financial system (often at the expense of the ecological system), greater socio-ecological transparency will advance the governance agenda. Customer interest will be more acutely aligned with societal and ecological health and even talent attractiveness will be reconstituted.

Scenarios for the impact of the interacting social, ecological and economic systems in the future of Africa reveal the need for a dramatic and innovative course correction. The current future, perpetuated by status quo bias and self-defeating short-termism, must now yield to the active innovation required for preferred African futures. New philosophies and methodologies which integrate value, values and valuations offer just such an alternative, desirable pathway to success – a most desirable advancement to what Agenda2063 describes as 'the Africa we want'.

The paradox of organisations sponsoring learning programmes for leaders without allowing them to explore the implementation of the learning content in its broadest possible contextual sense, is made patently obvious by the scenarios above. It is a self-limiting strategy by organisations to prevent such creative ideation and application to occur. Such exploration will provide great insight into growth and development for the organisation and will enhance the possibility of return from the learning investment. It is therefore reasonable, as posited in the introduction, to argue for the exploration not only of what leaders learn from their organisations, but also what the organisation learns from its leaders. Such exploration is truly systemic in nature, as it relates directly to the nature of the intersection between the system of the leader and that of the organisation. It furthermore induces a more meaningful balance in the power differential between the system of the leader and that of the organisation.

4.2.3 Crouching Tiger, Hidden Dragon: The Al-Aimmah Bridge Effect

The question may be asked with some justification why organisations so often fear the emergence of insight about themselves from the learning process. Is it because they fear a lack of control over learning outcomes? Surely organisations cannot possibly aim to control the thinking that leaders will experience as a result of learning. Is it because the complexity of possible learning outcomes is simply too vast to anticipate? It cannot be argued that the simple avoidance of complexity automatically makes matters simpler. Could it be that organisations simply want leaders to implement predesigned processes more effectively? This expectation flies in the face of the calibre of leader most organisations invest such great effort into through rigorous recruitment and selection. It may be that organisations simply lack the consciousness and insight about the process and tools to optimise creative application opportunities from learning; they may lack a sense of organisational self-awareness, which may indeed be addressed through Systemic Leadership Learning.

One phenomenon observed may be referred to as the *Al-Aimmah Bridge Effect*. On 31 August 2005 a group of thousands of Shiite Muslims marched over the Tigris River in Baghdad on their way to mosque. As they crossed the Al-Aimmah Bridge straddling the river, someone on the opposite side of the bridge shouted a warning that a suicide bomber was about to detonate a bomb on that side. The crowd immediately panicked in response to what they have learnt. Without any further examination of the facts (a typical behaviour of a lack of organisational self-awareness in times of crisis) the crowd turned on the bridge and forced their way back to the side from which they came. The gate had closed where they had entered the bridge and could only open towards the inside of the bridge. In the stampede that ensued, more than one thousand people died. Al Qaeda claimed responsibility for the attack. It emerged that there was no suicide bomber, and that simple fear drove the behaviour of the crowd.

The tragic events that occurred on Al-Aimmah Bridge are reminiscent of the behaviour of some organisations in response to learning. In the event described above, the crowd as a system self-destructed due to an irrational fear of the outside world – this is the Al-Aimmah Bridge Effect. An organisation that lacks the ability or determination to integrate new knowledge or learning into the boundaries of its system for fear that the new learning will destroy it, can often self-destruct in terms of its lack of retention of talented leaders and its inability to harness the innovation potential and creative application opportunities from the learning experience.

4.2.4 Legends of the fall: Anthropological perspectives on culture

Organisations are societies. Members have varying levels of commitment to the mores and norms of the social system, which is in constant flux as individuals enter and exit, and as perpetual restructure, necessitated by the context, renders all organisational architecture a mere temporal reality.

With AI as an undeniable force, such societies are rapidly evolving beyond social systems to become socio-technical systems. As these societies morph, the process of the formation of the psychological contract evolves equally. That contract, most tacit, may be viewed through an anthropological lens as one perspective on cultural sense-making.

If defined as the study of humanity and its distinctiveness as a species, such an anthropological lens is becoming increasingly complex through its socio-technical character. International work on organisational culture, especially on building cultures of creativity and foresight, has revealed a number of critical anthropological dimensions which may guide the learning process for senior executives:

1. Norms and ranges of acceptable behaviour, i.e. Overton window

2. Ritual, including celebrations of success and dealing with loss

3. Temporal dimensions, that is the way in which the culture deals with time. This is becoming increasingly important in a global, 24hour system of temporal reality. It includes:

    *   Flow and sequence
        *   Work schedules
        *   Meals
        *   Recreation
    *   Life stages (plan, birth/new entrant, toddler, tween, teen, adulthood, marriage, children, grandchildren, retirement, death)
    *   Cycles (nature, agriculture)
    *   Hours of privacy

4. Symbols, arts & artefacts

5. Beliefs and (indigenous) knowledge systems, including noesis as the thought process of perceiving reality.

6. Structures, especially the cha-ordic (that is simultaneously chaotic and orderly) nature of institutional architecture. This extends to social sub-structures, group formation and role definition.

7. Rules, laws and taboos, most of which are tacit and implicit

8. Security and threat as perceived by the group

9. Reward and punishment as agreed by the leaders of the institution.

Such an anthropological perspective advances a deep understanding of culture as both the sum and driver of behaviour.

Yet another undeniable factor that plays a significant role in the learning reality of the leader is the role of organisational culture.

One traditional way of understanding organisational culture is through climate surveys. The inevitable result of organisational culture/climate surveys is that, while tacit experiences become salient and unavoidable to senior leaders, these leaders often struggle to determine the exact implications for them as leaders – surveys make experiences clear, but seldom make any contribution to authentically address human concerns. This creates disillusionment for members of the institutional community and may, counterintuitively, exacerbate further disengagement.

Table 3 below offers a simple tool to help leaders take some degree of action in response to insight about organisational culture. It is important to note that leaders not only receive feedback about organisational culture, but also experience the culture in their engagements with others and continuously participate in the creation of culture. Because leaders are key system leverage points, they also drive and create culture.

Table 3: Response to culture feedback

	ON SELF	ON OTHERS
POSITIVE	Q1: Integrate	Q2: Leverage
NEGATIVE	Q3: Mitigate; Find contingencies	Q4: Invoke true selves of others

Actors in the organisational ecosystem simply experience the institutional culture differently. The table shows the positive and negative impact of culture (positive or negative) on the Y-axis and the impacted entity (leader or others) on the X-axis.

Quadrant 1 shows a positive impact on the self or leader. The leader who experiences this impact is advised to integrate the positive aspects of the organisation in which she leads into the dimensions of her own character. In this way, the leader creates congruence between the personality of the leader and that of the organisation. It may boost the leader's confidence to discover that there are even more opportunities to demonstrate elements of the true self and that these elements would align well with the positive characteristics of the organisation.

Quadrant 2 shows a positive impact of the culture (as created and driven by leaders) on others. This is system feedback to which most leaders are highly receptive. Executives should move beyond viewing such feedback as complimentary, and leverage the positive experience of others in an appreciate manner to create greater momentum in the interest of an even more conducive working environment, that is a containing system for work in which the structures and rules enhance the purpose of that system with integrity.

Quadrant 3 shows a negative impact of culture on the self/leader. Leaders in this quadrant may be tempted to protect themselves by closing their systems to the feedback received from their environment. This would deprive them from continuous feedback from the organisation and as a result leaders may soon find themselves isolated from the true dynamics of the organisation, including the lived experience of their stakeholders. These leaders are therefore advised to mitigate the negative impact of the culture on them by increasing the positive impact they have on the culture. While this may seem an exaggerated and even counterintuitive ambition, in practical terms this means allowing their own systems to permeate the organisation, that is to live more confidently the positive elements of their own systems. Finding greater strength to demonstrate more of the positive elements of the system of the self may be the single most valuable contingency to negative culture.

Quadrant 4 shows a negative impact of organisational culture on others. Leaders are, once again, often tempted to ignore these impacts and dismiss them as the musings of disgruntled staff who lack motivation. Leaders who observe such negative impact are advised to invoke the positive true selves of others. This means that they may gain great benefit from encouraging others not to withdraw negative statements, but to inspire others to demonstrate the positive aspects of their systems, thus integrating multiple positive partial views into a collective cultural whole.

The simple strategies proposed in response to the impact of organisational culture make a more positive organisational culture a distinct possibility, rather than a topic for intellectual analysis, broken down into boxes, some of which are deliberately ignored. It is a true movement towards the synthesis of the positive true selves as systems for staff and leaders at all levels.

4.3 AI Sense and sensibility: Content as Hyper-Fluid System

AI can produce rapid publication. The first determination for the selection of content from various sources is provenance - the quality of the source from which the content is derived. One potential critique on work produced by AI is that the Large Learning Model (LLM) must, by definition, have its own sources. One touted benefit of such models is the staggeringly large data sets used as inputs. But herein the conundrum may be found: is a larger data set necessarily better? Large, representative data sets have been assumed in classical research as a distinct advantage. But that was before machines interpreted the data. In other words, large data as benefit to classical authorship was static, passive and the subject of investigation of the author. This gave the author a degree of discretion on the selection of the data set. AI is considerably less discerning. And much of its sources are simply what is available in the public domain. That public domain has expanded to include almost any source. The risk is clear: indiscriminate data harvesting may simply produce an aggregate view. And when, as it must statistically, most data sets represent the average rather than the excellent, the authorship produced by AI is often exactly that: average. Not wrong, but not necessarily excellent. To put it bluntly, the average author must be average. The average author who self-publishes has not had to yield to pre-publication editorial scrutiny. AI is typically unclear on which data sets have been scrutinised editorially. Most of the internet is self-publishing. Therefore, most AI publications are, in a word, the average of self-publishing, and therefore lamentably tending towards the mean.

Within the context of the leader and organisation as interactive systems, the learning content proposed as curriculum for the learning process for leaders is also subject to the rules of system formation and as such deserves examination regarding its relative role in SLL. The learning content, too, is in a continuous dynamic interchange with the systems of the leader and organisation and, as can be seen below, also with that of the facilitator.

One of the main considerations behind the system status of learning content in SLL is that content for curricula appears somewhat random, i.e. there is no clear rule or process that governs the selection of specific content. Content may be selected from various sources, including:

- Articles in scholarly journals
- Articles in popular publications
- University and other education provider websites
- Books
- Other content-based websites
- Practical experiences
- Reference works.

Some additional principles for content selection are proposed for completeness, but these principles do not necessitate the inclusion or exclusion of any concepts or authors. In each case I question the usefulness of the principle identified.

Content selection principles may include:

Publication

Content selected for the curriculum must adhere to the minimum criteria of having been edited by a respected publisher in the field. This provides a natural pre-selection of the quality of content. The reality is, however, that many decisions in business are made based upon ideas and insights that have not been published anywhere, let alone in publications respected in a certain field. Many executives would argue that, by the time content or information is published, the competitive advantage for implementation is largely diluted.

With the opportunity for rapid publication through digital media, the requirements for what constitutes publication are also being redefined. A simple email by the CEO is often viewed as a valid publication and as foundation for substantial decisions. Thus, if organisations can make decisions based upon a very loose definition of publication, it may be asked with some validity as to what necessitates more formal publication for the purposes of learning. It is patently evident that people in organisations learn effectively without the formal requirements for publication often associated with formal learning programmes.

Recency

Content included for learning often needs to be published recently to demonstrate current thinking and research. While this principle is valuable for the understanding of current thinking, business problems do not limit themselves to current thinking. It should therefore not exclude more dated content that remains valid, whether published or not.

Another challenge to the principle of recency is that the content proposed may be so new that it has not proven itself in practice. The ideas may be revolutionary, but few longitudinal studies would exist to verify the long-term impact of implementing the proposed new ideas.

Respected publication houses and journals

Renowned publication houses or journals provide proof of robust editorial review and therefore qualified literature for selection. Of course, the respect journals have accumulated is measured by the quality of its contributors, and not through the profitability increases those journals have offered organisations.

Tenure

Content may be selected based on the fact that it represents ideas that have been in the field of study for a significant period of time and therefore appear to have proven itself as valid. It is blatantly obvious that this principle is in direct contradiction with the principle of recency – it is the very antithesis of recency. The question may then be asked whether any organisation could apply both principles in the selection of content. It is proposed here that organisations do so based upon a predefined definition of what is acceptable, that is, content is selected using both contradictory principles on the justification that the selected content serves the emerging insights of contextual dynamics and organisational purpose.

Relevance and quality of ideas

Content must be selected for its apparent match with perceived learning needs. This principle appears self-evident, until one considers that a systemic approach to content selection implies that interconnectedness may be observed between the apparent learning need and almost any field of study, let alone specific content within only one selected field. One example of this observation is the apparently universal application of certain elements of content for programmes with widely differing titles.

Author profile

Content is more likely to be suitable to organisations if the ideas were created by authors who have a certain standing in the field. This is based upon the assumption that certain authors have enjoyed acceptance and that their ideas are therefore more valid than those of less respected authors. Authors may be viewed as respected due to renown in the media, number of publications or volume of copies sold.

A similar challenge applies as for the principle of publication: the required speed of modern (and post-modern) business simply demands ideas that are likely to work, irrespective of whether they are the views of respected authors or junior level staff within the organisation. Most organisations have a pragmatic approach to learning: if it is feasible and return is most likely to exceed investment, it is worth learning about. This does not imply that all organisations implement good ideas without reservation – the dynamics of organisational politics, structural hierarchies and the slow movement of bureaucratic decision-making processes all contribute to the retardation of organisational responsiveness. Therefore, organisations should at least be willing to explore ideas on the basis that they are sound, and that the notoriety of the author is not a prerequisite for highly responsive organisations. What is required is executive discernment.

Common practice

Content may be included in the curriculum if it represents the common practice of other organisations in the same industry, particularly by successful organisations.

This principle introduces a degree of safety for content selection borne out by the fact that other successful organisations are doing the same. It is immediately apparent that criteria for sameness pose significant challenges to competitive advantage – if the organisation offers the same as other organisations, particularly successful ones with substantial infrastructure, the question may be asked with some validity as to the nature of differentiation the organisation brings to its leaders and the market. If, on the other hand, benchmarking is done with organisations who are in other industries and therefore non-competitive, a similar question may be asked about the value and relevance of the benchmarking process. In the reality of executive education, clients often appear to ask for:

- Content that demonstrates our complete uniqueness,
- Based on other organisations which are just like us.

The absurdity of the exercise cannot be ignored.

The principles noted above aim to highlight only the most salient criteria for content selection and does not propose to offer a complete list of principles in this pursuit.

It is clear from the discussion above that deep inherent contradictions exist between principles. The nature of these contradictions has led to the conclusion that content selection for learning purposes is, at least to some degree, a random process based upon the deeply held beliefs and typically unconscious assumptions of organisations and the academic exposure of facilitators. The mere fact that information has grown beyond all control in almost any conceivable field, coupled with the fact that no single organisation or facilitator could study all content, suggests that selection is based on grounds other than the mere validity of the content.

The characteristic of randomness in the selection of content is further exacerbated by the *random sequencing of content*, that is the linear process by which various elements of content is introduced into the learning journey. It is clear that no two content designers are likely to select exactly the same content, and then introduce it in exactly the same sequence.

In addition to random content selection and content sequencing in the learning process, different facilitators would also demonstrate content with the use of various didactic techniques, such as reading only, lecturing, Socratic questioning, group work, inductive or deductive approaches and other methodologies.

Add to the dynamics above the complexities of the personalities of the facilitators, the varying nature of organisations that commission learning, the philosophical vantage points of the universities or private providers and the diversity of levels, personalities and experience of leaders on the learning programme, and it becomes irrefutably clear that no two programmes focusing on seemingly similar learning objectives could possibly look exactly the same.

If a degree of randomness in content selection is indeed common practice in learning design, then it remains an even greater conundrum why content is not more closely aligned with actual needs of the organisations and their leaders – if content selection is somewhat random, it may as well include content that speaks to the real needs of its beneficiaries, rather than to the needs of removed and politicised executives or ivory tower academics.

Too often learning content becomes a law unto itself. It is validated as required learning by itself, the institutions that promote it, its authors and its long-standing presence in academic discourse.

It is proposed in SLL that the learning content should also adhere to the criteria of producing or supporting the identification of creative application opportunities from learning. It seems almost supercilious to propose this as a criterion, as application value seems the blatantly obvious initial purpose of the learning journey. Counterintuitively, experience and research seem to suggest that return on investment from learning may indeed be part of the original aim, but does not remain a consistent monitoring criterion throughout the learning process.

The most salient implication for learning content that emerges from a systemic perspective of the learning process is that the learning content has to integrate with the systemic realities of the leaders and their organisations, and must simultaneously create insights on emerging realities. To this end, learning content is not only a system in itself, but forms part of a greater system of elements of the learning process as macro-system. Such a systemic approach to learning immediately places the status of learning content below that of the leader and the organisation it should aim to serve.

In systemic terms, this means that the learning content is required to be permeable by the systemic realities of the leader and organisation. Content, from this perspective, is simply a sub-system, enraptured by the multiple containing systems of the leader and organisation. The implication of this reality is significant: learning content in SLL is continuously subject to the intellectual approval of the systems of the leaders and organisations. No matter what degree of research has been done to verify the learning content, it demands further design to integrate with the systems of leaders and organisations. In SLL, learning content is therefore not a law unto itself, but is subject to the rules and architecture of the systems of leaders and organisations. This principle is borne out by the phenomenon that no two organisations are exactly the same and that innovation is a pervasive demand on 21st century organisations.

The same principle applies for any organisation that aims to gain competitive advantage through innovation – doing what has been done before, and by extension, learning what has been studied before, may simply produce more of the same. Only through a robust engagement with the validity of learning content for specific leaders and organisations, can learning content lead to the identification of innovative application opportunities and add real and tangible value.

To view content as a system also implies that the boundaries of that system should remain permeable in order to ensure its requisite energy. Such openness is required towards the realities of the organisation, as well as the challenges and opportunities sensed by leaders in the learning process. At a meta-level content should also remain open to content, that is content is itself contained by various larger systems of content and interact with other content systems.

As an example, we may use the content selection for the development of SLL.

In the discussion on the challenges of validity above, I mentioned the conundrum of applying systems thinking in an attempt to justify a systemic approach. In alignment with a true systemic approach that allows for the evolution of systems and the emergence of system characteristics not present in the original design of the system, I am therefore drawn to various lateral links that may contribute to insight into the theory proposed in this book. In this regard, I have consulted literature from various fields including:

- Systems Thinking
- Leadership
- Learning/Education
- Psychology
- Sociology
- Business studies
- Philosophy
- And others.

Given the outline above, one way of creating the boundaries of the system of literature that applies to this research, is to examine where various fields of study might overlap and interact, as shown in the matrix below.

Table 4: Subject matter and scope definition

	Systems Thinking	Leadership	Learning/ Education	Psychology	Sociology	Business
Systems Thinking		6. Leading systems	11. Educational Systems	16. The psychology of systems	21. Sociological systems	26. The business world as a system
Leadership	1. Systemic leadership		12. Educational Leadership	17. The psychology of leadership	22. Sociological leadership	27. The business of leadership
Learning/ Education	2. Systemic Learning	7. Leadership Education		18. Psychology of education	23. Sociological education	28. The business of education
Psychology	3. Systemic psychology	8. Leadership in psychology	13. Educational psychology		24. Sociological dimensions of psychology	29. The business of psychology
Sociology	4. Systemic sociology	9. Leadership in Sociology	14. Educational Sociology	19. Psychological dimensions of sociology		30. The business of sociology
Business	5. Systemic business thinking and operations	10. Leadership in business	15. Education for business	20. The psychology of business	25. The sociology of business	

Table 4 above shows the integration between some of the most saliently related fields in relation to Systemic Leadership Learning.

While every point of integration may be expounded upon, it may not be essential in this context. Suffice it to suggest that the direct relevance has been colour-coded to provide some limitation of the potentially infinite scope, as indicated below:

- Cells shaded in **light grey** as indicated by this text, represent literature that is centrally relevant.
- Cells shaded in **medium grey** as indicated in this text, have intermediate levels of relevance to the main thesis of the book.
- Cells shaded in **dark grey** as indicated in this text, have only peripheral levels of relevance and may only be called upon incidentally for completeness.

In the deliberation of the selection process, content that shows the integration between various fields above was favoured over content that exclusively focused on one area, although such exclusively focused content was indeed consulted for clarity.

The implication is that learning content has to evolve through the learning process as the result of the continuous review of the systemic realities of the leader and organisation. In such a process, each group of leaders in each organisation co-designs and moulds the content to ensure that it addresses the unique challenges faced. If one accepts that (provided that the leader behaves and learns with integrity) in the mind of the leader the organisation forms part of the leader as supra-system, then the learning content is also subjugated to the leader as supra-system.

4.3.1 Don't stand so close to me: Proximity Perception Trap

It is often the intention of a systemic analysis (a noted potential contradiction) to identify relationships between various elements that initially appear to have no relationship. Systems thinking suggests that an event or change in one element may have an impact in the system that may be much greater than anticipated by the observer. This may be because of a lack of understanding on the part of the system observer, precipitated by the reality that:

• The observer did not realise that the event or change was within the boundary of a greater system,

• The observer could not see the connection between the elements of the event or change and other observed or distal elements, or

• The observer did not appreciate the full extent of the possible causal relationship between the event or change and the observed elements.

While such a call for systemic awareness is essential for SLL, the observer may also be lured into drawing a false connection between two elements, changes or events simply based on their proximity to each other. Such proximity may be based upon some of the scenarios identified below. These scenarios, once again, represent the most salient possibilities and are not proposed as a complete list. The scenarios include:

i.   Closeness in chronological timing, that is two events occur within a short space of time and the observer assumes they must be connected,

ii.   Similarity in terms of shape, size or appearance, that is two events occur that look similar and the observer assumes that they were caused by the same thing or that one was the cause of the other,

iii. Similarity in terms of context or conditions, that is two events occur under the same circumstances and a shared or causal link is assumed,

iv.   Similarity in terms of origin, that is two events are the result of the same action, and they are assumed to have the same intention.

The scenarios above are instances in which the observer may assume a link - often a causal relationship – between two events, changes or entities simply because they are in proximity of one another. This phenomenon may be referred to as the *Proximity Perception Trap of Systems Thinking*. Such a flawed assumption is a blatant misapplication and over-simplification of systems thinking and creates two significant problems:

i.   It assumes causal relationships (between events, changes or entities) that do not exist in reality. Such false assumptions may lead to the misallocation of resources to resolve problems that do not exist or cannot possibly be solved with the facilitation of proposed connections.

ii.   It diverts the attention and effort away from real insight and resulting synthesis of the systemic realities at work, which may lead the observer away from seeing relationships which are more systemically significant.

The implications for learning content are also significant. Facilitators and learning designers often believe that simply exposing leaders to learning content will automatically lead to the dissolution of problems. The reality is quite different and there is a notable implication of which both leaders and facilitators need to be aware: by exposing leaders to certain learning content, the mere juxtaposition of the content and the leader may suggest a causal relationship that does not exist in reality. As an example, a programme in financial management has the tacit implication that both the problem and solution reside within the financial management practices of the leader and organisation, while, in reality, the financial management practices may simply be a reflection of problems that occur elsewhere or skills deficits in other areas of competence for the leader.

4.3.2 Transformers: Content as System Inputs

Given the options for the relative system-level status of the leader and the organisation as outlined above, and recognising the self-perceived supra-system status of the leader during the learning journey, it may be concluded with some validity that the learning content serves as catalytic input to the system of the leader during the learning situation.

Table 5 below explores the relationship between the system of the leader and the learning content as provocative system input. It examines the implications for reciprocal openness of both the leader as system, and the learning content as both input and system. Note that no system is entirely closed or open, and that this implies a degree of flexibility in the application of the tool.

For the system of the leader to be open in relation to learning content, it means that the leader is both curious and receptive to learning content and will allow for the exploration of the implications of the emerging ideas. For the leader to be closed, it means that the leader prevents the learning content from entering that leader's system. Such leaders will avoid or even actively prevent themselves from engaging meaningfully with the content. In the words of the American author, Zig Ziglar, "If you are not willing to learn, no one can help you. If you are determined to learn, no one can stop you."

For learning content as system input to be open, it means that the learning content is sufficiently flexible to accommodate the realities of the leader and organisation. This means that, no matter what degree of research is represented by the content, if the reality of the leader's system is different, the content must aim to adjust to and serve that reality. In this scenario it is not the aim for leaders to memorise learning content. Rather, it is the aim of learning content to serve the objectives of the leader. This can be highly counterintuitive to traditional facilitators who see their role predominantly as subject matter experts.

For content to be closed, it implies a puritanical self-preservation on the part of the content. Admittedly, this assertion may sound strange and may imply the personification of the system of content to the extent that the content possesses purposiveness. It is stated in this manner due to the often-heated debates among scholars in defence of their espoused intellectual positions and academic masters. Should the leader challenge the content based on the reality of the structure and rules of that leader's system, such challenges are all too frequently dismissed as irrelevant to the content curriculum at hand.

Table 5: Learning content as system inputs

CONTENT AS INPUT	SYSTEM OF THE LEADER	
	Open	Closed
Open	Q1	Q2
Closed	Q3	Q4

Quadrant 1 shows an open system of a leader in relation to open learning content. This means that the systems are mutually receptive. Full integration of the learning content is possible in the system of the leader, with a reciprocal flexibility on the part of learning content to adjust to the reality of the leader's system. There is a risk to this mutual openness, in that both systems may be so receptive to the other's realities that both may be changed beyond the limits of control. SLL argues that such fear of loss of control must yield to the systemic preference for order rather than control. Autopoiesis, that is, systemic self-organisation, must be permitted to flourish during the fluid experience of learning.

Quadrant 2 shows a closed system of a leader in relation to open learning content. The only option for change in this case is that which exists in the content. The risk in this instance is that the only system change that occurs for the leader is that the leader increases in defensiveness based upon a dysfunctional suspicion of the learning content.

Quadrant 3 shows an open system of a leader in relation to closed learning content. This means that the leader is receptive to learning, but the learning content lacks sufficient fluidity to accommodate the reality of the leader and organisation.

In this instance, learning content is viewed as an additional tool, but will only be called upon selectively when the reality of the leader happens to overlap with the reality of the learning content. The risk here is that, should the leader allow the content access to that leader's system, and the leader's reality can no longer accommodate the content, it will fester in the leader's system, like a veritable learning septicaemia, until the system of the leader inevitably rejects the tenets of the content.

Quadrant 4 shows the closed system of a leader in relation to closed learning content. This means that neither system is receptive to the reality of the other. In this case, there may be a change in both or neither, depending on what may be referred to as *Approach Velocity*. Approach velocity may be defined here as the force with which two systems migrate towards each other. In SLL, this means that the force and authority with which leaders defend their position or the degree to which learning content is enforced upon leaders by more senior leaders or by inflexible but reputable learning institutions, authors or content disciples, will impact the extent to which change occurs in either system.

Even if change does occur, the risk is that such change will be superficial – no executive can be forced to learn, and no puritanical learning institution or educator will be forced to see the glaring deficiencies in their process or content. In a sense, this power struggle is similar to that shown above between the supra-system status of the leader and that of the organisation. In that case, however, learning content is implicitly viewed as a sub-system by leaders, while it may yet resist the realities of the leader as supra-system.

4.4 The phantom menace: The Facilitator as System

In addition to the significance of the leader, organisation and learning content as systems, the facilitator of the learning journey is equally a key system in the navigation of the ebb and flow of the learning process.

The facilitator in this context is defined broadly as the entire body of actors responsible for ensuring the meeting of the leader and the learning content. Thus, it may be a single facilitator or group of facilitators guiding meaningful dialogue in the "training room" (as many organisations outdatedly refer to learning spaces). It may also include the programme sponsors, researchers of the learning content, the programme designers and developers as well as those who manage the operations of learning. This broad definition is used for ease of reference to identify the entire group of people facilitating learning. It is noteworthy that it is often observed that peers are potential facilitators of learning, whether at higher or lower hierarchical levels. This is a significant insight into the systemic nature of the learning process, as peer executives may offer education, reading, experience and other exposure or intellectual virtuosity as strategic learning catalysts for the benefit for the newly formed learning system.

The facilitator, whether defined as the group above or as individual learning guide or coach, brings to the learning situation an entire system with its own structures and rules. The facilitator as individual is certainly likely to have a particular affinity for and depth of understanding of the selected learning content. The leader as system, on the other hand, wishes only to resolve pressing issues and perhaps identify some opportunities for growth or improvement in some element of work or context. This juxtaposition places great pressure on the facilitator, who may be tempted to extol the virtues of a beloved field of specialisation, rather than explore the reality and ambition of the leader. The facilitator thus risks behaving like a supra-system, and using learning content, about which they hold high expertise, as weapon to defend their own supra-system status with the audience.

Furthermore, the facilitator has a worldview, which may or may not be aligned with that of the leaders on the learning journey. Fundamental philosophical differences, such as an overall perspective of the aim of business, the role of humans in organisations or the institutional responsibility for the planet, may have a dramatic impact on learning effectiveness.

The facilitator further has ego, especially in the role of subject matter expert. Leaders who challenge this expertise with examples of exceptions from their own extensive executive experience may be disregarded if the facilitator drives the learning content as supra-system, thus compromising the possible dissolution of complex business challenges.

Such apparent competition for supra-system status diverts attention from the overall aim of learning: to improve the ability of the leader to lead people, process, technology and ideas towards more expansive interpretations of personal, social, organisational and planetary value.

4.4.1 **Soul snatcher: Responsibility of the 'facilitator'**

I only hope when I am free,
As they are free, to go in quest
Of the knowledge beyond the bounds of life,
It may not seem better to me to rest.

Robert Frost, Misgiving

Within the context of SLL, it is the primary responsibility of the facilitator to catalyse the positive evolution of the leader as system. It is therefore imperative that the facilitator recognises the leader as system, with a full understanding of the implications of this insight as outlined above.

The facilitator should consider the mind of the leader as one that potentially views itself as the supra-system in the learning situation. This means that the facilitator requires a deep appreciation for the structure and rules of that system. It further suggests a degree of humility on the part of the facilitator to view the learning content as servant to the leader as supra-system, rather than the leader as servant to the content.

In the above section on the leader as system, it was explained that the collection of leaders in a learning setting also creates yet another layer of complexity as this collection of leaders forms an emerging system, often with its own rules and structures, based on hierarchies, confidence levels of individual leaders, diversity of philosophical approaches to people and work and other dimensions. It is thus incumbent on the facilitator to appreciate the fractals of the apparently chaotic system created by the collection of leaders.

The facilitator is naturally responsible to serve the best interest of the organisation represented by the leader. This obligation may generate a moral tension for the facilitator, as leaders are humans, while organisations are devoid of the dynamics of human vulnerability and potential. This demands that the facilitator has an intimate understanding of the nature of those organisations, most notably in terms of their key current and future challenges as they relate to the overall focus of the learning content. This means that learning content also requires subordination to the organisation as system. The facilitator is further required, within an SLL framework, to move beyond the reactive response to challenges and explore the possible opportunities that exist for the organisation as well as for each leader in terms of that leader's potential contribution to the seizing of present and future opportunities.

It may be true in some cases that the facilitator lacks the required levels of knowledge for the optimal facilitation of dissolution of challenges and the identification of opportunities for the systems of the organisation and leader. It is certainly my experience, and I suspect this experience is shared by fellow executive facilitators, that in almost all learning engagements with clients, there is much more tacit complexity to the challenges than the initial brief to the facilitator seems to suggest. Organisations are often loath to share the full scope of challenges they face and appear, in some cases, to mask underlying problems through addressing superficial ones. The classical organisation preference for action over thought exacerbates this reality. The facilitator in such cases faces a complex dilemma: there may be a clear brief from project sponsors who pay for the programme, yet the system created by the collection of leaders in the room shows the emergence of characteristics that do not reflect the initial objectives of the brief. The dilemma goes to what would constitute integrity on the part of the facilitator: to drive the agenda of the sponsors or to support the growth of the leaders within the reality of their own systems.

The facilitator would be out of integrity if any of the two opposites were ignored. A systemic lens by the facilitator leads to the insight that both views, that of the sponsors and that emerging from the leaders on course, form part of a greater system – both views are elements of the system. It is imperative for the facilitator to observe this dichotomy and to confront the leaders present with the reality thereof. This provides the leaders present with the same systemic awareness. The realisation that there appears to be a contradiction in expectations then becomes a learning challenge for leaders to dissolve. The fact that the contradiction exists is in itself a characteristic of the complexities of the systems at play.

The facilitator in SLL is thus accountable to note with honesty the observable elements of the systems involved. This allows for more honest debate and a more realistic assessment of creative application opportunities. It generates a context that makes learning content relevant and impactful. The facilitator must demonstrate the courage to provoke leaders on the systemic implications of the learning content. The facilitator thus finds personal meaning formation in the realisation that she becomes part of the newly created learning system. Within that system, the facilitator plays a role in service of the supra-system. The facilitator is part of the system with clear responsibility to advance the systems of the leaders and the organisations they represent, just as they have responsibility to do the same. The alternative is a denial of the true characteristics of the systems involved.

Such an application is greatly aided by another responsibility of the facilitator in SLL, namely to encourage leaders to reveal their stories – the narrative of how their schemas came to be constructed. The facilitator requires the humility to recognise that leaders have their own stories based on unique experiences to which the facilitator was not privy. These stories, if delivered with integrity (which must be assumed by the facilitator) have the potential of forming the context for the facilitation of significant learning shifts.

Such awareness of real, underlying and systemic challenges leads to what one might refer to as *Real-Time Design*. This means that, as the system of leaders begins to show characteristics not evident from the initial brief and design of the learning programme, the facilitator is required to modify and adjust the design of the programme in real-time to ensure that creative application opportunities are identified that will add meaningful value to the leader and organisation. Such real-time design necessitates that the facilitator subordinates both her own system as well as the system of learning content to the systems of the leaders present, thus granting the leaders the supra-system status that they believe they have and increasing learning receptiveness.

In order to facilitate learning in this way, the facilitator needs a selection of critical skills. These skills are noted below.

4.4.2 Dr. Dolittle: Qualitative criteria for facilitation

The following qualitative delivery criteria serve as prerequisite for facilitators to work within an SLL framework:

Level of thinking

A level of intellectual processing at least matching that of the leaders is required from the facilitator. Critical here is the depth and clarity of cognition, that is the ability to decompose complex problems and even dissolve them where appropriate.

Co-Creating context

Facilitators are required to help learners to establish their place within their context, as well as the contextual relevance of the challenges under discussion within the greater organisation. The sense-making obligation extends to the pre- and sub-text dimensions described above.

Intellectual rigour

Given the predominantly linear, logical-analytical approach of business managers, the ability to echo the level of logical analysis of leaders opens the door for greater learning opportunity through systemic techniques once leaders are more receptive.

Exploring logical links

Moving beyond logic is essential for fluid learning support, as it is leaders' current logic that has created their current limited results, as evidenced by the fact that they require further learning.

Exploring lateral links

The exploration of options that are not immediately obvious is essential for further growth. The provocation of leaders by the facilitator to examine potential portable learning opportunities from other industries is a prerequisite for effective facilitation within an SLL framework.

Synthesis

The focus of this book is on the development of leaders of organisations. Therefore, it is essential that, while learning may be a virtue worthy of its own reward, organisations invest financially in the learning process and therefore require demonstrable return on learning investment. It is therefore essential that the facilitator not only proposes content, but also synthesises such content with the real challenges facing leaders. Even the best quality traditional facilitation only exercises synthesis at the level of content, that is synthesis follows analysis in a typical continuum that places learning content, rather than business solutions, at the forefront of learning priority.

Sensitivity

The traditional training model requires leaders to be attentive to the learning content. This misplaces content once again as the main focus of learning. Within SLL, the legitimate systemic needs of executives are paramount, as the measurable dimensions for effective learning will ultimately be the fulfilment of pre-stated and emerging learning needs and a meaningful shift within organisational systems.

SLL requires the facilitator to continuously monitor the learning needs of leaders. This is essential, as learning needs morph during the learning process. Traditional learning needs analyses end with the identification of (often stilted) needs prior to the learning process. In SLL, the facilitator recognises that leaders will reach insights during learning process that extend far beyond the appreciation of the facilitator. This is because leaders are continuously navigating their own system and trawling for insights into complexities that the facilitator cannot possibly comprehend at the same level of depth. It is not possible for the facilitator to fully appreciate the experience of the leader; not because of the lack of ability, but simply because the facilitator does not possess a perfect schematic match. If the reality of multiple leaders in the learning environment is then recognised, it is imperative that the facilitator shows immense humility, with a profound understanding that the challenges and intricacies of complex personal and organisational systems, merged with the unique system of every leader within the organisational system, renders it utterly impossible for the facilitator to propose ready solutions. The needs of leaders will therefore provoke and guide the learning process, while the facilitator, having proposed key content, reciprocates with provocation for meaningful ideation.

Chapter 5

PHOTO-SHOPPED

Visual experimentation with photography

Ah, when to the heart of man
Was it ever less than a treason
To go with the drift of things,
To yield with a grace to reason,
And bow and accept the end
Of a love or a season.

Robert Frost, Reluctance

Intellectual attention is at a premium. It is expensive and in desperately short supply. The assault on the senses from social and other media is relentless. Even behavioural science, with potential to inspire greater humanity, is employed as a mechanism for hijacking attention. And yet, there is no shortage of information. With memory having become a portable commodity, vast swathes of data are continuously employed as missiles for commandeering our increasingly fragile capabilities for concentration. Therefore, a learning deficit is no longer, as it once was, caused by a lack of access to information. This thesis is easy to prove: poor leadership decisions continue unabated around the world, while research expands exponentially simultaneously. An alternative paradigm of learning has therefore become essential for 21st century executive development.

Following the endorsement by industry representatives to examine the value of the theory of Systemic Leadership Learning, it was imperative to reference some of the developed insights from SLL through an engagement process that would operate at a more detailed level of insight.

One of the key tenets that emerged in the theory of SLL is that the leader holds a self-perception of being the supra-system during the learning experience. To test this assumption, it was imperative for the reliability of the research to identify a method in which leaders (both thought leaders and leaders of people and processes) could be provoked to explore their own systems during a learning experience in which their systems were isolated as far as possible, with minimal external input from learning content. If leaders could explore their own systems and as a result produce insights that would be unique to their systems, this would be a clear indication that the leader has both the ability and the inclination to view the system of the self as the supra-system during learning.

One challenge for such an experiment was to provide just the right amount of input to provoke leaders to explore their own systems, without allowing excessive external stimuli to dominate the learning process. If leaders could develop insights in a learning environment in which external learning inputs have been limited to the extreme, it would also support another tenet of the emerging theory, namely the principle of subordination of learning content to the reality of the leader.

An experiment was designed that would use photography as minimal input into the system of the leader as a means of inspiring leaders to explore their own systems. Members of a reference group once again consisting of industry professionals, organisational leaders and those responsible for executive development in their organisations were invited to a photographic exhibition as part of the research for this book. The event was entitled "Moments in a system". A copy of the invitation appears below.

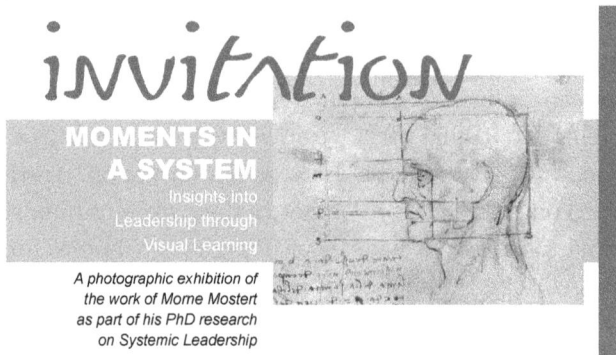

Figure 8: Invitation to photographic exhibition

The art form of photography was selected because of its nonthreatening nature. Neutral images could be presented to leaders, in response to which they would be invited to share the insights they gained through their personal navigation of their own systems. This neutrality of images as system inputs would mirror the leader's reality of confronting challenges "as they appear", that is, without prejudice and without forced perceptions.

Photographs are also clearly visual in nature. As such, the medium lends itself to the exploration of metaphor and consequential personal meaning formation. Such meaning formation by the leader would be a sign of the personal navigation of the leader's system. Photographs were therefore used as *system navigation tools*, that is the means by which leaders would explore their own systems in search of insights that may lie hidden or masked by an obsession with external inputs.

Furthermore, photographs offer vast opportunities to present contrast. In one image juxtapositions can be made of elements as diverse as order and chaos. In this sense, photographs offer multi-dimensional aspects of the same subject, which may be seen to echo the leader's experience of the complexity of challenges faced in organisations.

In order to find the correct balance between sufficient external input to provoke the leader on the one hand, and emphasis on the system of the leader on the other, the search was for *requisite thought architecture*, that is, the minimum input required into the system of the leader that would nevertheless provide the requisite framework and context within which leaders could respond from the vantage point of their own systems.

To this end, I selected photographs from my own photographic work from around the world that would lend themselves to this aim. Photographs were selected on two key criteria.

The first criterion was the degree of aesthetic elegance of the photograph. The motivation for this selection criterion was the optimisation of engagement in the photographs and the need to mitigate the risk of a lack of interest in the photographs by the reference group. Clearly aesthetic elegance is subjective in nature, but qualitative feedback on the photographs suggested that most members of the reference group shared the view that the photographs lent themselves to a degree of aesthetic appreciation.

The second criterion was that each photograph would contain the appearance of potential contradictions or paradoxes. The motivation for this criterion was that it might reflect the reality of leaders in the workplace – a great deal of the complexities leaders face at work is as a result of apparently contradictory elements in their systems as well as in the systems of their organisations. Their decisions are rendered more complex by the counterintuitive data they confront. The element of potential contradiction would present an intellectual conundrum and it was my expectation that such intellectual challenge would engage leaders and provoke them to insights of their own.

A total of twenty-seven photographs were selected and exhibited. The decision on the number of photographs was based on the desire to provide the members of the reference group with sufficient options to provoke the navigation of their own systems. Members of the reference group would self-select the photographs they wished to engage with. Qualitative feedback during a debriefing session following the exhibition revealed that members of the reference group were indeed attracted to some photographs and dispelled from others. Interestingly, the qualitative feedback also showed that the preference of individual members changed as they became more engaged in the process. The initial attraction was to the aesthetic elegance of the photographs or to a personal interest in the subject matter, while interest evolved into other photographs that offered more of an intellectual challenge through the contradictions the photographs would exhibit.

Having selected photographs based on the criteria above, I then added a simple title to each photograph. These titles were metaphorical rather than literal in nature as a means of provoking deeper thought processes for the leader.

In addition to the titles, each photograph was annotated by reference to two to three system sets represented in the photograph. These system sets were expressed in very simple language and consisted of two apparently contradictory concepts. As an example, in one photograph that contained an image of water next to an office building, the conceptual system sets identified included: fluidity and rigidity.

In order to complete the creation of *requisite thought architecture* as defined, a simple reflection sheet was provided. This sheet invited members to comment on two aspects, which were the same for every photograph, namely:

i. The implications of the photograph for their organisation in terms of the organisational culture, customers, strategy or any other aspect of their organisational experience, and

ii. The implications of the photograph for them as a leader.

An example of the reflection sheet appears below. Members of the reference group were asked to comment on a minimum of five photographs.

Table 6: Reflection sheet

REFLECTION SHEET
Implications for my organisation (e.g. culture, structure, customers, strategy, etc.)
Implications for me as a leader:

The process was that members of the reference group were first invited to simply experience the exhibition by observing the photographs. At this stage they were not requested to record any insights. The observable behaviour of members was noticeable discomfort. Discomfort is inherent in the learning process. The collision of the existing schema with a new insight or experience creates intellectual and emotional disruption. This is why learning often requires intellectual fortitude and curiosity to engage with the previously unexplored.

A video recording of the proceedings shows how the discomfort evolved into curiosity as the members started to read the photograph titles and the system sets present in each photograph.

Members were then invited to leave the exhibition room and attend a briefing session on the context and purpose of the process. Here they were provided with a brief explanation of the nature of the experiment. They were then invited to return to the exhibition room and to record their insights in response to each photograph.

They were also provided with an abstract of the nature of the experiment, which appeared at the entrance to the exhibition for their reference. A copy of the abstract is provided below.

Table 7: Abstract for exhibition

ABSTRACT
The idea This exhibition examines Systemic Leadership Learning, a concept for executive development that proposes that leaders learn with greater impact if they do so in a systemic way. Traditional executive development programmes emphasise text and content, with little regard for the reality of the leader. This often alienates the leader from the learning process and inhibits the potential ROI from learning. Finding other ways to learn is therefore imperative.
The leader as supra-system Mostert proposes that the leader holds a self-perception of supra-system during the learning process, that is leaders naturally subordinate learning content to their own reality. If this is true, the starting point for learning has to be the leader's reality, rather than the content selection and design. The challenge is to find a way that navigates the leader's system, without dictating the learning process, content or intended outcomes.
Visual input as system navigation tool The visual image offers one way in which to provoke and invite the leader to navigate the self and organisation as systems. The most salient challenges are most likely to rise to a level of consciousness, without threat, pressure or intimidation to admit failure.
Requisite thought architecture The proposed methodology raises interesting questions regarding the **risk of content as propaganda** for leadership. One challenge is therefore to provide **sufficient learning architecture that promotes self-navigation**, while allowing sufficient freedom of expression and self-navigation to insight for the leader. The photographs invite honest reflection and the supporting universal questions allow for **requisite thought architecture** within which the leader can move freely, formulate problems and safely communicate systemic implications and possible solutions.

The room was designed like an art exhibition, with photographs exhibited against the walls in frames. Some photographs were also hung on an industrial ladder, to support the idea of architecture of thought.

In addition to printed photographs, electronic photographs were also exhibited through projection onto a wall. Furthermore, a live video stream of the room was projected onto yet another wall. This moving image reflected events as they occurred in the room. This design posed interesting questions about the definition of a photograph as potentially dynamic. It also created a physical manifestation of a feedback loop: members of the reference group (a nascent social system like groups in a learning process) could see themselves in the video image while observing the photographs. They could, in other words, watch themselves watching themselves in a manner that mirrored (literally) both the patent and opaque circularity present in all systems. As they changed their physical movements, they could see the feedback of a change in the design of the room from the projected image. They were literally co-designing the learning experience for themselves and other actors in the system. The presence of a physical feedback loop in the room therefor supported the overarching theory of systems thinking that was being applied to the learning process. It furthermore supported the idea that the leader is an inherent part of the system, while retaining the discretion of freedom of movement, intellectual processing and expression.

Observable behaviour was noticeably different on the second encounter with the photographs. Members were more vocal and appeared more confident as they paused at selected photographs, reflected on the minimal input from the titles and system sets, and recorded their insights.

Following the second encounter with the photographs, members were once again invited to leave the exhibition for a debriefing session during which they were consulted on their experiences. Two key findings emerged as a result of this experiment:

i.   **Evolving context through incubation**

Members commented that their first visit to the exhibition room filled them with uncertainty, as endorsed by my observation of their uncomfortable demeanour. They commented that, while they enjoyed the photographs, they could not meaningfully engage with the questions asked. However, once the intellectual context had been created and they had time to consider the photographs again, they found it considerably easier to complete the reflection sheet regarding the implications for their own organisations and for themselves as leaders.

This suggested that, on the first visit, the requisite thought architecture had not yet been established and that time for incubation had not been sufficient. This illustrates the value of context and incubation time for the learning process. It also supports the value of requisite design of the system (however minimal) for the achievement of the learning purpose, despite the inevitable evolution that will occur in the learning process as emerging system.

ii.   Confirmation of the leader as supra-system

With almost no input provided other than the titles, system sets and abstract, all members of the reference group were able to generate insights about their organisations and about themselves as leaders.

There were no other learning content, notes or discussion questions. The organisations represented by the leaders present did not dictate any learning content. No lecturers insisted on the correct interpretation of theories. There was no assessment and no quality assurance process. And yet leaders learnt!

Learning appears to have occurred through the simple process of allowing leaders the freedom to be provoked and to engage with minimal learning input in the form of visual inputs from photographs. This provided the requisite thought architecture for them to navigate their own systems. The system of each leader was therefore perceived by that leader as the supra-system in need of elucidation. In all cases without exception, every member of the reference group was able to identify creative application opportunities from a nonthreatening and meaningful engagement with their own systems. This self-navigation process of their own systems as the supra-system during learning, led them to insights that they believed they did not have before the learning experience. They had therefore expanded their insight into their organisations and themselves as leaders, with only the requisite thought architecture.

It became clear that the exhibition of photographs allowed leaders to tell their own story, in their own way, based on their own experience. This could be done without fear of editing or ridicule, and made the learning experience personal and unique. Their recorded insights were the recording of the leader's story of a personal reading of the system.

This experiment showed that leaders have at the very least both the ability and inclination to perceive their own systems as the supra-system during the learning process. This finding poses interesting questions about the effectiveness of traditional learning processes in which learning content appears to dominate in the form of extensive notes, presentations, lectures, assessments and prescribed reading. Research shown above regarding the lack of return on investment from many traditional executive development programmes endorses the need for the exploration of new approaches.

It is not suggested that traditional methods are never effective. Nor is it implied that learning content cannot aid the learning process. What is indeed proposed is an additional approach and methodology in the form of Systemic Leadership Learning that allows leaders to experience the necessary respect for their systems as the supra-system during learning. With the appropriate integration of learning content as part of the learning process, leaders may be guided to even greater insights and may identify even more creative application opportunities as a means of advancing themselves and their organisations and thus ensuring return on learning investment, provided such content does not subordinate the leaders.

It also deserves mention that learning in the experiment above was an emerging property, not a pre-determined set of learning outcomes. The implications for the way executive programmes are designed are significant.

A valid conclusion to be drawn, as endorsed by the leaders present in a debrief of the experiment, is that leaders already have their own systems that require navigation through the learning process. Leaders are indeed their own supra-systems in the learning situation.

SLL suggests that the executive in the learning situation should resist this subordination, and should be encouraged to do so; to accept that the systems of the content, facilitator and organisation are not the containing systems for the complete system of the leader. The acceptance of such subordination of other systems will improve the engagement of the leader in the learning process, as the real challenges experienced will enjoy more prominence. The leader will not feel alienated by sterile learning content presented as the only truth and enforced in a pseudo-participative style. Instead, the leaders will derive confidence from the recognition that their systems are unique, and therefore require unique solutions, for which those leaders have the responsibility of dissolution. Paradoxically, the fluid freedom allotted in SLL therefore suggests greater rather than reduced responsibility for the leader.

It is often the case that systems thinking is confused with a laissez faire approach. Because of the alternative paradigm of structure and process present in systems thinking, those new to the field view it either as another set of engineering instructions, or a philosophy in which anything goes. Nothing could be further from the truth. Systems thinking demand very high levels of intellectual commitment. Because system architecture is often emergent rather than explicit, the deepest sense of curiosity and intellectual humility is required to enhance systemic understanding.

Chapter 6

WHIPLASH

Merging four fields of study

Much as I own I owe
The passers of the past
Because their to and fro
Has cut this road to last...
They have found other scenes
For haste and other means.

Robert Frost, Closed for Good

In SLL it is therefore critical to understand the dynamic interplay between the four primary systems of the Leader, Organisation, Facilitator and Learning Content. Each system impacts on and is itself mutated by each of the other major systems.

The cognitive twist is that this energised interplay only works, as is true for all systems, when its containing environment is conducive to its existence and potential. All systems have *multiple containing systems*, that is, they exist within the boundaries of more than one macro-system. In the case of SLL, the multiple containing environments are viewed as four fields of study, the appreciation of which greatly enhances the return on learning investment. These four fields are:

- **Systems Thinking** – the study of the nature of systems and, in this context, the implications for an alternative form of intellectual processing by leaders.
- **Leadership** – the study of the intellectual, affective and behavioural dimensions most likely to enhance migration of the system to a more preferable state.
- **Learning** – the study of how to generate and synthesise new insight.
- **Story** – the expression of narrative from a unique vantage point in a manner that incorporates multidimensional aspects of the leader's world, history and future.

Just like the four primary systems, these four fields of study engage in an ever-changing, dynamic dance, exchanging energy and redefining themselves and each other, while creating the evolutionary context for the four primary systems that also engage in constant mutual co-creation. This means that the overall learning system continuously regenerates into a system that demands ongoing re-evaluation.

The respective fields represented above are almost infinitely broad. This is partly due to the prolific publication in these fields, which in turn is driven by what appears to be a great need for clarification by those working and studying in these areas.

It has been the intention of this book to establish clarity on the main perspectives in the fields, but also to determine the extent to which the fields of leadership, learning, systems thinking and story have been merged. In the search for clarify on the state of literature, I have found the following:

The need for a dramatic paradigm shift in the field of executive development

Much of the literature that professes to show the need for executive development, in fact presents a view on the behaviour required from leaders in their leadership roles, rather than as students of leadership. Large research studies conducted with leaders seem to intend to define the characteristics of good leadership. The literature tends to suggest what leaders should *do,* while it is the intention of this book to show the way in which these abilities and behaviours may be learnt, perpetually and systemically. There appears to be some consensus and clarity on what leaders need to do, but little guidance on how these behaviours and abilities may be acquired through learning.

The value of Systems Thinking as an approach

The field of systems thinking is well explored, and large volumes of literature exist on the subject and certainly provide ample insight into the dynamics of systems thinking. There is furthermore ample exploration of systems thinking as applied to general organisational theory and even on organisational learning. However, there appears to be little that specifically explains the relationship between the systems of the leader and the organisation. The literature also appears to view the leader as sub-system of the organisation, and even of the learning content, while this book proposes that the leader has a self-perception of being the supra-system during learning. This systemic interchange appears limited in the literature. Equally, and perhaps for this reason, systems thinking is generally applied as an organisational tool, while this book aims to apply it to individual learning for executives.

Insight into the nature of learning for executives

The field of learning is, as with systems thinking, well represented by a vast landscape of literature. It is the intention here to explore from that landscape those insights that relate to executive development. In this domain, literature exists for the study of various methodological approaches for executive development. The most notable amongst these may be the literature on action learning.

There appears, however, some uncertainty about whether the current methods used for the development of leaders deliver the desired application of learning.

A need for a systemic approach to executive development

It was my intention to explore the literature landscape for work that may be similar to the theory proposed in this book. I could then build upon the work already done in this specific field.

Once again, extensive literature exists for the study of systems thinking as it relates to organisation behaviour. The notion that organisations may be viewed as systems and therefore adhere to the characteristics of systems is not a new insight.

But the view of the leader as system in the learning space is almost entirely absent from the literature on systems thinking. The notion of the leader as supra-system is therefore even more elusive. There appears to be a need, and there certainly is a gap, for literature that elaborates on the supra-system status of the leader as applied to the learning situation in a systemic way. Some authors may argue that their work infers this, but continuous mention of the leader's responsibility to somehow serve or fit into the system of the organisation would belie such a claim: the organisation is consistently viewed in the literature as the supra-system, into which the leader somehow has to fit and create value for the organisation. There is, admittedly, a notable exception in the world of coaching, in which coaches are encouraged to act in service of the leader and to 'get out of the way' of the leader's development.

Most literature seems to suggest that the leader is little more than an element of the system of the organisation. Despite this status ascribed to leaders, they are nevertheless given the responsibility for meaningful change. It is little wonder that studies reveal a serious lack in the return on investment from executive development.

The need for clarity on Mode 2 knowledge production

The literature reviewed shows a clear need for new methods of creating insight about the reality of the executive development industry. Despite this apparent cohesion in the recognition for the search of new methods of inquiry, not all authors agree on exactly how this should be done.

In each of these four fields of study a myriad of literature exists. For the purposes of this book, I have attempted to limit the study of these four fields to where they intersect, that is, those areas in each field that have a direct impact on each of the other fields. The diagram below shows the intersection.

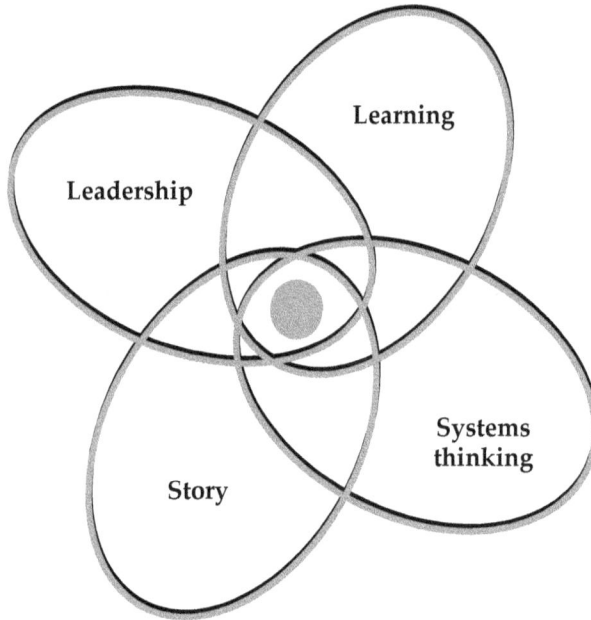

Figure 9: Merging four fields of study

The dynamic interplay merits some exploration. What the merger of these four fields of study implies, is that SLL seeks to examine the intersections of, for example, where leadership is exposed to learning; where leadership is learnt in multiple interconnected systems (which learning situation forms its own new system), where leadership has its own unique story worthy of recognition and other intersectionality. It further examines the space where learning happens systemically and where learning has and continues to create its own story. It explores the milieu where systems thinking informs the composition of the leadership, where systems thinking is learnt and where systems thinking informs the design, communication and co-creation of a personal and holistic multi-system narrative.

Chapter 7

THE FUGITIVE: EXECUTIVES AT SCHOOL

A portrait of divergence

Freedom to flash off into wild connection.
Once to have known it, nothing else will do.
When it's in you and in the situation.

Robert Frost, How hard it is to keep from being king

It is a fundamental principle of SLL that the leader represents a key system; an active and dynamic role player that shapes the learning process as it unfolds. For this reason, it is essential that we should understand the nature of the leader as system. As part of the professional work of many leadership consultants, they engage with leaders in a process of continuous exchange. This means essentially that they examine the objectives and frustrations of the individual leader and cooperatively navigate a route to improved success. Key to the success of this process is the ability of the facilitator to:

- Challenge the views and examine the quality of decisions of leaders,
- Continuously request the executive to define and design possible solutions,
- Insist upon brutal honesty at all times,
- Integrate various elements of information from the executive into cohesive structure of feedback and reflection,
- Identify and evaluate options as possible dissolutions to challenges,
- And, most significantly, provide support within the realities of the context of the leader.

The research conducted for this book has produced a framework that is applicable for use by facilitators of a wide spectrum of learning content. This model moves beyond the approach of group coaching, since it positions each leader as supra-system, rather than as sub-system.

The first step in the process is to gain a detailed and respectful insight of the reality of the system of the leader.

7.1 Braveheart: The executive reality

It is clear from the dialectic (exploring paradoxes in the discussion towards truth-finding and synthesis) on SLL thus far that this methodology positions the leader as the supra-system during the learning process. This supra-system status is allocated to the leader on the grounds that:

- It is the leader who is expected to learn, not the facilitator
- It is the leader's system that must internalise learning content and develop a degree of internal congruence between the personal views and experiences of the leader, the expectations of the organisation and the tenets of the learning content proposed
- It is the leader who has to ensure the creative application of insights gained during learning
- And, most significantly, SLL proposes that the leader takes a default position as supra-system during the learning situation.

Therefore, the other systems at work in the learning process, notably the organisation, the learning content and the facilitator, have to accept the reality of the leader as supra-system in order for these other systems to ensure optimal learning by the leader.

It is therefore critical that the reality of the leader is understood and appreciated at deep levels of internal systemic relatedness.

In my experience with a wide range of clients in a broad spectrum of industries and at various levels of leadership across the planet, almost all leaders experience typical dimensions of reality. These realities have a significant impact on the ability and commitment of leaders to learn. These realities also have a wide range of different impacts on various leaders, given the uniqueness of the system of each leader. Some of the dimensions facing all leaders are:

Mutiny of the Bounty: Incessant change

If there is one generic reality for all leaders that has become a truism of modern organisations, it is the experience of constant change. This is often driven by an increasingly sophisticated and demanding customer base, constantly changing local and international market conditions and the need for competitive advantage. It poses a challenge to the learning process, since, just as leaders have learnt new methods and approaches, conditions change that necessitate further learning and even un-learning, that is learning to reinterpret and even reject what has previously been learnt.

Locked up: Limited authority

It has already been highlighted that many leaders are, rather paradoxically, required to lead as followers. This means that they are described as leaders by their organisations but are simultaneously subjected to a host of organisational rules, policies, processes and protocols. The reality is therefore that almost all leaders have limited control over the scope of their decision-making and can exercise limited power over resources at their disposal, despite the quality of their ideas. The experience of having limited power and control has a significant impact on the potential for the identification and implementation of creative application opportunities, as the leader (within the confines of supra-system perceptions) may undervalue the learning process as having limited use, due to the fact that, even if the leader agrees with the content and possibilities highlighted, that leader may lack the power to ensure implementation – a frequent piece of feedback from executive development programmes.

X-Men: Levels of IQ and EQ

It is essential to note that the system of the leader operates in the presence of the systems of others, who may have some form of power over the leader. An understanding of the character and abilities of those around the leader may also provide great insight into the systemic reality of the leader.

One of the key variables in the systems of those around the leader is the level of their IQ, or Intelligence Quotient, that is essentially their ability to solve complex problems. Naturally, the IQ of the leader is also relevant to understanding the system of the self, but the IQ of those around the leader can have a great impact in terms of whether the leader's insights and ideas will find support for implementation. The ability of those around the leader to deal with complexity, take on serious challenges and apply their minds to solutions will have a noticeable impact on the leader's ability and willingness to identify creative application opportunities from learning. The stories of those who have risen to the top while their intellectual elevators have not, are too many to recount.

Another critical dimension of those around the leader is their EQ, or Emotional Quotient, that is emotional intelligence or their ability to interpret and act meaningfully upon their own emotions and those of others. One of the main reasons why the emotional intelligence of those around the leader is significant for the learning of the leader as system is that work is the main source of recognition for many executives. This means that leaders derive a great deal of personal confirmation from the content, quality and outcomes of their work. For other leaders to introduce a change to that work is therefore very likely to generate anxiety in the systems of those leaders whose work may be affected. The strategic navigation of the resulting dissonance from such change is a critical skill for all leaders, as change and innovation are critical to the work of all leaders. My earlier definition of leadership noted a migration from the status quo. The implication is that someone who simply implements processes without consideration of change or innovation in the interest of progress cannot be viewed as a leader for the purposes of SLL.

Raging bull: Relentless demand for higher performance

Linked to the three realities of the leader noted above, is the relentless demand for greater performance placed upon the leader by customers, shareholders, other leaders, staff, investors and other stakeholders, including social actors like politicians and activists.

One of the classical conundrums for leaders under such relentless expectations is whether higher performance implies improving of the status quo through improved efficiency or reinventing the status quo through innovation.

The former implies that learning for the leader aims to find incremental improvements at best. Learning in this context asks the leader to accept the fundamentals of the status quo, and to look for possible opportunities to leverage efficiencies. The challenge this presents to leaders in the learning situation is that they may be unsure about what to do with breakthrough insights reached during learning. It may lead to some disillusionment for the leader if significant creative application opportunities are identified, but the leader knows that breakthrough insights will not be welcomed by the sponsoring organisation.

The latter, namely improvement through innovation, allows the leader to gain the full benefit of the learning experience. It calls for an honest review of the way things are done and invites leaders to apply the full range of competencies that formed the foundation of their selection and appointment into the organisation in the first instance.

The departure from traditional executive development programmes should be noted here: an SLL-type programme is not limited to whether leaders have understood the learning content. Nor is it confined to whether leaders can find ways of applying the content. SLL encourages leaders to examine the systemic implications of their insights to migrate the system as the result of engaging with the systems of the content, facilitator, organisation and other leaders, as well as the broader ecosystem in which all these systems reside.

7.1.1 Shape of you: Perceptual Positions

The diagram below shows the three-dimensional framework created based upon the field work that formed the foundation for this book. According to the model, a leader may find a position on each of the dimensions. These are referred to as perceptual positions, since it is often the perception of the leader that will determine the leader's location on each dimension. The value of a three-dimensional model in this context is that it contributes to the sense of orientation and navigation that is essential for leaders to progress along their learning journey, albeit in a non-linear way.

The model shows a number of dimensions identified as key to the successful navigation of the learning process. Each dimension is represented as a continuum. This means that the leader may find a personal position along each continuum. Personal, individual positioning by each leader is essential and it is the role of each leader in the learning process to display sufficient honesty for meaningful self-assessment.

The model further suggests that each leader has a position on each of the dimensions. That means that each leader simultaneously has a position on all of the dimensions. This insight is critical as it serves to provide greater insight into the leader as system and moves beyond a crude traditional analysis of the leader as having a number of domains comprising identity, such as:

- Spiritual
- Intellectual
- Emotional
- Physical
- Social
- Cultural
- Professional

While the domains of identity highlighted above are undoubtedly valuable, the multidimensional model proposed here emphasises the areas critical to learning and perceives the leader as a complex system within the context of learning. The leader in SLL is permanently and simultaneously the collection of all comprising dimensions.

The model raises levels of self-awareness with regards to knowledge, skills, attributes and also examines the realities of other key stakeholders, some of whom are co-creating the learning process through design inputs or a physical presence on the course, and others of whom are wholly disengaged from the learning process. The leader is encouraged to honestly review personal levels of knowledge about the self and others.

Below is an outline of each dimension identified in the proposed multidimensional model. In each case, the leader is encouraged with the help of the facilitator and with provocation and guidance from the learning content and colleagues, within the context of the organisation represented by the leader, to consider the implications of that leader's position on the continuum represented by each dimension. Furthermore, the leader's relative position is afforded more detail through insights of the dimension in relation to at least two other variables, indicated in a matrix structure. This creates a number of quadrants, which are numbered from the top left quadrant to the bottom right quadrant. The letter "Q" indicates a quadrant.

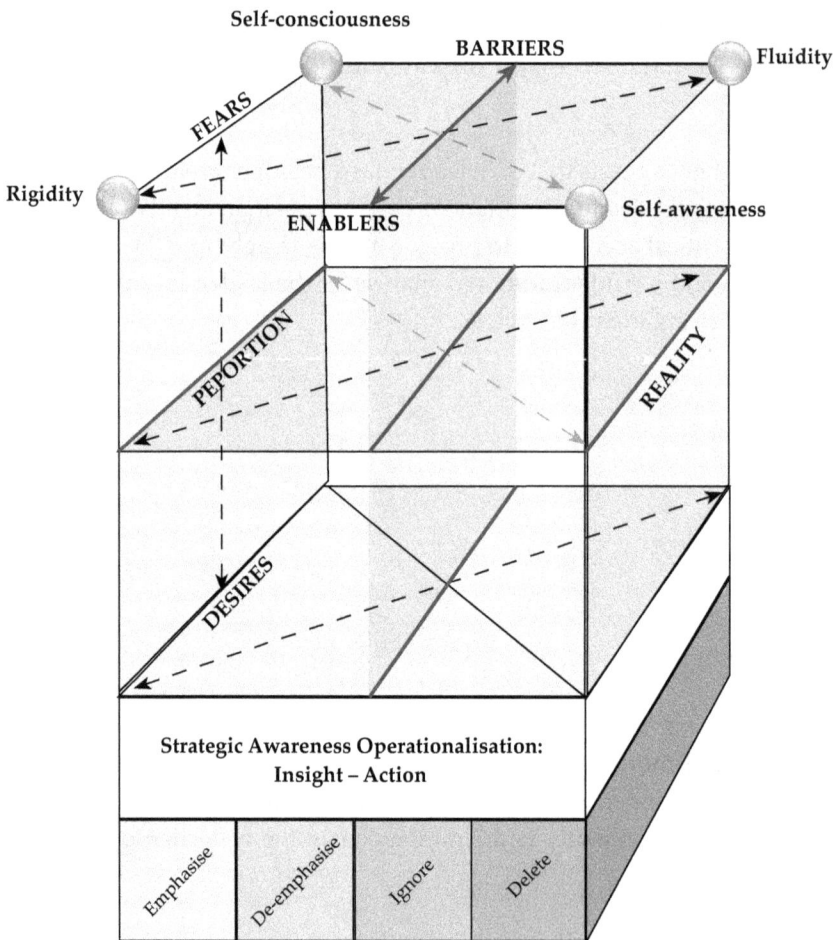

Figure 10: Multi-dimensional orientation framework

The dimensions are discussed in no particular order, as they are deemed as being at the same level of priority for the leader or at varying levels of priority depending on the leader's unique vantage point within a series of interrelated systems. It is further important to note that the model does not prescribe an ideal position on any of the dimensions for any leader, as the systemic reality for each leader may be different.

7.1.1.1 Despicable me: Fear and Desire

One of the dimensions identified is that of fears and desires. This dimension evaluates whether the leader's current behaviour is driven by fears, that is people or situations that represent a threat and should be avoided, or whether the leader is driven by desires, that is the leader is pulled towards the achievement of some identified or implicit goal. The distinction is significant, as neurological insights suggest key distinctions in subsequent behaviour.

Leaders driven by fear may behave evasively and defensively. They continuously attempt to avoid certain risks and base their plans on the avoidance of danger. It is clear that an approach driven by fear may ignore many opportunities that may arise for two reasons. The first is that opportunity may represent danger in the form of risk or challenge. The second is that opportunities may not represent fears and therefore may not be deemed worthy of neurological attention. At the same time, fear may be a valuable insight if it is limited to the identification and evasion of real and significant risk.

Leaders driven by desire often appear more positive in their approach. They have defined expected goals and outcomes and navigate themselves and their resources towards the meaningful fulfilment of these goals. The risk of this approach is that leaders may follow their goals blindly, without due consideration of the risks involved. They may also justify their behaviour based on the fact that it supports a stated goal, without appreciating the systemic realities of that goal.

Table 8 below shows an outline of typical fear and desire scenarios. It shows the implications of moving both towards and from fears and desires.

Table 8: Fears and Desires

	TOWARDS	FROM
FEARS	Q1: Negatively teleological	Q2: Fighting the negative
DESIRES	Q3: Self-determining	Q4: Self-defeating

Quadrant 1 shows a move towards or in the direction of fears. This is often caused by the power of negative suggestion, that is, there is so much focus on what to

avoid, that it ultimately becomes the only thing the leader spends any time on. It is described here as *negatively teleological*, that is the leader's behaviour is attracted to and aligned behind exactly what that leader is trying to avoid. Note: teleology in this context refers to the design and execution (by commission or omission) of behaviour by the leader in the interest of achieving a purpose.

Quadrant 2 shows a scenario of moving away from fears. The challenge with behaviour in this quadrant is that it is negatively formulated – it states what will be avoided, rather than what will be achieved. A classical social example is the fighting of crime. It suggests that crime will be fought, rather than that a safe society will be established. In social policy, similar language is found in eradicating poverty (rather than creating wealth), combatting disease (rather than creating health), opposing inequality (rather than establishing equity) and several others.

Quadrant 3 demonstrates behaviour that moves the leader towards desires. This is behaviour that is likely to achieve positive objectives. It is positively formulated and requires careful consideration of the exact nature of the desires. It should be followed by behaviour that is most likely to achieve the stated goals. It is recognised here that social systems are probabilistic in nature; not deterministic. It is for this reason that this text often refers to likelihood of results rather than linear outcomes.

Quadrant 4 shows behaviour that moves the leader away from desires. Such behaviour is self-defeating, as it creates distance between the leader and the goals. Clearly, no leader deliberately moves away from desires, but it often happens that leaders are diverted from desires by a preoccupation with other problems. Very often, leaders simply need to be made aware that their behaviour is deterring them from their stated goals – the simple increase in self-awareness is often enough for the leader to realign behaviour behind the stated goals.

The above is not intended to suggest that the achievement of goals constitutes a simple implementation process. The reality is that goals morph as the dynamic context shifts. SLL recognises the fluid nature of intentionality, but nevertheless proposes the pursuit of clarity of intention wherever it may be discovered. SLL is therefore not simply the binary opposite of programmatic goal achievement. It is not fatalistic. Nor is it nihilistic. It possesses the requisite pragmatism to investigate systems as they are, and acknowledges the possibility, and indeed the responsibility, for leaders to navigate systems to greater levels of preferability.

7.1.1.2   The big heist: Perception and Reality

Another dimension identified as critical to learning for the leader is that of perception and reality. This dimension is critical due to the potential impact it may have on leadership decisions. It is clearly essential that leaders should base decisions on reality, rather than perception, as the response of customers, staff, shareholders and other stakeholders will be based upon their reality, rather than upon the perception of the leader. Herein lies one of the great paradoxes of leadership: leaders must trust and believe their own judgement and demonstrate confidence, but should simultaneously be sensitive to the needs, perceptions and realities of multiple direct and indirect stakeholders in multiple containing systems.

Table 9 below shows some of the key considerations in the analysis of the perception and reality dimension. The implication is that views which are mere perceptions, while real in the owner of the perception, do not reflect the reality as experienced by others. As the table indicates, the leader should consider (with the help of the facilitator and guided by the learning content) the perceptions and realities both according to the leader, as well as according to other key stakeholders. In systems thinking terms, the leader is actively encouraged to gather multiple partial views as a means of evaluating assumptions. The obligatory difficulties for the leader present themselves clearly: how does the executive know whether perceptions are real and how does the leader decide on the reality status of the views of others? Which view carries more weight: the reality of the leader or the perceptions of others? They are, of course, potentially interrelated as the system of the leader's reality should be sufficiently permeable by the views of other stakeholders.

Many may argue philosophically that there is no objective reality and that all views are subject to a degree of relativism. It is not the intention here to prove the existence of objective reality, but to encourage leaders in the learning process to at the very least test the validity of their assumptions through robust engagement with the perceptual positions of the self and others in the system.

Table 9: Perception and Reality

	LEADER		OTHERS	
	By leader	Of leader	By others	Of others
PERCEPTION	Q1	Q2	Q3	Q4
REALITY	Q5	Q6	Q7	Q8

What the table shows in Q1 and Q5 is that the understanding of this dimension may be further refined by exploring the perceptions and realities *by* the leader *of* the leader and others as well as perceptions and realities of others by themselves. Both perceptions and realities may relate to the organisational environment, challenges, change or any other aspect of the experience of the organisation or leader.

Q1 shows perceptions by the leader that are subject to verification. As perceptions, and not reality, they often represent the myopia of the leader, that is, the leader's inability to see reality beyond the immediate view.

Q2 shows perceptions of the leader. These perceptions may be held by the leader or any other stakeholder. Whether these perceptions are accurate or not, it is imperative for the leader to be aware of them, as they will impact on the way in which others in the system may be engaged.

Q3 shows the views of others. As with the perceptions of the leader, these perceptions may represent the myopia of others, who see matters in a way that suits their own worldview.

Q4 shows the perceptions that are held *of* others, that is, the way in which others are perceived. These perceptions may be held by the leader as well as third parties and highlight the perception of stakeholders.

Q5 shows the true reality aspects in the working environment observed by the leader. This quadrant represents honesty and integrity by the leader in the assessment of the systemic environment.

Q6 shows the leader's true reality as seen by the leader. This quadrant describes a state of healthy self-awareness that allows the leader to gain self-insight. The leader can act and make decisions based on a true state of affairs, or as closely as that may be approximated.

Q7 represents the truth of others, that is, the way things truly are for them. Of late, this has become a highly contestable social dimension. This is critical for the leader to understand at a profound level, as the leader's decisions may impact on this reality, resulting in a feedback loop which will impact the likely success of the leader's decisions.

Q8 shows an objective view of others that may be held by the leader, or by the staff, colleagues, clients, peers or other stakeholders in relation to others. This quadrant may also explain the degree to which others understand themselves and those with whom they engage.

7.1.1.3   No time to die: Barriers and Enablers

The learning effectiveness of the leader is furthermore impacted by an assessment of the leader's engagement with barriers and enablers.

Barriers may be defined as any element, internal or external to both the system of the leader or the organisation, that may, in the view of the leader, prevent, limit or retard the progress or implementation of an idea.

Enablers may be defined as any element, internal or external to both the leader and the organisation, that may, in the view of the leader, advance, free up or accelerate the progress or implementation of an idea.

Table 10 below shows the assessment of the leader's relative position on this continuum in relation to whether the leader is moving towards or from barriers or enablers. As with a number of the dimensions identified in this model, it may appear glaringly obvious when reviewed on reflection. But the reality of many leaders is that a limited degree of self-awareness, driven by habitual over-emphasis of activity over results, prevents the leader from understanding personal behaviour and thus limits the opportunities for behaviour modification.

Table 10: Barriers and Enablers

	TOWARDS	FROM
BARRIERS	Q1	Q2
ENABLERS	Q3	Q4

Quadrant 1 illustrates the implication of a leader whose behaviour moves towards the risk presented by barriers. Leaders who demonstrate this kind of behaviour are investing their energies poorly, as the very thing they are trying to achieve is increasingly being prevented by their actions and decisions through circular causality. They are unable to observe this tendency, as they have multiple objectives and cannot identify behaviours that may be driving certain objectives while damaging others.

Quadrant 2 shows the reality of moving away from potential barriers. It is proposed that leaders display this behaviour as a means of self-protection; sometimes in an attempt to close the boundaries of their systems, thus limiting exposure to problems. While there may be value in this behaviour, it places the leader at risk of not confronting and engaging with the systemic implications of the barriers. Barriers exist as the result of other realities and these realities may be worthy of investigation. Avoidance of these realities may simply create an artificially closed system for the executive, and may lead to barriers reappearing through a systemic feedback loop that the leader has simply ignored. This would find the leader vastly unprepared for dealing with the realities of a barrier that can no longer be avoided. Recurring difficulties must be interpreted as the voice of the system shouting loudly and clearly: "Try something else! Be more creative! Expand your thinking!"

Quadrant 3 shows behaviour characterised by moving towards enablers. This means that the leader is harnessing the appropriate resources, physical, virtual, intellectual and otherwise, for increasing the probability of success. The leader is scanning the environment for supportive drivers of goals and is identifying and implementing synergies with the use of those enablers.

Quadrant 4 indicates behaviour that moves the leader away from enablers. This quadrant should not be confused with Quadrant 1. In Q1 the leader moves blindly towards barriers. In this quadrant, the leader is moving blindly away from those resources that may advance the achievement of goals. The leader is failing to capture the opportunities in the environment and is spending time on a less valuable activity. It is true that behaviour in both quadrants may be characterised as self-defeating, as it is the very efforts of the leader that in some way contribute to the retardation in the achievement of goals. Consciousness of the self-inflicted circularity may offer intellectual relief.

7.1.1.4   Skyfall: Rigidity and Fluidity

Given the great degree of complexity and challenge confronting leaders in the 21st century, and the concomitant personal challenges they have to experience, it is imperative that the leader considers personal levels of rigidity and fluidity in the navigation of the learning.

Rigidity describes a degree of inflexibility or refusal to adapt to demands and pressures by stakeholders. A leader high on rigidity demonstrates an over-attachment to the way things have been done before and are being conducted at present. Such a leader favours proven recipes over innovation and risk. It is clear that high degrees of rigidity may limit progress and learning, as learning is by definition the exploration of what is new and potentially different from what has been done or known before.

An approach characterised by rigidity also insulates the leader as system. It closes off the system of the leader and prevents the leader from venturing and exploring other means of achieving goals and certainly, and in extreme cases, precludes the leader from defining new opportunities entirely. It thus prevents the leader from progressing both in terms of process (the way things are done) and in terms of content (what is done). A classical example of such behaviour may be found in Founder's Syndrome, that is, the founder of an organisation, unit or idea who is closed to new ideas and refuses to take input and advice from others. The founder believes blindly that only the ideas that created the organisation and brought it to its current state are valid and worthy of further investment. Such leaders are not responsive to the demands and opportunities of their multiple containing systems. They may have been strong founders, but are not the best candidates for reinventing through innovative sigmoid curves.

The complexity of a product range, varying client needs, the challenges of staff performance, the requisite financial investment spread, and the sheer scale of operations required to compete in complex markets, characterised by continuously emerging technologies and variations in the competitive landscape, often prove too much for such leaders of organisations that at one point seemed infallible. Consider, for example, the number of once great organisations that have driven their old business models into oblivion during the global financial crisis that started in 2007 or the ones who were unable to adjust to the demands of the covid pandemic or the global ripple effects of the Russian war in Ukraine.

I am not proposing that some degree of firmness about intentions is devoid of value. In fact, robustness of approach and a degree of confidence is essential to success. What is proposed is that the leader becomes aware of potential personal levels of rigidity and examines the value and risks of such convictions within the ever-changing systemic context of the multiple containing environments of the organisation.

Fluidity, on the other hand, refers to a leader's ability to demonstrate flexibility and adaptability. It also alludes to a leader's inclination to explore and learn new things. In this sense, it is an indication of the willingness of a leader to maintain an open system – one that is at least partially receptive to inputs from others.

Table 11 shows the dimension of rigidity and flexibility in relation to behaviour under conditions of risk and safety. This differentiation is important as the behaviour of leaders may change depending on the degree of pressure they experience. Behaviour in conditions of risk tends to be more closed, while conditions of safety tend to allow for more openness.

Table 11: Rigidity and Fluidity

	IN RISK	IN SAFETY
RIGIDITY	Q1	Q2
FLUIDITY	Q3	Q4

Quadrant 1 shows behaviour of rigidity under conditions of risk. Once again, the leader may be justified to show some resistance to change during risk, since the leader is attempting to protect or defend personal, social or organisational interests under these conditions. One of the risks of this behaviour, however, is that the leader may hold an external locus of control, that is the leader's behaviour is the result of predominantly (or even exclusively) external factors, rather than the result of the leader's internalisation of learning. This could lead to a habit of reactive behaviour and may prevent the leader from learning about what is required to guide the organisation out of the impending risk.

Even if the leader is intent on self-protection or is determined to protect the current interests of the organisation, rather than access new opportunities, the option may still be open for the leader to identify possible contingencies. This presents an opportunity that is slightly less open, but at the very least it explores alternative courses of action. It may even be argued that conditions of risk represent the greatest need for openness and learning, as it is exactly the old habits and previous strategies of the organisation that have created the conditions of risk. For the leader to close up their personal and organisational systems and behave with rigidity may therefore, in certain cases, be the worst behaviour to display under conditions of risk.

Quadrant 2 shows behaviour of rigidity under conditions of safety. This behaviour may, at first glance, appear incomprehensible and unlikely for leaders, but closer investigation may make such behaviour defensible.

Such conduct is typically found in leaders who lack the confidence to venture. This lack of confidence may, in turn, be the result of the leader's own lack of self-esteem, or may emanate as the result of a working environment that punishes risk and castigates failure. Thus, while external business conditions may be safe from risk, the internal organisational environment may present risk to the leader's behaviour. Similar internal self-destruction has already been alluded to in the description of the Al-Aimmah Bridge Effect above.

Quadrant 3 shows behaviour of fluidity under conditions of risk. This behaviour illustrates an internal locus of control, that is, the leader's behaviour is driven by internalisation of thought and insights, and is not exclusively driven by the risk factors in the external environment. As with all behaviour, this conduct introduces a number of risks: the leader may be so enamoured of that internal thought process that external factors may be ignored.

It is advisable for leaders in this quadrant to remain open to external factors that may impact upon the system of the leader or the organisation. Such leaders will also benefit from consolidation of processes and protocols to ensure that the organisation is safeguarded against risk.

Quadrant 4 describes behaviour of fluidity under conditions of safety. Fluid behaviour is most likely to occur under safe conditions, as these conditions provide the optimal opportunity for exploration with limited risk. Leaders under such conditions who do not demonstrate fluidity are unlikely to do so under any conditions. They are in effect depriving their organisations of the benefits of innovation and organisational learning, even during periods of relative security.

Leaders who do seize the opportunity for exploration have developed the requisite confidence for bold action. An enabling environment will offer the necessary support to allow leaders the freedom to explore under these conditions, providing ample space for speculation, exploration and anticipation of potential future risks and opportunities.

7.1.1.5   Unhinged: Self-Consciousness and Self-Awareness

Another dimension that is critical to the synthesis of the system of the leader in the learning situation is that of self-consciousness and self-awareness. This continuum examines the degree of self-insight on the part of the leader. It is essential due to the fact that it is ultimately the leader who will be required to find creative application opportunities from the learning content and experience. While it is important for the leader to understand the environment, the leader must also gain insight into the internal personal landscape to optimise for new insights. Note that, while this dimension is applied to the leader, it may be equally applied to organisations as systems.

Self-consciousness may be described as that state in which the leader becomes aware of personal differentiation from others, where this difference has not been internalised and integrated into a coherent and dynamic system of self.

Self-awareness, on the other hand, describes a state of being in which those distinguishing elements of the leader's complete make-up as leader, as well as those elements that are similar to others, have been synthesised into a coherent and congruent construct of self. It is a state in which the leader is aware of personal style and mode of behaviour as it may relate to:

- Decision-making
- Engagement with others
- Need for structure
- Physical characteristics
- World view and philosophy
- Culture
- Behaviour under stress or in crisis
- Problem-solving orientation
- Taking of responsibility
- Learning style
- Personality
- Intelligence

- And any other variable of the leader's overall personal system that may impact the leadership style of that leader

Table 12 below shows the integration between self-consciousness and self-awareness in relation to whether the leader has a sense of comfort or discomfort with the state of being.

Table 12: Self-consciousness and Self-awareness

	COMFORT	DISCOMFORT
SELF-CONSCIOUSNESS Activity; my appearance; reactive; self-obsessed; incongruent with self	*Q1: Dishonest with self*	*Q2: Revert to known & proven; unwilling to venture*
SELF-AWARENESS Process; my impact; proactive; self-integrated; congruent with self	*Q3: Self-determining; personal mastery and performance wellness*	*Q4: Receptive to learning*

Quadrant 1 shows a leader who is in a state of self-consciousness (as defined above), but who behaves as though the leader has a sense of comfort with this state. Such a leader displays a lack of honesty with the self and therefore represents a state of false self-awareness, that is, the leader is in a state of pretence and false modesty that prevents the leader from gaining real and profound self-insight from learning. Such leaders are unaware that they may be closing themselves as systems and that they may be depriving their own systems of valuable energy for self-renewal and sustainability. They may find themselves suddenly on the verge of entropy without having monitored the gradual decay of their personal systems.

Quadrant 2 shows a leader who is in a state of self-consciousness, but has a degree of discomfort with this state. Such a leader may have been made aware of unusual or even deviant behaviour, and may even have realised the impact it has on others, but has not yet taken action to internalise the learning in an attempt to modify such behaviour. For leaders with true intent for learning, this may be an interim phase on their learning journey toward self-awareness. Leaders who feel overwhelmed and threatened by the provocation to their degree of self-insight, may become defensive in response. They may, as a result, revert to the known and "proven" elements of their behaviour, that is, those characteristics of their behaviour that they believe gave them the success and position they now hold. Such leaders are unlikely to venture and explore the full potential of the available learning journey by actively closing themselves up as systems.

Quadrant 3 shows a leader in a state of self-awareness who has developed as sense of comfort with the self-insight gained though learning and reflection. Such leaders have moved beyond self-consciousness, in which they became aware of their identities and the characterising behaviour they display, and have internalised meaningful learning. These leaders may be conscious of gaps in their competency make-up, but they have taken action to migrate their own systems towards vibrant growth. They do not view learning as threatening, but as a means of introducing dynamic energy into their systems. Leaders in this state may be described as possessing personal mastery, as they have a degree of honesty about themselves and continuously take action to enthuse their systems through learning. All systems, whether mechanical or social, are in need of re-energisation, and the system of the leader is no exception.

Quadrant 4 shows a leader in a state of self-awareness who has a degree of discomfort with this state. While the discomfort may be distressing to the leader, that leader is nonetheless receptive to learning. This is different from Quadrant 2 in which the leader has discomfort with self-consciousness, in the sense that the leader in Quadrant 4 has already made the decision to learn and grow, despite the discomfort experienced. Leaders in this quadrant have not yet internalised learning or took action such as those in Quadrant 3, but their intent allows their systems to be open to the dynamic energy represented by the potential of learning.

7.1.1.6 After we collided: Spectrum of Change

It is furthermore proposed that the leader also has awareness of the degree of change that both the leader and organisation have experienced in the recent past, the current degree of change as well as the anticipated scope of change, however unpredictable it might be. It is important for the learning process that the leader appreciates such change, as insight into flux dynamics may in turn provide great insight into the degree of receptiveness and the approach the leader has towards the learning opportunity.

Table 13 below shows the degree of change as high, medium or low on the X-axis and the area of change, whether in the self or the containing and related environments, on the Y-axis.

Table 13: Spectrum of Change

	IN SELF	IN ENVIRONMENT	
		Expectation from others on self	Change in others or environment
HIGH	Q1: Developed identity	Q2: New perception of self	Q3: New role for self
MEDIUM	Understand impact	Understand impact	Understand impact
LOW	Understand source	Understand source	Understand source

Quadrant 1 shows a leader who has experienced a high degree of change in the self. The exact reasons for the change should be explored, as the nature of the change may impact the degree of receptiveness of the leader. Consider, for example, a leader who has undergone a high degree of change as the result of being redeployed into a new role. This leader who has navigated the change successfully will have made great strides into developing personal adaptability and learning about the new challenges the new role may present. Consider now such a leader attending a change management programme with a focus on convincing leaders of the benefits of change – such a leader has already experienced the process and has already accepted the change. The programme may therefore offer little value to that leader and may even appear insulting.

It is therefore clear that insight about recent change for the leader is not only required by the leader, but also by the facilitator of learning. It is further essential, as proposed above, that learning content itself should display the characteristics of a complex adaptive system so as to accommodate the learning needs discovered by the leaders and facilitator during learning.

The leader in such a situation may benefit from adapting behaviour in congruence with self-insight gained from the learning process in relation to insights gained from recent, current and anticipated change.

Quadrants 2 and **3** refer to change that occurred not in the leader but in the environment. The first change, proposed in Quadrant 2, describes a change in the expectation that others have of the leader. This typically occurs where there has been a change in the constellation of the leader's stakeholders. There may have been a change in the network or immediate colleagues of the leader, or the ownership of the organisation may have changed. Another example is that the customers or suppliers with whom the leader engages most frequently may have changed.

The leader develops a new self-perception, as influenced by the new expectations on that leader. It is essential for such a leader to test the motivation for the changed expectations others have, as it may be due to a change in their needs, rather than the result of a change in the leader. The leader in such a situation may be well advised to adapt behaviour with a clear insight into the nature of the new relationships and expectations.

Quadrant 3 describes a change not in the leader (Q1) or the expectations of others (Q2), but in the nature of others or in the systemic environment of the leader.

An example of this from my experience is a trade union boss who became a CEO. In this case, a trade union managed the interests of their union members and also administered the benefit funds of their members, including the pension fund and medical aid funds. The head of the union realised an opportunity to strip out the benefit fund administration offering from the union and form a separate company to offer this service back to the union. This would allow the newly formed company the commercial opportunity to administer benefit funds for other clients as well. As a result of the formation of the new company, the role of the leader changed from that of a union boss to that of a CEO of a commercial enterprise. While the union used to be an organisation under his control it was now a client of his, and thus it determined the service levels it expected of him. One of the union executives now became the union boss and relationships were dramatically redefined. It is clear from this example that it was predominantly the nature of those in the containing and related environment that changed, thus impacting on the learning requirements placed on the leader.

It is essential that the leader gain insight into the nature of a change in others or in the environment, as these elements form part of the system of the leader – the leader must accept the definition of a personal system as extending beyond the self and including contextual components and relationships. As a result, it is essential that the leader develops a new role identity and acquires a sense of comfort with the new role.

A leader in such a situation may benefit from a review of system dependencies in the new system. The System-dependency Analysis below provides further insight.

Whenever executives experience change, if they are ostensibly driving it themselves, they will inevitably experience both a sense of loss and a sense of gain. The sense of loss is the result of those parts of the system that served the leader in the past but are no longer within the boundaries of the leader's system. It is important that the executive recognises this loss, as the leader may be prevented from directly harnessing these elements as resources in future.

As per Table 13 above, for instances where the degree of change is only moderate, it is essential that the leader explores the potential impact of the change. It may not require dramatic self-transformation on the part of the executive, but demands at least a deep understanding of the system implications of the change.

For changes of which the impact is low, it is proposed that the leader has, at very least, a clear indication of the source of the change. This may not be easily determined, as complex systems may hide triggers to change. The leader would be well served to identify at least one trigger of change. A detailed systems analysis may not be required, and certainly a complete redefinition of the self would be an over-reaction and place too many demands on the leader, as minor changes occur almost continuously. A clear understanding of the source of the change may accelerate the leader's insight into the change and will guide the leader should the change evolve (as aggressively purposive systems tend to do) to become greater in impact.

The sense of gain may be found in the rationale of the proposed change. It is clear that the rationale for the change may not have been designed around the needs of the leader, but rather based upon the needs of the organisation or the emergent flux in the organisational context. The challenge for the leader experiencing change is therefore not only to cope with change in terms of redesigning processes, but also to identify the personal gain that may be derived as a result of the change, such as learning, new relationships and influence.

Table 14 below describes the loss and gain that may be the result of the change in relation to the risk and benefit associated with the change.

Table 14: Loss and Gain

	RISK	BENEFIT
LOSS	Q1	Q2
GAIN	Q3	Q4

Quadrant 1 shows the risk associated with the experience of loss, as defined above. Risks that may feature in this quadrant are associated with the loss of resources no longer under the control of the leader. The leader may undervalue the loss of these resources or may be unaware of the loss of resources until the need to harness them recurs.

Quadrant 2 in the table above describes the benefit that may be derived from a loss. Examples of elements in this quadrant include the removal of damage, risks, destructive forces and any other damaging elements of a system. It is important to note, however, that these elements did once serve a purpose in the system and were connected to other elements in the system. Therefore, the removal of these elements is likely to impact several other elements in the system due to the inevitable interconnectedness.

Quadrant 3 shows the risk associated with gain. Often gain can be viewed one-dimensionally, without leaders being fully honest about the risks involved in the gain. Acquisitions are classic examples of risk emanating from gain – holding companies acquire other companies, but also take on the debt and risk inherent to those acquired organisations. This is one reason why many organisations follow a strategic policy of organic growth, which provides greater insight due to the incremental and heuristic nature of the expansion of the organisation as system.

Quadrant 4 shows the benefit associated with gain. This is perhaps the most obvious domain of the table, as leaders do not usually note the benefit of something in their favour when the overall experience is unfavourable. What is perhaps less clear to leaders is the shadow side of the benefit, that is, the concomitant elements of gain such as described in the Authority Paradox. What is likewise unclear to many leaders is the full benefit, as opposed to the obvious benefit. The full benefit requires a detailed exploration of the gain on the part of the leader. It requires leaders to ask questions about the full systemic benefit and the alternative value of gains beyond the obvious. The exploration of greater synergy is one clear option for the examination of benefit beyond the obvious.

7.2 The Fast and the Curious: Personal Responsibility

This was a thing we could not wait to learn.
We saw the risk we took in doing good,
But dared not spare to do the best we could.

Robert Frost, The Exposed Nest

While insight about the self and the environment is essential for optimal learning, it is also essential that the leader should take action as the result of learning. The leader has to define a personal responsibility for the application of learning opportunities gleaned from the learning process.

Table 15 below shows the responsibility of the leader towards the self and towards others, as constituted by stakeholders of the leader. It also shows the responsibility to gain insight and to take action, both of which are viewed as valuable behaviours by the leader.

Table 15: Personal responsibility from learning

	LEADER'S INSIGHT	LEADER'S ACTION
TOWARDS SELF	Q1: Learn	Q2: Identify objectives & Implement
TOWARDS OTHERS	Q3: Empathetic understanding	Q4: Communicate

Quadrant 1 shows the leader's responsibility towards the self to gain insight. The behaviour required from the leader in this quadrant is to learn. Such learning may be focused on the self, the environment or any of the stakeholders or other elements in the containing or related environments of the leader. Insight in this context is seen as a precursor of action, and is therefore essential for meaningful action to follow.

Quadrant 2 shows the leader's responsibility towards the self in relation to action to be taken. Leaders are required in this quadrant to translate insight into action. In its simplest form, leaders in this quadrant are required to identify specific objectives as a result of their insight and to start the process of implementation for the achievement of those objectives. It is essential that insight should translate into action as the leader is compelled to achieve results by a myriad of stakeholders, as proven above. In SLL it is essential that leaders explore the systemic implications of their actions, and that they should not act simply as a reaction to learning or because their organisational cultures favour a bias for action.

Quadrant 3 shows the responsibility of the leader towards others in relation to the required insight about them. The leader in this quadrant is required to develop an empathetic understanding of others. This means that the leader must gain a full appreciation of the realities of others. This insight is essential due to the fact that these "others" form part of the system of the leader and will therefore impact upon the leader's system. Developing a deep appreciative understanding of the realities of others will provide the leader with greater insight about:

i. How to navigate engagements with them

ii. The likely expectations and resulting reciprocal impact others may have on the system of the leader.

Quadrant 4 shows the responsibility of the leader towards others in relation to the action the leader is required to take. In simple terms, it is the leader's obligation in this quadrant to communicate, with the full and complete meaning of the communication responsibility.

Communication in a systemic sense means gaining insight into the relative significance of people and events as nodal leverage points within the system. It requires the leader to engage others not only on the leader's views of the system, but also on the nature of others as systems in their own right and their (albeit partial) view of their role within the system. This will, in turn, provide the leader with valuable insight regarding the optimal way for the continuous and living design of the system.

It is clear from the outline above that, while learning often emphasises insight, SLL encourages leaders to move beyond insight into *systemically informed action*. This move towards action should not be delayed until leaders have left the learning situation, but should be identified and even planned at a high level during the learning situation, while the leader can still test the systemic reality against the learning content, the experience of the facilitator and the experience and insights of the leader's peers on the learning programme. Therefore, insight in SLL is not limited to an understanding of the learning content, but explicitly extends to insight about the systemic implications of learning content for the systemic reality of the executive.

7.2.1 Deep impact: Scoping the learning scene for results

One of the key considerations for the decision on the selection of learning content and the expectations organisations have of leaders, is the overall impact the organisation expects the learning process to produce. Paradoxically, the very mention of the expected outcome of the learning process can create confusion, even for senior executives. It appears as though the learning process is often the aim in itself – training departments have to prove that they have done training, and that is what they do. The dialogue on expected final outcome seems to disappear as soon as training starts.

Given the reality that it is the leader who experiences the learning process, and not the leader's staff, the organisation or other stakeholders, it follows that whatever impact will result from the learning process, will be the direct result of the leader's engagement with the vast array of components in the system. In this sense, creative application opportunities from executive development are therefore dependant as much upon the leader's ability to understand, challenge and internalise learning, as it is upon the leader's motivation and ability to give life to the insights gained from learning.

The learning process will have an impact on three broad spectra of the leader's system in the workplace, which, as the diagram shows below, may be characterised as:

i. Self-impact

ii. Impact on others

iii. Strategic-reciprocal impact

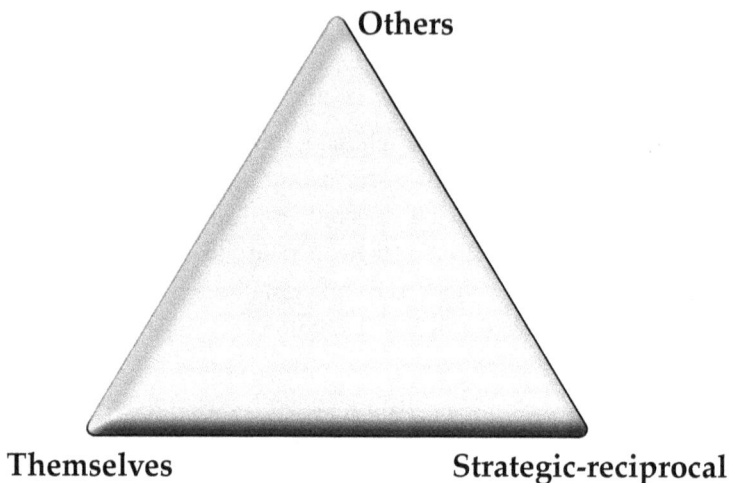

Figure 11: Impact Scope Analysis

The diagram shows the three areas in a triangle because of the interrelated nature of the three areas of impact, as outlined below.

Self-impact refers to the changes that will occur in the leader as a result of the learning process. This may influence the leader's competence related to the leader's knowledge, skills, attributes and perspectives in a myriad of ways. It is clear that self-impact will ultimately impact others, as leaders continuously influence others as part of their leadership role as significant actors in the organisational system.

Impact on others relates to the motivation and ability of the leader to impact other stakeholders as a result of the leader's insights reached during learning. It is clear that the successful impact on others will ultimately, through circular causality, impact the leader, as the leader is part of the system and is thus impacted through the continuous feedback loop that permeates the system – leaders are not immune to the reality of circular causality that flows from their own decisions and actions.

Strategic-reciprocal impact is a phenomenon observed as a further possibility that extends the scope of the impact of learning. This phenomenon occurs when the leader, as a result of insights reached, researches the realities of the organisation as system as a means of exploring that leader's potential for having an impact beyond immediate teams or processes under the leader's control. A leader who pursues strategic-reciprocal impact attempts to identify opportunities that will advance the organisation without having to be in control for the full implementation of the opportunities identified. This is not to be confused with a lack of responsibility – quite the contrary. Such a leader takes creative intellectual responsibility for full-enterprise strategic risk and opportunity. It is partly an altruistic pursuit, as the leader's own team will not gain the resources for the management of the initiatives that will drive the opportunity identified. But such work may also be seen as being done in self-interest, as any benefit bestowed upon the organisation as a result of the leader's insight and drive for the opportunity, will ultimately be reciprocated through indirect benefit back to all the leaders of the organisation - thus the terminology of strategic-reciprocal impact.

7.2.2 Edge of tomorrow: Strategic Awareness

While self-awareness is essential as part of the leader's competency set, the role of a leader extends far beyond an understanding of the self to an in-depth appreciation of the intentions of the organisation. If one accepts the tenet that it is the leader's role to align people with the strategic objectives of the organisation, it is essential that the leader should have high levels of clarity about these objectives. Strategic awareness therefore forms one important containing system within which self-insight has to be contextualised.

The strategic executive must integrate self-insight with insight about the organisation.

7.2.2.1 Scenario Dependency Matrix

One tool developed for the analysis of strategy and the improvement of strategic awareness is the Scenario Dependency Matrix. It provides a simple, yet dynamic instrument for the balancing of possible scenarios. It was developed as a tool for learning in response to confusion that leaders often experience when more than one variable impacted on their strategies, which becomes immediately and undeniably apparent through systemic awareness. It is one way for leaders to avoid being paralysed by the complexity of multiple permutations.

Table 16 below shows the condition on the X-axis and the consequence on the Y-axis. Conditions refer to one set of possible scenarios and are prerequisites for the occurrence of consequences. Consequences, in turn, are the direct results of the meeting of the conditions identified. Both conditions are expressed positively and negatively.

Table 16: Scenario Dependency Matrix

CONSEQUENCE	CONDITION	
	If This...	**If Not This...**
Then That	Q1: Positive Mutual Conditionality	Q2: Alternative Conditionality
Then Not That	Q3: Mutual Exclusivity	Q4: Negative Mutual Conditionality

Quadrant 1 shows a scenario of *Positive Mutual Conditionality*. This means that a certain consequence is directly dependent on the occurrence of a specific condition. The occurrence of the condition will automatically lead to the identified consequence, whether directly or through a delayed ripple effect in the system. This type of "if... then..." conditionality is vastly overused and often lacks the probabilistic nuances required from a deeper appreciation of uncertainty. Consider, for example, the notion that, if we develop our leaders, they will be more productive. The reality is often that 'development' may simply mean course attendance. Not only does this not deterministically lead to improved productivity, but it may, counterintuitively, lead to leaders being exposed to ideas during training that alert them to the futility of their attempts at work.

Quadrant 2 shows a scenario of *Alternative Conditionality*. This means that a certain consequence will only occur if a specific condition does not occur. An example may be the belief that we will only improve performance if we do not accept errors. In reality, errors are a normal part of exploration in the system. In the absence of exploration, new ways of improving performance are not investigated, which may result in perpetuating current practices and patterns of behaviour.

Quadrant 3 shows a scenario of *Mutual Exclusivity*. This means that the condition and the consequence are mutually exclusive, that is if the condition occurs, the consequence will not take place. This is differentiated from Quadrant 2 in the sense that, in Quadrant 3 the condition does indeed occur, while in Quadrant 2 it does not. Consider, for example, the assumption that, if we hire people with lower academic qualifications, our values will not flourish. This fallacy is not uncommon in traditional work environments where academic qualification is equated with almost all virtue at higher managerial levels. Some leading global technology firms are good examples of where this fallacy no longer exists. The reality is that personal value systems operate quite independently from the vast majority of values required for business success.

Quadrant 4 shows a scenario of *Negative Mutual Conditionality*. This means that if the condition does not occur, the consequence will also not occur. This is different from Quadrant 1 in the sense that, in Quadrant 4 the condition does not occur, whereas in Quadrant 1 it does. An example here may be the belief that, if we do not communicate the strategy, staff cannot not hold us accountable for its implementation and consequently we will not disappoint their expectations – a perverse tactic often employed in environments of great uncertainty. In reality, the absence of communication on strategy creates a vacuum, which increases the very uncertainty this tactic was hoping to prevent. A positive example may be that, if we do not engage customers in the design process of future product ranges, they may feel disengaged from our offering.

It is clear from the above examples that causality deserves closer scrutiny during the learning process.

7.2.2.2 Lost in translation: Customer concerns

Unless the programme is about customer service or strategic access to the customer, executive development can be deafeningly silent on the impact on the customer. Such vast literature exists on the subject of the relationship between organisations and their customers that only a brief contextualisation within SLL will be done here.

The key implication in SLL for customer engagement is that, if the leader can be the supra-system during the learning situation, then the customer may well have a self-perception of being the supra-system during the service engagement.

The implication of this insight is that the leader with systemic awareness can appreciate the fact that the experience of the customer will be different from the experience of the leader – glaringly obvious when expressed in this manner! The leader is therefore required to examine in some detail the nature of the customer as system and respond to needs as they emerge from that system, rather than blindly pushing solutions based on the reality of the system of the leader. This has significant implications for learning, since the trap in learning is often that the content and facilitator, and not the customer or leader, dominate. Through SLL, strategic decision-makers are also alerted to the reality of the customer's customer – an insight from the examination of multiple containing systems.

7.2.3 What we do in the shadows: Operationalisation

While the effectiveness of the learning process is essential for the internalisation of learning content, it is critical for return on learning investment that specific creative application opportunities are identified. There is growing disillusionment with so-called leadership coaches and leadership experts who expound, Oprah-like, on the virtues of congruence and integral living and leading, while businesses burn as customers' needs are neglected and projects fail.

The multi-dimensional orientation framework proposed identifies four generically applicable options as responses to strategic awareness reached. The leader only exercises these options once substantial insight has been gained as a result of the other dimensions in the framework. This ensures that the leader avoids emotional decisions and allows for options that will serve the leader's true preferred state, based on honest reflection and significant self-insight. The options are explained below.

7.2.3.1 Emphasise

It is essential that the leader moves beyond an intellectual understanding of challenges and creates plans that may give life to those insights. This means that the leader should harness resources and align them behind the strategic intentions based on the insights reached from learning. The call to "emphasise" implies that additional time and resources should be dedicated to the intention.

Leaders do indeed often gain great insight in the learning situation, but they then frequently allow these insights to dilute into the day-to-day activity of managing operations. All thinkers have had this experience: wisdom floods the mind with sudden delightful surprise - a delicate insightful whisper in a storm of mundaneness - only to disappear just as quickly and mysteriously as it arrived. These day-to-day operations aim to retain current processes, rather than improve or redesign them. As a result, insights reached during learning often evaporate and seldom attain creative application in the workplace. Emphasis requires additional focus and investment of time and effort. Taking a conscious decision to emphasise certain intentions increases the likelihood that further value-adding, ripple-effecting action may be taken.

7.2.3.2 De-emphasise

Leaders often comment during learning that certain projects receive attention and resources beyond their value to the organisation or its people. This may be due to the personal ambitions of certain powerful leaders in the organisation, or may be the result of the legacy of leaders who have already left the organisation, the ripple of which is experienced far beyond its origin. Such disproportionate emphasis can become an organisational habit, and may be allocated to certain kinds of projects simply on the grounds that it is the dominant accepted culture at that organisation.

In SLL, leaders may gain insight on the disproportionality of resources allocated as the perceived value of high-profile, well-resourced projects may emerge to be false. This should not mean that these projects have to be removed in their entirety – they simply need to be adjusted and given an appropriate resource allocation within the systemic constellation of projects which 21st century organisation run in simultaneity. In practice, this suggests that parallel projects may be viewed as parts of a socio-organismic system, the nature of which implies that growth in one may imply adjustment or even cessation of another. The temptation for 'more' is falsely intuitive. It drives complexity and often taxes decision-making beyond the intellectual capability of even the most talented executives. This process is referred to in the framework of SLL as the process to "de-emphasise" disproportionately supported projects. It should be noted that this does not mean that leaders should pretend, in an analytical either...or... manner, that these projects no longer exist, since even after de-emphasis they will remain in the systemic reality of the leader.

7.2.3.3 Ignore

It may become clear in the learning situation that leaders have been focusing on entirely the wrong aspect to address a certain challenge – this is often the case when a systemic lens is applied. Their focus may have been skewed by personal ambitions or legacy policies that have created myopia for leaders and caused inappropriate strategies.

Companies often believe, for example, that attracting talented graduates present them with the opportunity to recruit from the base for more senior positions in the organisation. The language often heard is that 'we need young, vibey, funky, bright staff.' The reality, however, is that the true nature of the work in many work environments is highly repetitive and in no way represents the ambitions of 'young, vibey, funky, bright staff.' This assumption then often proves to be false when it is realised that the average period of tenure is exceedingly short, which means that graduates do not enjoy the environment and do not stay in the organisation long enough to be promoted. Some clients now actively ignore graduates in their selection criteria.

This strategy to "ignore" certain aspects that deserved special attention in the past, allows organisations to focus on more strategically significant risks and opportunities. They no longer need to be blinded by deeply held perceptions that prove to be false as a result of learning.

7.2.3.4 Delete

The last option proposed in this framework involves elements that should not be de-emphasised or ignored, but actively deleted in their entirety. This call to "delete" certain projects, processes, beliefs or risks encourages leaders to take bold steps to align themselves with their strategic intent and the insights reached from learning.

It implies the complete removal of certain elements of the organisation, whether at a small or macro-level. This action should not be limited to the removal of energy from that element with the aim of causing its gradual demise, since the slow process of deterioration may impact negatively on other elements of the organisation as the component decays. Consider, for example, the required action to deal with a senior leader who has repeatedly proven to be a destructive force and active barrier to advancement for the organisation. Allowing that leader to simply be ignored, allows for the rest of the organisation, especially the team led by that leader and the internal and external customers served, to be negatively affected by the presence and decisions that leader is still able to make during the remaining tenure. It may be more advisable to remove the leader from the organisation completely in order to remove the threat posed. Even then, such "deletion" should be done with the insight that the leader may once again impact the organisation in future, as that leader will form part of an industry, as its containing system, in which the organisation aims to thrive.

The call to "delete" should not be read as an attempt to close the organisation's system and deprive it of life-giving energy. Rather, it is a redefinition of the system boundaries of the organisation to limit the impact of destructive forces. Deletion also provides intellectual space for the dissolution of other challenges.

7.3 Levelling up: Learning System Levels

It is an established tenet of SLL that the leader holds a self-perception of having supra-system status during the learning situation. In practical terms, this means that the leader will tend to subordinate the systems of the organisation, facilitator and learning content to the realities of that leader's own system, including their systemic insights and perspectives.

The risk of holding such a perception appears significant: do leaders believe that they are more prominent than the organisation? The table below shows the balance of supra-system status between the organisation and the leader. It demonstrates the implications for the status of learning content in scenarios where both the leader and organisation act as supra-system and sub-system in the learning situation.

Table 17: Learning System Levels

	ORGANISATION AS SUB-SYSTEM	ORGANISATION AS SUPRA-SYSTEM
LEADER AS SUB-SYSTEM	Q1: Content as default supra-system	Q2: Content as propaganda
LEADER AS SUPRA-SYSTEM	Q3: Content as agent provocateur	Q4: Content as irrelevant; Power struggle emerges

Quadrant 1 shows the implications for the status of learning content if both the leader and the organisation act as sub-systems in the learning situation. The implication here is that dual sub-system status of the leader and organisation creates a supra-system vacuum. In this case, this vacuum will be filled by the learning content. This means that the learning content becomes the supra-system, to which both the leader and organisation are subordinated.

Such subordination of the systems of the leader and the organisation furthermore implies that their interests are not served. Learning content becomes the system that shall be served best. Therefore, any challenges proffered by the leader in the learning situation may be denied on the grounds that the challenges do not fit in with the system of the learning content.

Quadrant 2 shows the implications for the status of learning content if the leader is the sub-system in a process where the organisation is the supra-system during learning. The result is that the interests of the leader are subordinated to those of the organisation. This appears counter-productive, as it is the leader who is required to learn and to apply the learning within a personal and organisational context. Learning content in such a scenario is viewed as propaganda, that is, learning content aims to convince the leader of the reality of the organisation, irrespective of the leader's real experience of that reality.

The leader's reality is once again ignored in this scenario, and content serves as the flag bearer of messages by the organisation – content is presented as being above the review of the leader.

Quadrant 3 shows the implications for the status of learning content where the leader is the supra-system, and the organisation acts as sub-system. In this scenario, the reality of the leader is paramount and becomes the system to be served by the learning process.

One might argue that this places the leader in a position of power that may lead to abuse of the learning situation. This argument is easily countered by the philosophical vantage point that the leader in the learning situation behaves with integrity, and will therefore automatically pursue learning that will improve leadership and institutional effectiveness. There is, in reality, no viable alternative - the learning system cannot be designed with any other philosophical foundation that questions the integrity of the leader, as this would create a flawed design process *ab initio*.

In a scenario where the leader is treated as the supra-system, the leader is at liberty to mould learning content to meet the exact needs faced by typical patterns displayed by the multiple components in the system of the leader. The learning content in this situation is viewed as *agent provocateur*, a tool for the accelerated accomplishment of the insights of the leader and the identification of creative application opportunities. The content bounces like a particle into the system of the leader and both systems are potentially impacted by the energy-generating collision. This introduces a high level of authenticity into the learning process and creates the foundations for real and meaningful advancement of the leader and the organisation.

Quadrant 4 shows the implications for the status of learning content in a situation where both the leader and the organisation behave like the supra-system. The implication here is that the two systems become embroiled in a struggle for supremacy. Consequently, each system defines itself as independent through the formulation of its boundaries, since the rules each system create as criteria for incorporation of the other system into itself, prevent the healthy integration of the two systems. Both systems behave defensively and reduce their permeability to protect their supra-system status. Leaders view content as attacking, and organisations interpret the emerging insights of leaders as defensive and even as signs of insubordination.

The ultimate result is that the learning content becomes irrelevant, since neither system is sufficiently open to allow for the dynamic free-flow and interaction of ideas. Such learning interventions deliver almost no return on learning investment, as very little learning occurs – the majority of energy is spent on self-justification and the falsification of the claims of the other system. A prime example of such behaviour is found in cases of restructure, where organisations defend their decision (often made without immersive research) and leaders opposed to the restructure spend their energy on discovering the flaws in the arguments of the organisation in defence of the survival their own systems.

7.4 Dangerous Liaisons: System Dependency Analysis

Systemic Leadership Learning encourages all role players in the learning process to gain a deep insight into the reciprocal implications of recognising each role player as a system. As stated repeatedly, it purports that the leader perceives the self as the supra-system during the learning situation. This is done mainly because it is the leader who must do the work and who experiences the learning process - learning cannot be experienced on behalf of another. As the leader does not learn or lead in isolation, it is therefore important to examine the relationships of dependencies between the system of the leader and the other systems involved in the leader's world of work.

The nature of the other key systems in the learning process (organisation, facilitator and learning content) has already been expounded upon above. Despite the fact that the leader may view the self as the supra-system during learning, the reality of organisational strategy translated into day-to-day operations may imply that the leader is not always the supra-system for operational implementation purposes. This poses a *learning status paradox* to the leader: during the learning process the leader is the supra-system, while for the purposes of implementation of learning insights other systems may be higher in status.

To gain greater insight into the types of dependencies that the leader may experience for the implementation of learning insights, a simple diagnostic tool has been developed in order for the leader to analyse the nature of the dependency that the leader has upon other systems in the workplace.

7.4.1 The maze runner: Direct and Indirect Impact

The diagram below shows the Systems Dependency Analysis tool. The framework works on three dimensions.

INDIRECT IMPACT

DIRECT IMPACT

Sources		DEPENDENT	CO-DEPENDENT	INTERDEPENDENT	INDEPENDENT
	Vision and growth				
	Influence				
	Existence				
	Functional excellence				
	Execution and functional outputs				

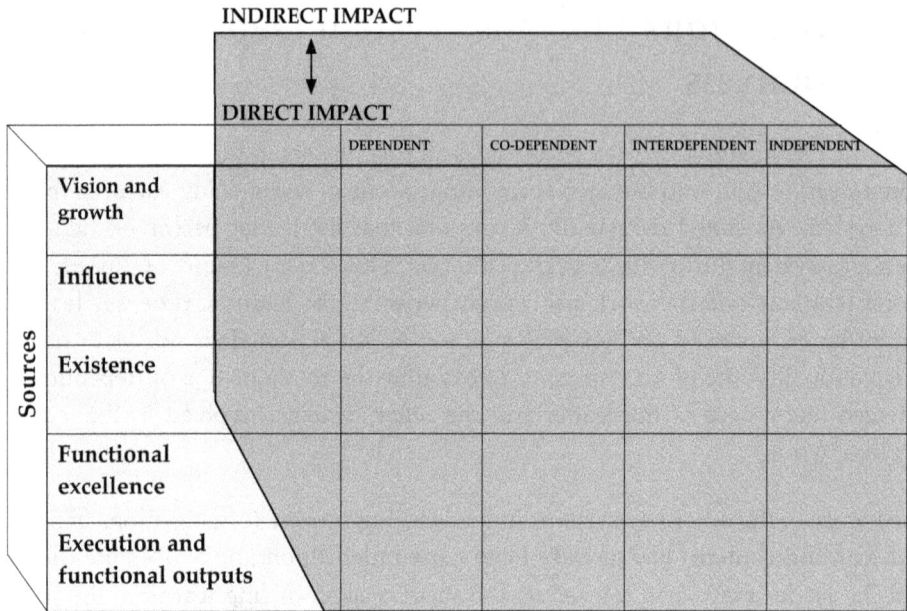

Figure 12: Systems Dependency Analysis

The diagram shows that the reciprocal impact between the leader and other systems in the workplace may be direct or indirect. One might refer to the system that creates the first action as the *originating system*, whereas the system that perpetuates an impact generated by the originating system may be referred to as the *intermediary system*, since all impacted systems in turn impact at least two other systems and are therefore *conductors of impact*.

Direct impact occurs where the leader takes action (based upon learning insight) that results in change in systems without the use of what has been described above as intermediary systems, i.e. systems that convey the impact from the leader to other systems. Similarly, another system may have a direct impact on the system of the leader without the presence of an intermediary system.

Indirect impact occurs when the leader takes action that has a change on another system only as the result of a reaction by an intermediary system to the action of the leader. It may therefore appear that the impact on the final system is caused by the intermediary system, but actually it is the result of the leader's action. Similarly, another system may cause an impact upon the system of the leader by first impacting an intermediary system, which then reacts and exerts an impact on the executive.

It is clear that one action may impact upon a number of intermediary systems before the leader is impacted or before the leader impacts a distal system. It is therefore essential that the leader should appreciate the level of directness of impact as well as identify the originating system that impacts on that leader (where possible), as this will largely influence the response the leader will have in terms of the impact reached. Failure to identify any of the intermediary systems may lead to uninformed decisions that will, in turn, affect yet more unintended intermediary systems and may not resolve the problems created by the originating system.

Is it possible to identify the final system that is impacted by an action of an originating system? One reason for the validity of this question is the fact that systems outside the boundaries of the system under review may be impacted. Another reason is that one action ripples through various systems and may transform these systems in ways that are difficult to recognise as the direct result of an action by the originating system. Even with the advent of entropy in the originating system, the impact of its actions prior to entropy may well outlive the originating system. Consider, for example, the impact of decisions made by CEOs who are no longer with an organisation. It appears, therefore, that such a system (which may be referred to as the end system) may only be identified within a very specific context and within limited measurement criteria – the impact of an action by an originating system may in fact survive in perpetuity through the impact it has on other systems.

7.4.2 The best of me: Sources of Dependency

Systems may be dependent on one another in various ways and for various reasons. The model proposed shows five sources of dependency; aspects that describe the successful functioning of the system. It is essential that executives recognise the type of dependency that they have on other systems, as this will inform their decisions about other systems and will shape their engagement with those systems.

As the diagram indicates, the most fundamental aspect for which one system may depend upon another is the very existence of the system. In such a relationship, a system cannot survive without the presence and contributions of another system. Naturally, this requires that the dependant system is open to the supporting system. Leaders who fail to recognise their dependency on other systems, may make decisions that will create disengagement for those supporting systems and as a result cause the demise of the system of the leader.

Another aspect for which leaders may be dependent upon another system is execution and functional outputs. In such a relationship, the leader can exist without the other system, but is unable to execute learning insights and as a result cannot produce creative outputs from operations. This implies a requisite degree of cooperation between the two systems. An example of such dependency is the relationship between the leader and the organisation – only within the context of the organisation is the work of the leader translated into the execution of meaningful work. Without the framework of the organisation, the leader's work is a random collection of activities, only potentially coherent within the mind of the leader.

The next source of dependency that the leader may have on another system is functional excellence. This means that the leader can exist and even function at a basic level without the other system, but is unable to create outputs of the highest quality without the contribution of the other system. An example of such dependency is the relationship that exists between the system of the leader and the system of technology support that serve as tools for functional outputs. Such tools allow the leader to migrate basic operations to higher levels of excellence.

The next source of dependency for the system of the leader is influence. This refers to the ability of the leader to create an impact on others. This source of dependency extends beyond the ability of the leader to deliver functional excellence. The leader now aims to create excellence in others through meaningful engagement. It is saliently obvious that such a relationship is dependent on the existence of "others", which may allude to any of a range of multiple stakeholders in the broad definition in the leader's system. One example of such a relationship is that between leader and staff.

The next source of dependency for the system of the leader is vision and (notions of) growth. This refers to the ability of the leader to articulate an image of the preferred state. The need for such a leader is now beyond the achievement of excellence by the self and even beyond the inspiration of excellence in others – this leader is exploring new frontiers of possibility. This source of dependency also alludes to the ability of the leader to grow in terms of personal competencies to lead in the new state of being.

Once other sources of dependency have been fulfilled and once stakeholders have been engaged to a critical level of influence, the main subject upon which the leader is dependent for the fulfilment of this source of dependency, is the system of the self. The leader is ultimately, therefore, the supra-system during learning. The exploration of new frontiers is the ultimate expression of an unquenchable desire to learn. It is therefore the emerging characteristics of the leader's system that will drive the accomplishment of the new state.

7.4.3 Types of Dependency

He runs face forward. He is a pursuer.
He seeks a seeker who in his turn seeks.
Any who seek him seek in him a seeker
His life is a pursuit of a pursuit forever.

Robert Frost, Escapist - Never

Given the nature of direct and indirect impact and the elements for which a leader may be dependent upon other systems as described above (see Figure 12: Systems Dependency Analysis), further insight could be gained into system dependencies from examining the types of dependencies that may exist between the system of the leader and other systems in the leader's ecosystem. Each source of dependency described above may be fulfilled depending on the nature of the type of dependency that exists between the system of the leader and another system.

Types of dependencies refer to the nature of the relationship between the system of the leader and other systems, with specific reference to those elements of the leader's reality over which the leader does not have complete autonomy, that is, elements over which other systems may exercise significant influence. The diagram indicates four foundational types of dependencies.

One type of dependency is described simply as dependant. This means that the system of the leader cannot display certain characteristics without the existence of the other system, although the leader may be able to display other characteristics for which there is no dependency.

Another type of dependency that may exist for the system of the leader is one in which the system of the leader and another system are co-dependent. This means that, not only is one system dependent on another, but each system is dependent on the other for the same characteristic to emerge in both, that is, they are dependent on each other for the same outcome.

The next of type of relationship of dependency may be described as inter-dependent. As with a co-dependent relationship, two systems that are interdependent in SLL are both dependent on one another, but in this case the dependency is driven by different objectives. An example of such a relationship may be that between the leader and a provider or vendor of services. The leader is dependent upon the provider for the service, while the vendor is dependent upon the leader for value creation in the provider's business.

The final foundational type of dependency that may exist for the system of the leader is that of being independent. This means that both systems can display certain characteristics without the existence and/or functioning of the other system. Naturally, careful consideration must be given to whether such independence is possible within a complex ecosystem.

An example of misreading levels of dependency may be found in the 21st century global phenomenon of coalition governments or governments of national unity.

It is clear from the taxonomy of dependency above that two systems may be in more than one type of relationship of dependency, that is, they may be independent for certain dimensions, but dependent for others and co-dependent for yet more areas of focus.

It is critical that the executive creates a map of both the types and sources of dependency with actors in the ecosystem, as this will provide invaluable insights into the nature of the relationship with other systems and will, as a result, inform the nature of required engagement with those systems.

Chapter 8

THE PHILOSOPHER'S STONE

Mind, set and match

They will not find me changed from him they knew –
Only more sure of all I thought was true.

Robert Frost, Into My Own

Learning occurs with apparent randomness. While the process may be designed for linearity, with modules and concepts in neat, tidy timelines, learning is emergent, surprising, even delightful and frequently disruptive. Yet the mind of the executive presents a mental architecture within which all successful learning must occur.

Rogue thinker: Lost in paradigms

Paradigms create reality. As patterns of thought, paradigms are the most frequently repeated cognitions. They are often difficult to define, and may, like Young's double-slit experiment, exhibit contradictory properties when closely observed. They are, however, the fundamental substance of decision-making. So intimate is their relationship to decisions, that it may even be argued that decisions are the mere expression of paradigmatic embeddedness. Decisions, active or passive, shape behaviour. And since it is habitual behaviour which constitutes culture and create results, paradigms cannot be ignored when executives are embarking on a journey of learning which may challenge their most treasured beliefs.

If it is possible to transcend the banality of the general social call for a 'paradigm shift', it may then be possible to examine the nature of current dominant paradigms as a means of discerning more precisely where and how such a shift may occur. While a kaleidoscope of paradigmatic options is always simultaneously present, a selection of paradigms is posited below, which may cast a light on key questions for the future of executives, their organisations and the ecosystems which contain them. While discreet paradigms are identified below, the reality is that they interact in a dynamic system in which they exhibit fluidity and permeability by other paradigms.

Teleological paradigm: So, tell me what you want

A contextual definition of the teleological paradigm may be found in the underlying purpose to which an entity aspires or what it hopes to achieve, that is its needs and wants. Goals, aims, ambitions, targets and objectives are all examples. Executives often display what might be termed as negative teleology, that is, they are clear on exactly what they do NOT want. Positive teleology, by contrast, inspires greater clarity of thought and facilitates neurological attention towards the achievement of purpose.

Axiological paradigm: The good, the bad and the ugly

The axiological paradigm may be described as the explicit and implicit preferences of an entity. This includes two key dimensions. The first is ethical in nature and asks: what does the entity view as morally just? The second dimension is aesthetic in nature and inquires: what does the entity regard as attractive and aesthetically pleasing? For the strategist, axiological disfavour should not *per se* signify low market appetite. In other words, the fact that executives may not find a creative application concept attractive, does not imply the absence of a need to advance the implementation of that activity. Organisations often miss a strategic opportunity by allowing axiological bias to shape the design of curricula.

Doxological paradigm: What a fool believes

This paradigm investigates the set of beliefs that guide purposive behaviour. It is, in a general sense, the panacea of paradigms; the paradigm that contains the set of all other paradigms. Ontology is the supra-system of belief in the origin and nature of the universal order. In a specific sense, it is more akin to values and principles of conduct. A key question here may be simply: What do we as a social system believe? This is especially relevant in relation to the role of businesses in society, the marketed value of their product portfolios and the relationship they intend to have with the planet.

Ontological paradigm: What is this thing?

This paradigmatic frame probes the nature of things as well as their origins and definitions. It extends to the formulation of boundaries to determine discrete distinctiveness and classification of entities as distinguishable from others. It includes the continuum of realism to nominalism as it interrogates the extent to which characteristics of an entity are the result of the very nature and origin of that entity or whether such characteristics are so named through the perception of observers. Religion and, more recently, spirituality, is the *locus classicus* example. More secular examples of this paradigm are found in deceptively simple questions, in need of surprisingly profound answers: What is a business? What is a society? What is a successful executive? What is high performance? It is doubtful whether clear agreement is reached between the business and its executives prior to commencement of learning.

Epistemological paradigm: How do you know?

This paradigm investigates the nature and validity of knowledge. It interrogates the creation of new knowledge as well as the expiration of perspectives previously deemed to have been valid knowledge. Epistemology is concerned with the nature of evidence posited for new knowledge. It further examines both the provenance and methodology employed to reach conclusions offered as knowledge. An extension of this paradigm includes in its boundaries the selection and evaluation of knowledge deemed as suitable, thereby rendering it closely related to the axiological paradigm. One key question in this regard may be: What is the foundation for knowledge and the design of curricula that includes the explicit prominence of social dimensions and the de-selection of 'business learning for randomly defined knowledge'?

This author must therefore declare his own paradigmatic vantage point: his background is shaped by international business and advisory services in the strategic and cognitive domain, both in the developing world of Africa but also in the developed economies of Western Europe. The framework submitted here is therefore deeply influenced by the mind of a strategist, whose aim often is to enhance competitiveness in meaningful ways. The criteria of competitiveness may be interrogated in two ways. Firstly, it could be determined to what extent a business competes with other business broadly within its sector. Secondly, it explores the extent to which businesses enable greater competitiveness for their clients. The emphasis on competitiveness appears at first glance to be at odds with more recent trends in collaboration, but the argument that collaboration denies competitiveness is fundamentally flawed as it is most unlikely that all entities in any sector could ever form an alliance. Even if they attempted to do so, the acerbic criticism they would face would be for non-competitiveness. Every system has an external environment, in which entities outside the boundaries compete with each other or with that system.

Executives often have a keenly developed sense of the suitability and defensibility of knowledge proposed by the learning situation. In an attempt to avoid the scientific interrogation of knowledge, many facilitators of learning have opted out of the brutality of scientific rigour, and have adopted a misguiding didactic of simply debriefing the views and insights executives already possess. This does little to advance the scope of knowledge and inhibits creativity, which demands knowledge expansion.

Minervalogical paradigm: Let's get creative

Named after the Roman goddess of art, the Minervalogical paradigm defines the belief systems related to creativity and innovation. It employs dimensions such as the levels of appreciation for creativity in the system. It asks whether creativity is an authentic value, or simply a vacuous organisational call. For a sound paradigm of creativity to flourish, organisations must simultaneously believe in the importance of exploration and robust interrogation, which is why learning is so naturally aligned to creativity. Beyond mere creative adventures, executives must demonstrate wilful integration of new ideas into the fabric of the system.

Temporal paradigm: What time is it?

The temporal paradigm inquires into the belief held regarding the nature of time. This paradigm is repeated in the section on an anthropological perspective of culture, as time can be treated quite distinctly in different social systems. One may think of the temporal paradigm in three dimensions, namely whether the institution believes that the nature of time is linear, spectral or circular.

i. **Linear**

A paradigm of linear time emphasises linear planning. It follows recipe-type processes and believes in the inevitable domino effect: cause leads to eventual effect. It is patently obvious that examples of linear exist. Sequence is a classic case: the house must be built BEFORE it can be painted. But linear time exists within in much broader and more intricate reality of temporal perspectives.

ii. **Spectral**

Entities with a spectral belief of time exhibit parallel processing. This is often associated with higher order intellectual processing. It may induce greater levels of complexity due to the simultaneity present in such organisations. It demands a careful consideration of how attention is distributed and presents an intellectually taxing experience of time for executives. The dilemma with this paradigm is the phenomenon described by Linda Stone, advisor to the Hidden Brain Drain Task Force, as 'continuous partial attention'. In the functional version of a spectral perspective, time is viewed as a river delta of expanding possibility. The art lies in balancing divergent and convergent intellectual processing.

iii. **Circular**

Circularity is typical of a more systemic paradigm of time. The reason for circularity is the unpredictability of interconnectedness. All causes have multiple effects, and all effects have multiple causes. Simultaneously, all causes possess their own multiple causes, and all effects create their own multiple effects. Such multiplicity of causal relationships generates what Fritjoff Capra calls 'hidden connections'. Within these opaque relationships, invisible connections are formed which produce counterintuitive results, that is effects which appear to oppose logical thought processes and surprise the linear causal perspective.

One fascinating example of a circular paradigm of time is found in the beauty of the ancient wisdom of African perspectives on time related to both nature and community. Those of African intellectual persuasion often consider the role of and their relationships with ancestors. The circular paradigm of time is demonstrated through the aspiration to become a good future ancestor: while ancestors clearly represent the past lineage, they are deemed to be active in the present, and offer guidance to the living for present conduct in order to be respected figures in a time yet to come, at which point in the future those now living in the present, with guidance from ancestors of the past, will represent an emergent body of ancestors who will guide those yet to be born.

The temporal paradigm also concerns relative movement in relation to time. Some organisations believe that time is static while they themselves are mobile. Such organisations describe themselves as 'moving towards the future'. Conversely, organisations which see time as mobile view the future as approaching. They will frequently be heard observing that 'the future is coming'. Occasionally, the latter paradigm may be abused as an escape from responsibility. In classical complexity theory, executives are encouraged to view the entire system as dynamic, that is the executive, organisation, content, 'facilitator' and time are all in a perpetually evolving dance.

Structurological paradigm: Can I draw you a picture?

The nomenclature here is deliberate. The intention is to distinguish between structural as a simple descriptive treatment of structure, and 'structurological' to indicate the deliberate study of structure.

One key distinction between analytical and systemic paradigms of structure, is that analysis favours control. It asserts that power, rules, direction and intervention offer the shortest path to success. By significant contrast to control, a systemic paradigm invites order. In this context, order refers to the emergent quality of complex systems by which structure is created by the system itself, rather than being enforced upon it from the outside. This requires a deep curiosity and respect for the natural, inherent dynamics of the system. One clear advantage is the phenomenon of self-organisation (autopoiesis) exhibited by the system. This requires wisdom on the part of the executive for dancing with the natural energy of the system.

One disturbing example of the absence of such wisdom and the insistence on an interventionist approach is the dramatically damaging impact many organisations have had on the natural ecosystem over the last century. This led to exponential risk in planetary tipping points from which it may be impossible to recover. Order further relates to the structural dimension of allometry. The later is a form of biomimicry, in which notions of structure may be learnt from biological systems. It refers in particular to the study of the relative change in proportion of an attribute compared to another one during organismal growth. Elements of living systems typically *in relation to* the other elements of the system of which it belongs. Allometrical perspectives of structure offer significant insight for the contextual responsibilities of executives.

There is a connection between this paradigmatic frame and the temporal paradigm in the sense that time may be viewed as a form of structure. In the structurological view of time a distinction may be drawn between sequential structure, which is akin to linear time, and flow structure. The latter extends beyond even circular perspectives. It allows for the supreme level of variability. This version of the structurological paradigm subscribes to the emergent qualities and creative potential of hyper-fluidity. Elite performers in arts and sports induce in themselves a similar mental experience when they appear to perform at the very highest levels. They enter a different mental realm in which the need for structural analysis disappears, while combining extreme clarity of focus with apparent effortlessness. The traditional experience of time to which they are accustomed seems to disappear as they flow through time in ecstasy-like expression of their highest capabilities.

Anthropological: Living in the land of the common people

This paradigm describes the thought patterns dominant in beliefs about fellow humans. Two key dimensions of this paradigm are highlighted. The first is related to the axiological paradigm above as it interrogates whether dominant thought patterns of the executive or organisation perceive humans to be inherently good or evil. It may seem strongly expressed, but the stakes could not be higher. In environments where people are viewed with deep suspicion, trust is rapidly eroded. These environments also find it more palatable to mistreat people or to value them for their productive outputs only. By contrast, where humans are viewed with inherently benign beliefs, talent and potential are more likely to flourish.

A second dimension of the anthropological paradigm is that most pervasive quality of human nature, what Hugo Grotius in 1625 (variously attributed to Cicero and Seneca) described as *appetitus societatis*, the need and affection for society, that is, the presence or company of other humans. It is a tension as old as humanity and its endeavours that enterprises need humans, but not all humans value each other's company. And some value the absence of others of their species. The argument is not that misanthropy is the only alternative – human relationships are far more complex than that simple binary.

As technology encroachment escalates, the anthropological paradigm will confront executives with deep questions about their need for others. As AI spreads its influence on task execution, executives will need greater self-awareness on their anthropological paradigmatic orientation, especially in those cases where AI is presented in human form, such as the early examples of the Saudi Arabian hyper-humanoid robot, Sara.

The last two paradigms are loosely borrowed from the study of certain types of theology. They are not included for any reasons of faith, but because of the profound nature of their probing interrogation.

Eschatological paradigm: Is this the end?

In simple terms, eschatology concerns itself with an investigation of the end state, the final and ultimate end of humanity. In the context of this book, it is used as provocation to consider whether executives hold beliefs about how things will end. There are various significant implications for learning. If a fixed belief is held about, for example, the end of the organisation, then learning will be viewed as pointless. Once a sense of inevitability permanently resides in the mind of the executive, openness to learning suffers a sudden death. They may play the game of participating in what appears to be learning, but no real cognitive shift will occur.

This paradigm is related to the mindset dimension of voluntarism and determinism. Voluntarists believe in the power of purposiveness. They hold that people can and should make choices, and that choices shape results. While this is an empowering view, it does incur two substantial risks. The first is that they may, in extreme cases, lack empathy and understanding for the reality of others. The second is that they may suffer from the cognitive bias of control illusion, by which they believe that their current and future reality is and will be the result of their choices, while the hyper-complexity of their systems simply does not yield to such mechanical choice-making.

Determinists diverge from this view and believe in the power of circumstance and conditioning. Their view is that people are essentially the result of their backgrounds, experiences, opportunities and exposure. While this view may demonstrate higher levels of empathy, it risks blindness in regard to the role of agency and responsibility for more preferable futures.

Soteriological paradigm: Rescue me

In executive leadership terms, soteriology may be viewed as asking simply: Who will save us? Soteriology concerns itself with the rationale, likelihood and method for deliverance. A few dimensions govern this paradigm. The first is whether salvation will come from the self or from an external party. In organisational terms, this may mean whether executives believe their decisions can create a more positive reality or whether they expect governments or investors to save them. This may sound extreme, but examples are everywhere. Consider, for example, the bailouts large financial institutions enjoyed from governments following the global financial crisis, large proportions of which were paid out as bonuses to executives. Consider, as another example, the insistence of certain countries during the covid pandemic for free access to vaccines, while politicians in those countries were unwilling to invest in science and technology prior to the pandemic, and even made themselves guilty of corruption. Consider, also, how many founders of start-ups expect investors to save them from obscurity.

Another dimension is the tension between faith and deeds. In recent self-help developments, many have underlined the importance of belief and even faith in success. The view seems to be that beliefs firmly held will somehow manifest in successful results. By contrast, others believe in the power of meaningful action as the best way towards success.

Yet another dimension is whether executives believe that salvation is even possible. Akin to the polar philosophical orientations of optimism and pessimism, certain executives may already, even prior to learning, have decided that the personal or organisational outcome is either salvation or doom. Naturally, this will close the boundaries of their minds and will retard learning dramatically.

Paradigmatic consciousness could have a significant impact on the creative return on learning investment. Blindness to paradigmatic embeddedness will skew the learning design and will limit learning to superficial learning theatre.

A catalogue of mind: The Mindset Index

No need for us to rack our common heads
About it, though. We haven't got the mind.
It best be left to great men of his kind
Who have no other object than our good.
There's a lot yet that isn't understood.

Robert Frost, The Literate Farmer and the Planet Venus

Our current epoch appears to pose novel questions. The attempts at answers by those who dare to lead are often inane, trite and self-aggrandising. For senior executives who have to make significant strategic decisions, insight into their own mindsets and those of their stakeholders offer unique advantage.

The mind presents an enormous and exciting next frontier of investigation. It retains a mysterious quality which enlivens the curiosity. With a world in hyper-flux, senior people around the world are making decisions affecting millions of others and countless ecosystems, and the nature of those decisions arise from the mind. To uncover the mind would be to reveal the quantum reality of the impetus for decisions.

Despite its frequent use in common language, the concept of the mind does not yield easily to definition. In one sense, the mind is viewed as a location – the place where all intellectual and psychological processes occur. It is often viewed as a collection of operations, including those as diverse as reasoning, emotion, motivation, imagination, consciousness, perception, awareness, memory, and other functions.

From work around the globe, I have been intrigued to observe the mind of executives at work. As executives' learning processes deepen and they become engrossed in the journey of sense-making, lively debates would often break out spontaneously. I observed that patterns of vantage points would emerge from the executive dialogue, whether in Geneva, London, Rome, Dubai, Saudi Arabia, Jordan, Azerbaijan, Kuwait, Paris, Tokyo or Kigali. This universality of perspective from around the world provoked a deep curiosity in me to investigate the architecture of the dialectics. From this field work emerged the need to record and name the nature (rather than the content) of the constructs engaged. As the collection grew, it seemed to settle at 48 constructs that appear to be repeated with surprising frequency. It became clear that to create a taxonomy, the 48 constructs could be organised on 24 polar scales of continua, because of the oppositional nature of the debates. Such nuance was required as executives, even when they agree, may hold views that are at various levels of extremes, with some leaning gently in one direction, while others, although in agreement, were more extremist in their perspectives. Thus started the basic architecture of an instrument to define and measure the fascinating domain of mindset.

Against the background of this field work, the concept of mind emerged as distinctly abstract – a dematerialised construct which must be differentiated from the brain. Tremendous advances have been made in neurology over the past two decades, including mapping the physical structures of the brain and locating certain functionality. This has encouraged many in the general world of leadership development to investigate so-called neuro-leadership, which aims to explain the concept of leadership by referencing brain stricture and functionality of its parts. Practitioners would often use language such as that leaders are 'wired' differently – a patently outdated conception of intellectual processing. They might add, for example, that an emotional response means that someone has 'literally' flipped their lid, referring to the 'short-circuiting' of the pre-frontal cortex. It is often interwoven with a vast array of neuro-trash, including the delusion that some people are right brain and others are left brain. As a humble scholar of thought processes, I have found such mechanistic brain-based approaches to learning rather trifling. To use a trite analogy, it is like teaching someone to swim by pointing out the rivers on a map on the grounds that the location for swimming is the watery parts. Locating the operation says almost nothing about its requirements for excellence.

While the brain presents the physical architecture (no matter how indefinable), the mind may be seen as an emerging property of the hyper-complex functionality of the brain. This is an important distinction, as it departs from a functionalist perspective of the mind and recognises its fluid and nuanced character.

Executives are often in the game of getting results, however those outcomes may be defined. There is always a current set of results – the most recent measurement of intended outcomes. It is reasonable to investigate the sources and drivers of those results. Naturally, systems are complex, and no simple cause-and-effect relationship may be found. But it would be difficult to pretend that results are not produced, among other things, by behaviour. It is the repeated patterns of behaviour, particularly in relation to the strategic context, which establish the results. The notion of the relationality of behaviour and context is facilitated by decision-making. Such processes may be implicitly derived from passive drivers such as habit and culture. Emotion would naturally play a role. But a more conscious executive would wish to make explicit the precise decisions taken, and choices made for the purposes of strategic intent. Thus, with results emerging from behaviour, in turn driven by decisions, whence the method and content of the decision-making process. It is posited that these decisions, while subject to many influences, including emotion, are the result of what may be described as mindset.

I must recognise the work of the American psychologist Carol Dweck[4], who highlighted the importance of mindset in her book published in 2006. A useful contribution, her work may, I humbly suggest, have fallen prey to the curse of the binary in the interest of popularisation. In the canon of "Women are from Venus, Men are from Mars", Dweck presents a false binary: that mindsets are fixed or fluid. Into these two categories she forces the vast array of human decision-making – a blatant over-simplification for popular consumption and ease of recall, albeit one important dimension. I further posit that she imposes a judgement on mindset and argues for one mindset, that of the fluid, to be the only path to success. The mind is simply far more beautiful and nuanced than such a singular categorisation could indicate. Nevertheless, her work supported the spotlighting of the mindset in the world of success theory.

Indexing the mind is no simple endeavour. It is useful to set down the datums which recognise the fluid dynamics, including:

i.   The human mind is complex and multi-dimensional

ii.   Humans cannot be boxed

iii.   Everyone is special, at least in their own minds

iv.   Ipsative assessment has limitations (like all other forms of assessment)

v.   Philosophy is fluid and contextual

vi.   Relativism and contextuality is ever-present, so it depends!!

vii. Thinking, like all behaviour, forms patterns.

As the process of procuring an index of mindset developed through the empirical process described above, the early design and consultation process with industrial psychology professionals produced several conceptual conundrums. It is in the nature of work which spans an array of disciplines that definitional aspects and distinct conceptual provenance will create cognitive disruption. Therefore, it may contribute clarity to attempt isolation of the assessment of mindset as distinct from other psychological constructs. In order to achieve this, I shall make use of negative definition, that is describing the perspective of mindset based on what it is NOT. The paradigm of the emerging Mindset Index is that mindset is NOT primarily concerned with:

iv.   Neuro-architecture

v.   EQ

vi.   IQ

vii. Personality

viii. Career interest

ix.   Competence

x.   Values

There are, admittedly, large batteries of assessments for the dimensions above, but none of these concepts capture the intention of what is to be measured by the Mindset Index.

The construct of mindset may be understood in four primary ways. The first is the view that the mind has set, like a jelly, or worse, like cement. This indeed has reference to the work of Dweck above and may be, to use her language, fixed, suggesting unresponsiveness to risk and opportunity.

The second, much more expansive perspective of mindset, is that the mind operates in sets, a series or cluster of concepts which seem to arrive together whenever one concept is referenced. This relates to the mental phenomena not only of denotation but also of connotation, in which related ideas are invoked as one concept is raised. Implications and tone, both overtones and undertones, associated ideas, suggestion and insinuation all form part of the set of ideas catalysed by one concept.

A third notion of mindset is the idea that the mind may be purposive, that is the mind focuses itself towards an end. This is related to the teleological paradigm. The mind sets course. It sets sail. It sets direction.

Finally, mindset may be conceived of as calibration. In this sense, the mind sets the standards and norms. It is clear from successful executives that they have a clear sense of the measurement of excellence. The mind sets the intended calibre of what it examines.

The four conceptions of mindset help to arrive at a more discerning view of the concept and may assist executives in cultivating a comprehensive understanding of mindset. Against the background understanding of mindset, the 48 constructs on 24 polar continua reside.

It became clear that the 24 polar continua may be structured on seven domains. These domains of the Mindset Index are:

i.   People – Foundational thinking about engaging with other humans

ii.   Agency – Beliefs about the role of the self as system and its actual and potential impact on the world

iii. Knowledge Processing - Foundation tenets about how to acquire, store, access, share and interpret learning

iv.   Enactment – Deeply held methodological views on how new learning may be applied for advancement

v.   Expectations – convictions of what the future may hold and how to interpret it

vi.   Essential thinking – the methods, likelihood, purpose and definition of purpose

vii. Reality – critical conceptions of what may be deemed as real

It is within these seven domains that the 24 polar continua are structured.

For those curious about the levels of validity and reliability to which Mindset Index (MI) complies, an expose is provided as an addendum.

The Mindset Index aims to provide insight into the emerging dimension of mindset. Naturally, mindset is a construct in and of itself. It is defined within the instrument, and only dimensions identified are subjected to assessment. The instrument offers scientifically validated assessment scores across a range of dimensions of mindset. Test-takers are free from external interference during testing and may respond freely to a randomised set of questions.

Organisations may therefore find confidence in the results produced by the Mindset Index. The world is in hyper-flux. For such a world, mind intelligence is essential. The alternative is the blind navigation in exacerbated risk. The Mindset Index offers a unique insight into the mindset of current and potential stakeholders in order to enhance strategic decision-making and foresight.

One of the weighty challenges of a systemic endeavour is to create an elegant synthesis from the surprisingly disparate and divergent components within multiple containing and overlapping systems, of which the mind is but one. The challenge is, to borrow a phrase from the nursery rhyme, to put Humpty together again.

SLL is systemic by definition, most notably because it examines the interconnectedness of multiple containing and temporarily overlapping systems related to executive development. The interactive complexity that emerges from such a study is counterintuitive, since the purpose of exploring the interrelatedness is, of course, to aid understanding in order to design and facilitate learning for more meaningful results. The practitioner in the field (whether researcher, leader, learning designer, facilitator, coach, mentor, consultant or learning quality assurer) should not be overwhelmed simply because it appears complex or non-linear, but should actively seek to make sense of the interrelated reality in which the practitioner is also an active organism. Such sense-making inevitably leads to sensing opportunities for enhancing both the learning experience and its returns, whether financial or otherwise.

Given the diverse and systemic nature of the proposal of SLL, it is essential to translate the comprehensive models and frameworks into workable and practical principles and processes that render them user-friendly for industry leaders and executive development professionals. This is essential since, in the final assessment, this book positions itself, among others, within the containing system of Mode 2 Knowledge Production, which necessitates industry engagement and absorption.

Simultaneously, one should be acutely aware of the risk of employing a reductionist approach characterised simply by analysis to achieve a "bottom-line effect" – such an approach would be inherently contradictory to both the qualitative research methodology as well as to the intention of the book to promote a systemic approach to the learning process for leaders. A similar risk lies in designing a "step-by-step" guide, since such a process is almost inevitably a linear one, or at best a decision-tree. Those in the broad field of executive development must caution against the significant risk of becoming 'learning technicians' – an approach to learning design and facilitation which is procedural and protocol-based, and which undermines the potentiality of systemic learning.

The dilemma of a systemic reality juxtaposed with the need of industry leaders and development practitioners to follow processes may be resolved by identifying a suitable starting point for the learning process. In SLL, this starting point is an understanding of the systemic learning dynamics within a learning process.

Within this systemic approach to learning, a key tenet is that the leader has a self-perception of being the supra-system during the learning situation (whether formal or informal). The recognition of leaders as systems, indeed as supra-systems in their own perception during learning, is a fundamental tenet for an approach to executive development based on SLL. It is indeed a prerequisite of SLL that the system of the executive is recognised and understood in its full creatively systemic reality.

It is this reality that creates the context for the systemic learning needs of the leader. Such learning needs emerge as the result of an in-depth understanding of the system of the leader and the non-linear evolution of the learning process in which the leader is paramount, although patently contained within multiple systems.

Learning content in itself is also an evolving system, while being simultaneously a system input into the system of the leader. Content should therefore be sufficiently permeable in its boundaries to allow for the self-organising system of the leader to display potentially unique insights.

The model below shows the integration of the four systems of the Leader, Organisation, Facilitator and Learning Content. It demonstrates the interconnectedness of these systems and sets them within the systemic context of the fields of study of leadership, systems thinking and learning, supported by the use of story. In SLL these fields, are also interconnected, and in addition, each of the fields has an impact on each of the others.

The model is shown in the shape of a molecule, in order to underline the principle of quantum-connectivity and the multidimensional systemic reality of the emerging learning process as proposed in SLL.

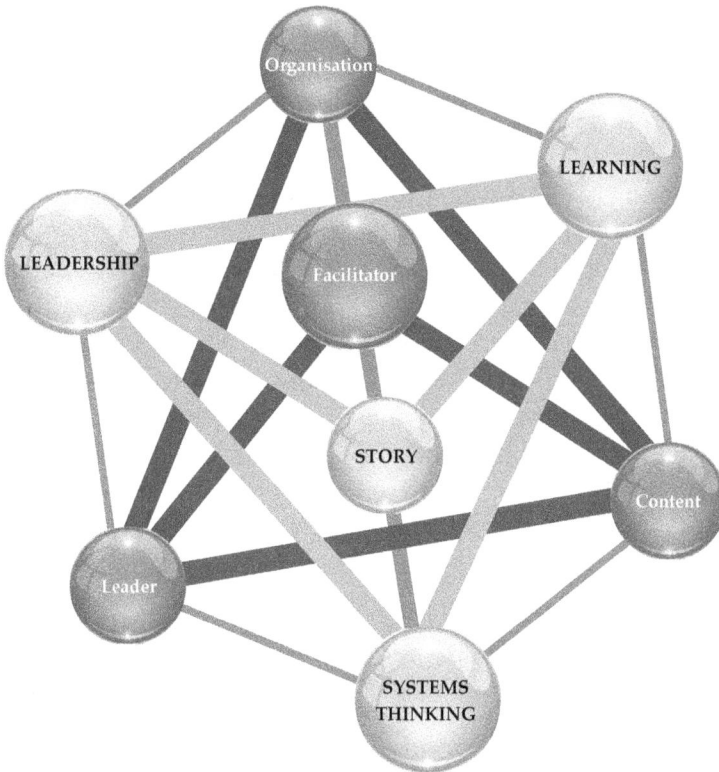

Figure 13: SLL Supra-model

The quantum quality of the model is supported by the graphic representation as a mandala, a concentric diagram used as an aid to meditation in the Hindu and Buddhist traditions. Mandala is a word from Sanskrit that means 'circle'. The connectedness between Eastern mysticism and 21st century paradigms of Western science have been investigated thoroughly. Symbolic of this relatedness is the dancing Shiva featured at CERN, the European Organization for Nuclear Research in Geneva. Lord Shiva is shown performing the Nataraj dance, a symbol of Shakti, the life force. The most salient connections are the very notions of interconnectedness, dance, the theatre of the parts in the whole and the multiple partial views which constitute that whole [in Hinduism through the Creator (Brahma), the Preserver (Vishnu) and the Destroyer (Shiva)]. In Buddhism such holism permeates the entire tradition. Triangularity appears in the three jewels of Buddhism, also known as the Triple Gems or Triratna, these are the Buddha (the teacher or exemplar), the dharma (the teachings), and the sangha (the community). These three pillars of Buddhist faith and practice represent ideals that Buddhists strive to embody. They are primary acts of the Buddhist faith that guide the learning journey towards nirvana, with suffering and its causes elegantly balanced by the cessation of suffering - the eightfold path which shows the way. Other spiritual traditions echo the visual evocation of the mandala. In Islam, geometric art uses the circle and variations in its deconstruction as symbol of the universal unity of creation. The five pillars – the declaration of faith (shahada), prayer (salah), almsgiving (zakat), fasting (sawm) and pilgrimage (hajj) – constitute the basic norms of Islamic practice and lends beautiful extension beyond the geometry of the four geographical directions by inspiring five-sided polygons to echo the pillars. Islamic art also features the Khatam, the eightfold pattern, and illustrates it through rich superimposition of myriad geometrical interactions.

It is perhaps the work of Lau Tzu in Taoism which illustrates the nature, and possibly the origins of systems thinking in the most striking way. Credited as author of the Tao Te Ching in the sixth century BCE, Lao Tzu lays the foundation for the principles of balance, interconnectedness, sensitivity, consciousness and circularity so crucially needed in our emerging understanding of the role of the executive in complex organisations, and the role of the organisation in the containing planetary ecosystem. Those who favour a more rigorous protocol orientation for an elegant society would do well to consult "The Analects" of Confucius roughly a century later.

In the case of the SLL supra-model, the graphic representation is aimed at the simultaneous focusing and stimulation of the mind. From the perspective of a mandala, the model has four access points, namely the four interacting systems, interwoven with four other gateways, namely the four fields of study. These gateways support a systemic principle which may be described as Multiple Access Points. It suggests that ingress to the system of executive development may be gained through various apertures in the system, depending on the permeability of the system boundary.

In the case of the SLL model, various mandala-type circles have been employed to create an overall circular effect. In this sense, it may also be viewed as a fractal - parts of a whole which resemble the same whole. Suggesting that each part contains each other part, they thus display self-similarity.

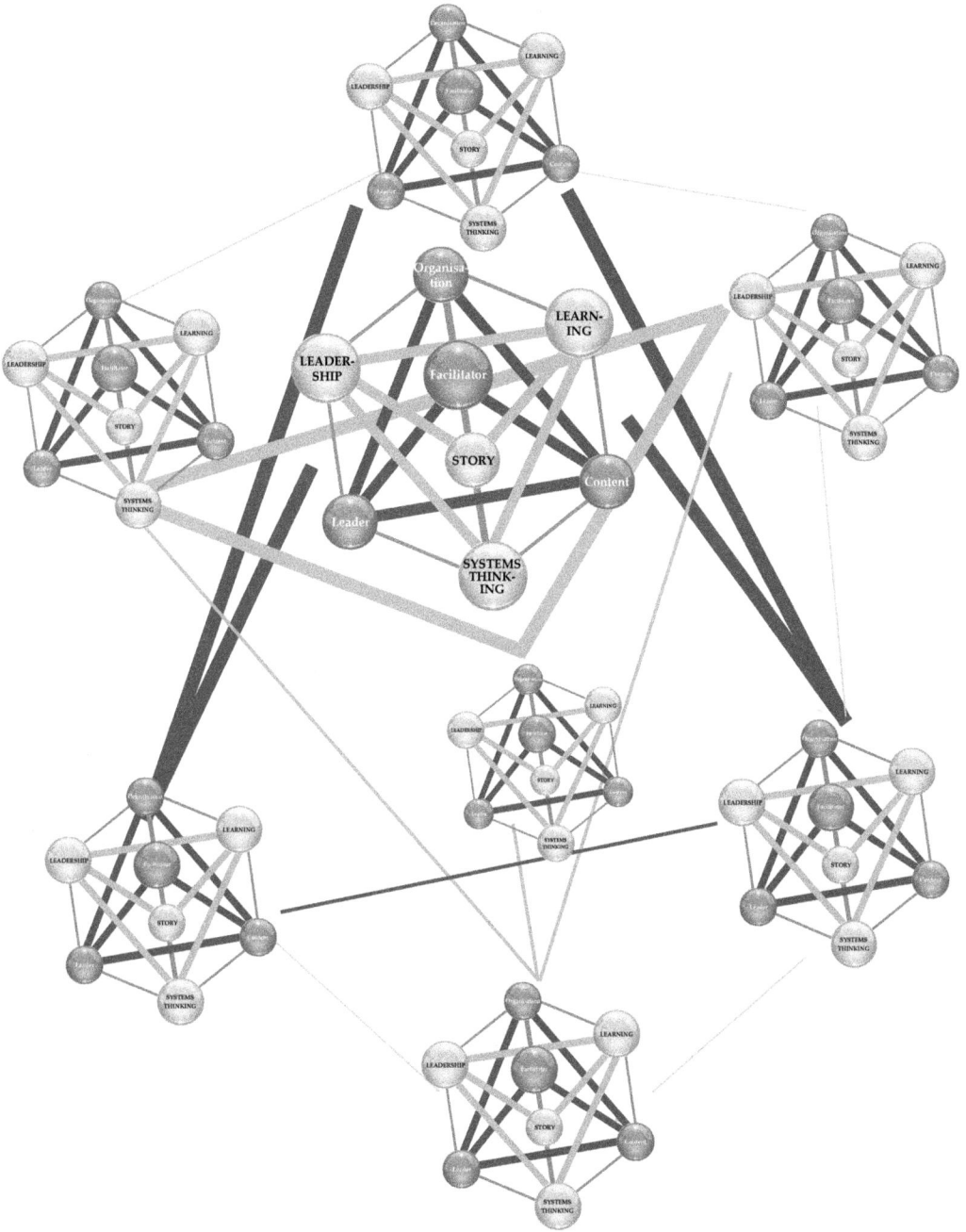

Figure 14: SLL supra-model as fractal

Chapter 9

AVENGERS: THE END GAME

The end of the affair:
The Appreciative Disruption Framework

Much of the development of senior leaders is undertaken by schools of business. C-suite responsibility in the procurement of learning services for executives, often residing in the Chief Learning Officer (CLO), has a valid claim to distinctiveness through the significant and direct impact on the development of people. When those people are executives, CLOs often look to business schools as higher order learning partners. As business schools experience their own accelerating change, within the context of rapid organisational, social and planetary transformation, the nature of the future evolution of this education-based relationship deserves significant investigation.

In the interrogation of the *raison d'etre* of business schools, it may be asked with reasonable justification whether business schools perpetuate the *status quo* for the role of business in society, however that role may be perceived, and whether it is indeed their mandate to do so. Are business schools complicit in the assumed damage to society, perceived to have been caused by four dramatic industrial revolutions? To what extent are business schools responsible for the implicit global crisis in sustainability, poverty and inequality?

Simultaneously, and in the interest of the balance of argument and the prevention of prejudicial thinking, a more fundamental and even less frequently entertained question may also be posited: are business schools intended for business? What do current designs in business school vision, management, didactic methodology and curriculum design suggest as the purpose of business schools? The answer to these questions may seem intuitive, but recent trends in the evolution of business schools suggest that a rather more counterintuitive and nuanced response may be required. Among such trends are several noisy signals in business school behaviour: a distinct social orientation, a penchant for public appeal and a sense of social activism that aims to redirect the pursuit of business to be defined as more socially minded, open and receptive to a wider spectrum of social entities and ambitions.

Business schools have also laboured towards their own transformation, with recent inclinations that include the favouring of social innovation, environmental consciousness, general self and community leadership, personal mastery, emotional intelligence, coaching, cultural sensitivity, corporate social responsibility, well-being, philanthropy and ethics as either modular offerings or (the much-touted) cross-cutting, transversal themes in their product portfolio.

The salient quandary appears to be that business must shrink its own footprint, while simultaneously labouring under rapidly rising pressure to create employment, drive participative growth, regenerate the planet, all while increasing their tax contribution. The apparently balancing forces probing such schools to participate in the establishment of a more equal and just society and even make reparations for historical inequity, leaves many senior executives with profound conceptual conundrums. A trite response is the assumed systemic retort that inter- and intra-societal dynamics in a state of well-being would lend their own health to that of business. Another popular view is that business is not separate from society; that business is *in* and *of* society, not *for* society.

But does this recent shift in the business school landscape from business to society deliver what business, and indeed society needs for various paradigms of sustainability? Or have business schools donned the cloak of social activism and taken a self-anointed moral superiority with the oft concurrent claim that business has a great deal to learn? Has academic humility, once a cornerstone of intellectual pursuits, succumbed to good intentions and naïve notions of social re-engineering through some of the most influential people in society - the clients of business schools - all the while charging exorbitant fees for prophetic and normative insights of business scholars on what business should be in a new dawn of professed egalitarianism?

Intuitively, values founded on social interest are desirable, or at the very least preferable to the rampant individualised cordoning off of business benefit. And there is extensive evidence of global malfeasance, environmental damage and social exploitation to necessitate a shift in the fundamental moral operating system of the business fraternity. The role that global business school education has played in the shaping of executives at the helm of such deviant enterprises is indubitably a worthy subject of investigation. But are business schools not, paradoxically, placing their own intellectual integrity at risk by purporting to offer business services, while in reality selling a re-packaged range of social development services? Such explicit manipulation of the privilege of learning facilitation must pose significant questions of the moral standing of business schools to make such claims. Are business schools not falling prey to the same moral questionability that is so frequently and publicly attributed as a malaise of business? If any other form of enterprise were to obfuscate its own product mix by labelling those products incorrectly, consumer protection bodies would rush to the rescue. Are business schools pretending to be *for* business, while offering something more akin to tendentious social re-engineering through their development of current and future leaders? This risk is made poignantly plausible by noting this disturbing reality: it remains possible, in many business schools, to obtain a doctorate degree, whether DBA, D.Comm. or Ph.D., without ever having been responsible for a profit and loss statement (P&L). The resulting implication is that, in many business schools, it is still conceivable for said doctorate to become a business school professor.

To escape this moral conundrum, a model is proposed as a guide for the structural and didactic design of possible business schools of the future.

The Appreciative Disruption Framework

In order to navigate the complexity of the paradigmatic landscape above, business schools may be well advised to acknowledge their prototypical vantage points – the leading schools are indeed expected, by a multitudinous and growing array of social activists - to be the very vanguard of societal development, a bulwark against the tyranny of antiquated shareholder value orientations and abuse. One way in which this may be achieved is to commence with the admission that learning, if not an intervention, is at the very least, and perhaps by definition, a form of disruption. That disruption, for scholarship to occur, is not optional but essential. Disruption in this context is not intended in the sense that it disrupts an entire existing market, supply chain or value ecosystem. It is defined here as a perturbation of the intrapersonal, interpersonal and organisational constellation of epistemology – the interconnected system of conscious and unconscious, familiar, favoured and known but ignored notions of knowledge - by the introduction of new concepts and frames by which risk and opportunity are understood and decisions are made within the context of more preferable futures. This definition may, at first, appear utilitarian to those who value learning for its own sake, but it should be noted that the procurement of higher learning from business schools is, at least in large-scale organisational supply chain terms, a transaction, the exact terms of which are often unclear beyond *prima facie* exchange of money for qualifications and learning. It is perhaps the definition of 'learning' in this transaction that is most perplexing. If dominant perspectives and processes of learning were to be maintained, the experience may be deemed to be more akin to propaganda than erudition. Learning that serves exclusively to confirm existing perspectives and knowledge pools is little more than the gentle stroking of executive egos and the propagation of organisational prejudice. The phenomenon of business school professors praising executives simply for being honest in class has been well-observed.

However, one may enquire as to the directionality of the perturbation presented by learning: is it directed at the most efficient achievement of business objectives or is it a subversive attempt to manipulate learning for the purposes of aligning the client with the assumed model – the paradigmatic schema - of a particular business school and its leading scholars?

One way of assessing the latter inclination may be to examine the extent to which business schools learn from businesses in a ratio of the time spent on 'teaching' executives. Naturally, leading business schools conduct extensive, robust and high-quality research. But the slightest intellectual honesty would acknowledge that the research question or target of investigation is often inspired by the curiosity of the researcher, rather than being at the behest of a business. Many may argue that curiosity-driven research is the very cornerstone of academic freedom, and that the researcher should be at utmost liberty, unencumbered by the mundane needs of business. But what of the inverse as a test of their own intellectual honesty: would they afford the same latitude to business in corporate research and development projects and budgets, or is such intellectual libertarianism the exclusive purview of the intellectual classes in universities?

While it may be common cause that the client attends the business school to learn, business schools should be less confident that the client demands teaching, let alone instruction, and would be well served to note a patent disregard by the client for normative preaching at the far end of that continuum.

If one accepts the premise that learning is indeed a form of disruption, however gentle or aggressive, then the requisite ethical sensitivity is required for meaningful engagement with the executive. For this reason, an appreciative form of disruption is proposed. This implies that the business school approaches the executive with an enquiring mind, not an instructive one. The self-proclaimed intellectual agility of universities, where robust debate and critical reasoning are comfortably at home, should find such a welcoming approach remarkably simple, if not second nature. In this approach, the business school actively seeks out potential value in the executive and organisation during the learning process. The Appreciative Disruptive Framework below proposes an evolution of levels of engagement at the intersection of the needs and intentions of five complex systems, namely:

i.   the business school

ii.   the executive

iii. the client organisation

iv.   the society

v.   the planet

One indicator of focus in such a constellation is the distinction between internal and external referencing. Internal referencing implies that the main focus of intervention is at an intrapersonal or intra-organisational level. It is posited that internal referencing has been the staple of much executive education for the last two decades. It is oriented towards enhancing greater understanding of the self (whether personal or organisational), often grounded on the argument that this is done as a means of removing obstacles to progress. The theory seems to be a self-contradictory assumption that, to get the self out of the way of progress, the self must be pre-eminent in all forms of investigation.

At this juncture, it may be useful to distinguish more clearly between the teaching process, the learning process and the resultant insights and actions from both teaching and learning. Patently, teaching is centred on the curriculum and style of the business school, often embodied by its professors, while learning is housed in the intention and competence of the executive. Insights from learning extend beyond the learning and teaching process to include the sub-atomic-particle-like collision of new knowledge with previously held insights and convictions, as described in SLL theory above.

Actions taken manifest in the behaviour of the client once the school has taught, the client has learnt and insights have been gained as the foundation for action. Naturally new action, at least for the conscious executive, would also lead to new learning and insight. At this point the 'teaching' process is often blind to the systemic implications of actions taken.

Figure 15 below shows the Appreciative Disruption Framework. The framework is proposed as a taxonomy for structural and didactic design by schools of business. The design process refers to both curriculum (content) and learning process (method). Taxonomically, both business schools and executives may evaluate their own needs and intentions. For each level, the business school should consider the extent to which this demonstrates its own style, approach and identity, informed by its philosophy, and whether executives are on the same level in their assessment of their own needs, typically driven by their relative location in their organisational or individual career life cycle. A potential mismatch between business school and executive would exacerbate the ethical dichotomies described above. The degree to which business school paradigm and executive need are in harmonious design may suggest a necessary shift by either party. In other words, it is not suggested that business schools somehow pander to executive needs, but rather that intellectual rigour and epistemological robustness inspire a meaningful meeting of minds, means and methods for the success of both parties.

External referencing

Leading
Taking a premier position among leaders in the contextual environment
Shaping trends in systemic landscape through inventiveness

WINNING WITH FLAIR & VIRTUOSITY

ON THE FIELD & IN THE GAME

Competitive
Contextual orientation
Challenging for leadership in selected areas

External referencing

Internal referencing

Developmental
Growth orientation beyond status quo ante
Exploring new avenues of efficiency and effectiveness

COACHING & GYMNASIUM

Internal referencing

Curative
Approaching a former norm (status quo ante)
Towards homoeostases

CARE & MEDICATION

Internal referencing

Rescue
Short term salvation
Survivalist crisis aversion

HEROES & EMERGENCY ROOM

Internal referencing

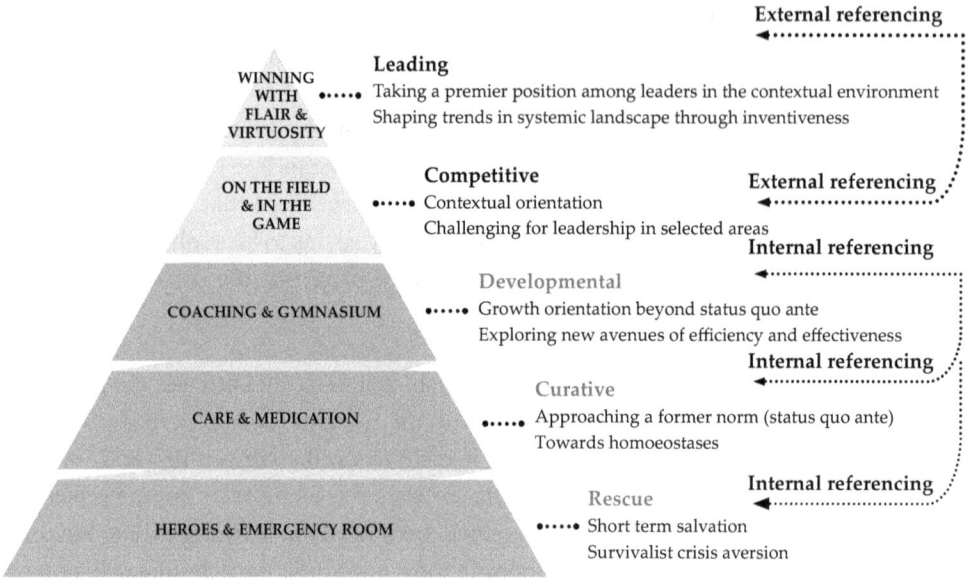

Figure 15: The Appreciative Disruption Framework

At the level of internal referencing, the business school may offer rescue. The client business or executive is deemed to be in crisis and the school presents learning as a means of survival. The implication is that either learning or the resultant insights and actions from learning have the potential to avert or ameliorate the crisis. The effect is often short-term and offers rescue from an immediate threat. Typical circumstances at this level include a complex merger/acquisition or business rescue. A metaphor for this level is that the business school acts as a hero, while the archetype of the patient in the emergency room reflects the status of the executive.

At a next level of internal referencing, the business school intervention is curative in nature. At this level the learning engagement attempts to move beyond rescue to elevate the executive towards a former norm of acceptable performance. The target is to get back to the *status quo ante*, a state of performance that existed at a former time, from where the executive's performance has slipped but towards which that executive is aiming to return in order to rediscover homeostasis. Typical context here is a recent client history of gradual decline without clear diagnostics for the downward trend. Metaphorically, the business school offers good quality care to the patient who has now left the emergency room and is in hospital.

The final level of internal referencing may be described as developmental. Here the business school is oriented beyond care to ensure progress to a level that exceeds previous performance. The orientation extends beyond balance towards various paradigms of growth. It explores new avenues of both efficiency, that is doing things better within current resource and method constraints, as well as effectiveness, that is doing more preferable things for greater impact and with superior resource sensitivity. Metaphorically, the patient has left the hospital and the business school behaves like a coach, while the client is strengthening muscles and fitness in the gymnasium.

The value of internal referencing can be significant. It shows respect for the internal dynamics of the executive and enables the client to recover and grow. But it is submitted here that internal referencing alone is not sufficient for either competitive sustainability or sustainable competitiveness. Competitive sustainability implies that plans and practices and their impact do not endure at the expense of business viability, while sustainable competitiveness suggests that competition should not counterintuitively and ironically destroy the business itself through direct organisational suicide or by systemic circularity through social and planetary destruction. Since both sustainability and competitiveness can only be defined and tested in relation to the behaviour of the executive in the systemic context, it is essential that business schools enable executives to move to external referencing, where critical self-awareness and balanced health must graduate to 'active exposure and participation in the arena'.

Therefore, at the first level of external referencing, the business school enables the executive to be competitive. As mentioned above, while collaboration is a noble pursuit, all activity competes, even if only against the opportunity cost for failing to enact alternative action choices. Even if all business schools on earth could collaborate, they would, as a collective, compete with other learning priorities and institutions. Even if all businesses on the planet could collaborate, they would compete with any entities that are not defined as businesses. Even more pressingly, the reality of the executive is that competitors abound, and in that world, a lack of competitiveness is tantamount to a lack of sustainability. One definition of a competitor in this context is any entity that acquires resources which, in the view of the business, should be within its own control. Such resources may be financial, but could also include talent, time, technique, technology, security, reputation and other indicators of value. It is often at this level that socially-minded academics and spreadsheet-minded business executives collide. It is proposed that the dissolution to this often tacit ontological conflict on the nature of business and society is found in the exploration of philosophical honesty, rather than in a payer-payee tussle of will.

At this level of business competitiveness, business schools therefore facilitate a contextual orientation. This is done in order to enable the client organisation to compete for leadership status in selected areas. Metaphorically, the client has moved out of the gymnasium and is now in the game; competing on the field of play, well outside the comfort of self-referencing and reflection. With the salient reality of several professors lacking competitive experience on the field of play, the complexity of the business school-client relationship demands the delicate navigation of values (the axiological paradigm).

At the apex level, the business school catalyses true leadership. Both the executive and organisation develop the capacity to lead both people and market segments. This supports the client to take a premier position, even among other leaders in the contextual environment through discernible, and distinctive *savoir faire*. At this level, the executive expects learning that drives the capability to not only follow but shape significant trends in the systemic landscape through inventiveness. To extend the metaphor, the client is now not only challenging for leadership but in reality, winning a selection of battles with both flair and virtuosity. Both client and business school are nonpareil, and learning has finally enabled executive and organisational leadership.

Are business schools for business? A rich paradigmatic constellation problematises this apparently simple question. The Appreciative Disruption Framework is posited as a means for business schools and their clients, whether executives or organisations, to explore an integration of explicit and emerging needs. Hierarchical conceptual models have limited application due to their apparent rigidity. For that reason, the model is proposed as a spectrum of possibility, rather than levels of attainment. The drive is toward appropriacy, rather than superiority. Offering rescue-based or curative executive education when competitive leadership is required would not only be insufficient, it would constitute, in the view of this author, an immoral peddling of tendentious curriculum. It is therefore humbly submitted as a potential technique for enhancing moral clarity in structural and didactic design for business schools, as it exposes partisan curriculum through an appreciation of the systemic reality and learning journey of the executive. It presents a fluid but nevertheless ordered taxonomy by which business schools may reassess their own market positioning and value proposition to clients in a way that exhibits the highest levels of intellectual integrity.

One future scenario therefore sees a spectrum of business schools emerging, quite possibly on each of the levels of appreciative disruption. In one explorative scenario of the business school constellation of the future, business schools for business may be complimented with business schools for:

- society
- individuals
- non-profits
- universities
- governments and
- any other form of entity.

The future of business schools, then, is similar to the future of any social system: it will be, at least partially, subject to the moral and intellectual quality of decisions. It is at this juncture that professionals in executive development, whether in the client or the educational institution, have a distinct opportunity – some may argue 'obligation' – to challenge the product offering and delivery methodology of business schools. Executives must hold business schools to account for matching client life cycles and systemic realities with inventive learning structure, curriculum and experience. Such C-suite accountability for learning procurement cannot afford to surrender the future of their organisation to the blanket philosophies of business schools. They must hold such schools to account for the truism that the future will not happen 'to' business schools to the extent that they will be absolved of moral responsibility for service delivery through internally oriented design.

Rather than asserting claims of superior moral advancement for the justification of curricular, didactic and related designs, business schools must recognise their own paradigmatic podia and gage the contribution they intend to make with enhanced lucidity and higher order justness. The Appreciative Disruption Framework offers both business school and executive a decision-making framework for learning success.

Quantum of Solace

He knew a path that wanted walking;
He knew a spring that wanted drinking;
A thought that wanted thinking.

Robert Frost, A Lone Striker

The dematerialised realities of executive development remain opaque. At the current inflection point in our social and planetary evolution, it is the ability to learn with consciousness of potential intersectionality and systemic relatedness which will differentiate the excellent executive of the future.

The world of the executive of the 21st century is utterly demanding. Learning lends essential energy. It opens avenues for intellectual exploration which offers reinvigoration of the executive mind. What is yet to be learnt is always an order of magnitude greater that which has already been discovered. The future is all that remains. Beyond oppositional analysis the executive requires propositional imagination. It is my humble wish that the random assemblage of warring conceptions above may offer the discerning executive a quantum of solace in a world of hyper-flux.

10. ADDENDUM

This addendum offers further original work by the author as elucidation on the text above. The addendum contains six parts:

i. Systems Thinking: The SODCAST Framework

ii. Futures Thinking: The Mostert Method

iii. Futures Bias Barometer

iv. Interrelations and research validity of the Mindset Index

v. What will the humans do? The 10Ps Framework

vi. Bespectacled strategy – advanced spectatorship through 5 'spections'

10.1 Systems Thinking: The SODCAST Framework

Introduction

Since this methodology forms the dominant architecture of Systemic Leadership Learning, a guide to systems interrogation is proposed below. It is known by the acronym SODCAST, that is, Systems Oriented Design for Complex Adaptive Systems Technique.

Forms of cognitive processing are distinguished by, among other things, the nature of questions posed in the structured method of inquiry. Below is a series of questions that stimulates a systemic approach to cognition. While questions are presented in sequential format, questions may be addressed in any order depending on the level of understanding of the system. The framework is introduced by the three Ackoffian questions, and acts as a guide to produce a rich-picture map in the specific form of a MCS (Multiple Containing System) Diagram.

Pre-examination

Systems thinking deliberately problematises both the wicked problem (messy, fluid and dynamic) selection and definition. Due to organisational bias for action, coupled with misplaced pragmatism, recurring problems, in which the 'system' is advising of its own dysfunctionality, are often fertile ground for initial exploration. Honesty and social consensus are key drivers of enhanced problem/solution clarity. Examples of interrogation at this stage include the following problem discernment questions:

- What exactly is the issue?
- Is there social honesty and consensus on the definition of the problem (with symptoms) to be addressed or opportunity (with promise and expectation) to be accessed?
- Why now (time?)
- Why here (location)?
- Why with these role players (social)?
- Why in this way (appearance)?

In an era of hyper-disruption, it is noteworthy that ecosystems with the requisite degree of interconnectedness are simply more sustainable. The art and science of ecosystem design is therefore essential to flourishing in the 21st century.

Questions: The Six Wards of Systemic Inquiry

The SODCAST framework is fluidly structured on six non-sequential wards of inquiry, i.e. broad domains of investigation. The rationale for nomenclature is (as always with systemic inquiry) multi-fold. It evokes the notion of an area or region, alluding to a cognition precinct, an expanse of the intellect defined by a temporary but discreet boundary. In architecture, 'ward' also references a section or division. Etymologically 'section' heralds from the Latin 'to cut', while 'division' has its origins in the act of dividing. While these concepts are more typically associated with analytical segregation and taxonomy, it also illustrates the paradox of parts within a whole, and the whole formed from parts. This is evident from the use of 'ward' in buildings, indicating rooms within a section, that is the holon identified as part of a whole, while itself containing other parts. In the geographical sense, 'ward' evoked, significantly, the notion of location and directionality. The senior executive is called upon to think with omni-directionality, that is a circumspect, holographic perspective towards the preferred synthesis of systemic redesign.

"Ward" is also used to denote someone under the custodianship of another. The metaphorical value here lies in the call for agency in thinkers and decision-makers, i.e. thinking is, at least to some degree, within the control of the thinker. Conscious cognitive processing is the ward of the philosopher, a role all decision-makers play, whether tacitly or explicitly.

The six wards of systemic inquiry are articulated below.

1. **AWKWARD** - the deliberate problematisation of the problem in terms of identification, definition and scope

2. **UPWARD** – the shifting of attention to multiple containing systems (MCS), that is, apparently away from the problem

3. **INWARD** – elements inside the MCS

4. **OUTWARD** – the other parts in the MCS

5. **WAYWARD** – the distal distortions and remote rebounds from nodal systemic surprises and reframing

6. **FORWARD** – the realisation of opportunities for systemic redesign and inventive synthesis

These spatial-temporal directional cognitive indicators are in stark contrast to those of classical Analytical Thinking, which may be crudely summarised as Backward, Inward and Downward.

AWKWARD

1. Are we asking the right questions?

2. For whom is this a problem?

3. Who benefits from this problem?

4. Is this the real problem? (Note: Guard against simple Root Cause Analysis)

5. Why do we have this problem at this time, in this place, in this way?

6. Why have we taken so long to notice and respond?

7. Which method of inquiry did we use to arrive at our problem definition?

8. Can we accept that having a problem is not the problem – we are simply attempting to upgrade the quality of our problems?

UPWARD

1. Which **multiple containing systems** is this **a part of**? / Of what is this an example/typical/exemplary? / To which group does this belong? Where is this located? For a **lateral (rather than medial**, i.e. towards the centre) option: What would be an extreme good/bad example of this? What would be an abstract containing system with lateral examples of this problem?

    *   What is the purpose of the **containing system/s**, including the **supra-system**?

    *   *NOTE:* Consider abstract systems, such as quality, speed, time, cost, behaviour type, etc.

INWARD

2. What is the **role/function** of this issue within that purpose? If it were/not working, what would it do within the purpose?

    -   Is it **fit for purpose**? If it is, but still appears dysfunctional, what does this reveal about the containing system?

        ◦   Formulating the issue as the current problem may enhance understanding of the current system.

        ◦   Formulating the issue as the ideal may enhance opportunity sensing and inspire design of the desired state. Formulation of the issue as a proposal will enhance scenariofication.

    -   Should the (dysfunctional) behaviour not make sense in the apparent supra-system, then **in which system would it indeed make sense and what does this reveal about what is dominant**?

OUTWARD

3. What are the **other parts in the containing systems** & **What ELSE** is going on?

    -   What is/should be the nature and quality of **relationships/connections** between

        ◦   this issue and other parts in the containing system/s?

        ◦   the other parts and the selected containing systems?

        ◦   the parts in various containing systems?

    -   Which **Multiple Partial Views and stories** should we consult, incorporate and synthesise to ensure requisite variety? Consider the **Four customers**: Who are the multiple:

    -   Buyers (decision-makes)

    -   Payers (funders)

    -   Users (applicators)

    -   Beneficiaries (winners of 'currency', such as Money, Time, Security, Anxiety reduction, Effort, Opportunity, Reputation, Data)

Consider the Drama Triangle: Who are the multiple:

-   Persecutors

-   Victims

-   Rescuers

-   Who are the main actors?

- Who is the supporting cast, such as the quirky best friend or the mole or the muscle?
- Who dies first?
- Who will still be there in the final scene?
- Who will be the last man standing?
- Who is implied as the next generation of power?
- Which of the **multiple access points** are ignored and how else could we enter or navigate the system? Where are the **multiple helms, bridges, nodes and levers?**
- Where and with whom do we need greater **immersion** to gain more **empathy** of real needs?
- How can we redraw the **boundaries** to access and leverage key parts and exclude (in bounded equilibrium) **emerging redundancies?**
- Where is the issue or where are we too **open or closed** (due to overconfidence or ignorance)? How do we ensure openness that enables **activation of better options?**
- How should we or other parts **feedback and feed-forward** to avoid untested assumptions & isolation?

WAYWARD

4. Which **right questions** are we not asking and which **right things** are we not doing (**errors of omission**), possibly due to **deficiency-centric** rather than **idealised approaches?**

- Which potentially **tendentious, specious, often mendacious hypothesis-testing** approaches should be replaced by **truth-seeking/sense-making** ones?
- Where are we observing or experiencing **counterintuitive results**, e.g. where continuous improvement retards the whole, and how could **creative discontinuity** help?
- **Under which conditions** could the **opposite also be true?** What **multiple realities** are we ignoring?
- Where should **circular, heuristic & safely random approaches, mindful** of **uncertainty & emergence,** replace linear overdesign (clouded by a need for linearity, exactness and anxiety-reduction)? Where could we experience the **remote/distal rebound effect?**

5. What will be the **ripple effect/2nd and 3rd effect** of our various options? How will these systems **evolve into non-linearity, tipping points & amplifying effects**

in the **As-It-Will-Be-state**? What are the systemic implications? Ask 'What will happen?' rather than 'How does this work?'

- Where should we play and explore **in future** to increase **sustainable 'probability' in the system evolution**?

- What will the **humans choose** to do in **socio-technical** challenges, given the Ten P's & what will result?

- How can the issue, system or response be energised and how can we prevent a loss of **energy**?

- Which distal signatures, shadows and footprints reveal which (distal and proximal) counterpoints in the system?

FORWARD

6. Which **rules**, including tacit, implicit and meta-rules, could facilitate the new design despite the potential for increasing the number of elements in the system?

    - Which **segmentation/segregation/taxonomy** (done to counter anxiety, promote certainty and reduce complexity) could be hurting us? Which **sub-optimisation** is making us sub-optimal?

    - Which insistence on factors that yield to the senses should be placed within the context of dematerialised elements?

    - Stand back. What do you see? Which **patterns**, e.g. ethos, sub-optimisation, should we stop/start/change/continue/create in order to avoid the current future-state and increase **probability** of the preferred future-state?

7. **Synthesis:** How could we ensure a **fractal** organisation? If we took a sample of our work, what would it suggest of the whole organisation?

    - How could/should these elements all be connected or disconnected sufficiently, and **what does/may indeed connect them all**?

    - Which action/structure/icon or artefact could act as a **strange and powerful attractor**?

    - Which **analogical thinking** or **depictions** could synthesise what analysis could not?

    - Can we recompose/synthesise/restructure/reconstitute/redesign this into a cohesive whole to serve or facilitate the purpose and **preferred state** and avoid the **will-be state/base case/current future**?

    - What requires **attenuation** in order for the system purpose to experience **amplification and valorisation**?

- **What would make viability and feasibility possible and/or failure impossible?** Which **contributively disruptive iterations** would make dysfunctional repetition impossible and serve probable and natural system fluctuations?

10.2 Futures Thinking: The Mostert Method

Similar to the case for systems thinking above, a method has emerged from global field work with senior executives which has allowed senior leaders to engage interrogatively with their personal, organisational and contextual futures.

Various methods exist for the production of scenarios. As always with futures thinking, the method is produced by the dominant philosophy and perspective. The method below is a hybrid model, inspired mainly by the emergent qualities of systems thinking concepts, such as multiple causality and reinforcing inflection points, together with cognitive processing that emphasises imagination, that is, the search, generation and consequences of imaginative (non-re-solutioning) creativity. It is further hybridised by its character: it is presented as strategic foresight, that is it operates optimally at the intersection of strategy and futures thinking. One clear distinction from strategy is that foresight proposes multiple futures (informed by Futures Science), but advances institutional normative futures, beyond contextual explorative futures, informed by strategy.

Emergence refers to the notion that scenarios cannot be observed at the start of the process. They make themselves apparent only as intersections of drivers are explored.

The method is also strategy-oriented, rather than pure futures-oriented. This means that it is characterised by an attempt at narrowing ranges of possibility, relative probability and strategic choice, while advancing opportunities for agency of the executive and organisation. The future is too often exonymous, that is, it is described by outsiders, foreigners and strangers to the intended future. When social systems develop a sense of deep agency, and sense the opportunity to design the future, the future becomes eponymous, that is, it refers to the designers after who imagined and created it.

The aim is NOT to produce the method of a futures technician. Conscious flair, philosophy and disposition are critical for method effectiveness. The futurist, compared to MBA counterparts, wishes not only to improve or change the world. At the imaginative end, futurists also wish to create and invent the world, save for those who see their role as merely cautionary. The futurist, then, aims to liberate the executive and organisation from pervasive hysteresis, i.e. the perceived perception of past- and path dependency. One perspective on futurists is that they are essentially evolutionary ecologists, not historic essentialists. They investigate how systems may develop over time. In this way, futures thinking and systems thinking are closely related, and indeed grew up in the literature to some degree.

The method, therefore, is systemic rather than analytical, strategic rather than purist, artistic rather than mechanistic, cognitive rather than emotive, inductive rather than deductive.

The foresight-informed strategist must suspend judgement for as long as possible and resist the intellectual temptation for predictions of premature conclusions. Immersion in the process with a light touch and fluid mind will aid futures discovery.

Process

1. **Create a multi-minded expert panel**. Strategic foresight is a 'team sport'. For a comprehensive perspective which increases the probability of sensing opportunity and risk from a holistic perspective, convene a group of diverse thinkers and role players (Multiple Partial Views) to contribute their insights. All thinkers can enlighten your own dark corners through respect for a kaleidoscope of other disciplines. It introduces the requisite variety essential to all successful systems. Ensure that at least one member is a beneficiary, one is a funder/investor, one is a user, one is an activist (i.e. agitator for change) and one is a leader in the system. Consider the use of the Four Clients Model, that is Buyer, Payer, User, Beneficiary.

2. **Problematisation**. Define the problem or issue of which future there is requisite curiosity. Consider defining the solution version of the problem as a possible problem statement, but caution against tendentious thinking in solution mode in which a singular or selection of solutions exist. Use a filter, such as the Tenology Paradigm Framework, geographical location or public/private sector. This allows focus and clarity on the real need.

3. **Horizon**: Select a horizon at any range beyond the immediate future. Possibility expands in direct correlation with the distance of the horizon, although select possibilities may also expire. Thinking beyond the typical or current cycle may also act as a means of horizon selection. This is because planning for the current cycle is typically complete and may cloud futures thinking. Horizons for futures thinking are both shortening and lengthening. Current indications are at least 12 years.

4. **Redeeming the past**: The industry saying goes, "Futurists have many faults, but living in the past in not one of them". The has its role in comprehending the future, but it is the one place where no-one will be going. The futurist therefore

resists the temptation to treat the past in its romanticised, nostalgic form as a kind of 'retropia'. The past of the challenge at hand, however severe, must be confronted with the five dimensions of the O-PATCH Framework for sense-making of the past. Consider:

i. Origins (of the issue and its current organisational, conceptual and social context. If it is a recent innovation, which may not have had its origins in the organisational or geographical location, consider the origins of containing systems.),

ii. Patterns (repeated behaviour including reactions to typical stimuli),

iii. Attitudes (mindsets, orientations, emotions & alliances),

iv. Traditions (icons, rituals, customs),

v. Cultures (national, regional, ethnic, organisational).

Overlaps may occur between OPATCH elements. Analytical classification of past elements into OPATCH clusters needs not occur. The purpose of this is two-fold: 1. to bring the past into the decision space and 2. to release the psychological ghost pressure of the past. This may include catalysing freedom from nostalgia and romanticisation.

1. **Paying attention to shape-shifting**: with a trans-disciplinary perspective, **what are the significant recent shifts from the past**, incl. flows of power (e.g. political, corporate, sectoral, etc.), finance (e.g. investment, divestment), talent (sectoral or geographical migration), attention (shifts in focus and pervasiveness), etc.? What is increasing, decreasing, dying or coming into being? As a guide, consider using dimensions from the **InCOME PRESCRIPTS-5i Framework.**

   Note: One insight which often emerges at this stage is that the past is not the present. There is often a commensurate realisation, therefore, that the present, equally, does not have to be the future. The futurist must caution against status quo bias, in which the dominance of the presence in the minds of decision-makers is perpetuated into a view of the future. The present is not the symmetrical axis of time, since the future will not resemble the past, nor the present. Even if nothing changes, things will be different.

   Beware: status quo bias.

2. **Driver identification (Missiles):** In the spirit of multiple causality, identify the key drivers (at least 6) which will impact on the futures of the selected issue. Which forces will shape the future? Caution against using the issue under investigation (or a variant thereof) as a driver as well. Include drivers that are:

i. Internal, that is inside the traditional (operating) boundaries of the issue or entity that wishes to flourish in the future, and within the boundaries of entity choices or behaviour

ii. External, that is the transactional and contextual environment of the issue or entity under investigation

3. **Relative Impact**: Prioritise the relative impact of the drivers, irrespective of whether the impact is positive or negative. This is essential as perturbation either way will influence the evolution to alternative futures.

i. Identify the top two internal drivers, and

ii. Top two external drivers.

Note: Avoid responding with personal preference or personal value system, e.g. ethics or aesthetics (unless these examples are very likely to have significant impact). The question interrogates the scale of impact, not the level of personal preference.

Note: As prioritisation unfolds, clarity on the definition of each driver should emerge.

4. **Spectrum**: A range of possible futures always exists. Create a continuum/ spectrum of possibility for the top two (2) internal & top two (2) external drivers. Consider continua on:

I. a numerical scale, such as 0 – 100

i. percentage

ii. participation level

iii. shift relative to present, either percentage-wise compared to present or qualitative e.g. extinction-dramatic decrease- decrease-same-increase-dramatic increase. (Note: status quo anchoring may lead to status quo bias).

iv. qualitative scale (None – Low – Medium – High – Extreme – Exclusive). Note: although it may be within the realm of possibility, it is unlikely within the realm of plausible future realities that the entire spectrum from zero to 100 or None to Exclusive will be relevant for any driver. Explore whether any drivers could be polarities of one another. If so, produce the continuum with these two drivers on opposite ends, and select the next driver into priority.

Note: the wider the range of realistic possibility (as opposed to dream-based possibility or 'magical thinking'), the greater the likely uncertainty.

Note: do not rate the impact of the driver – this was done in the previous step. Instead, rate the spectrum of what this driver could look like at the time of the horizon.

5. **Convergence**: Scenarios emerge at the intersection of drivers. Intersect the top two external drivers to commence explorative futures.

6. **Story**: Describe the narrative of each quadrant. Consider hitherto unincorporated drivers and/or critical agents, including agency. Identify key actors [e.g. government, customer, investors, suppliers, talent, regulator, bourses (incl. sovereign & corporate bonds), media, military, professional bodies, educational institutions, competitors, multilateral treaties, investment shifts, M&A, new entrants, demographics, economic cycles & shifts in debt, liquidity, growth and well-being]:

   - current actors and
   - emerging actors
   - internal actors
   - external actors

Describe the probable behaviour in each scenario. Consider the role of dis/incentives and possible mis/alignment, e.g. market vs political views as well as the probability of contagion in industry, regional, and international contexts. Consider trade-offs and short vs longer term risks and benefits, e.g. impact of market short-termism, short-term political gain vs underlying (China-type) long-term gaming. Consider old allies, emerging alliances and growing fissures between 'elephants' (big players) and social cohesion, within the context of green signals. Consider how the status and influence of actors might change, e.g. actors who used to be central will become peripheral, while erstwhile fringe players may become central.

7. **Choice:** Add an internal or purposive (organisational teleology) driver in each quadrant and describe the emerging eight (8) scenarios.

8. **Prioritise the probability** of the eight scenarios for a selected entity. Scenarios should always be imaginatively possible, that is, they should be outside the boundary of normal projection, without suffering disconnection from decision-makers.

9. **Prioritise the preferability** of the eight scenarios for a selected entity.

Note: In relation to steps 9 and 10 above: for multiple partial views, identify discrepancies between different entities, e.g. how might labour aspire to different futures from government or business?

WARNING: *When the scenario viewed as most probable aligns too perfectly with the most preferable, a paradigmatic blind spot has occurred.*

10. **Name and iconify** the top four (4) most probable scenarios.

11. Compare probable with preferable scenarios and identify design or other action elements for narrowing the deviation. Include comparison of the most probable and preferable with the current future and design deviation closure.

12. Identify agility elements, i.e. what is universally included/excluded in all of the top four (4) scenarios, and make explicit which actions (such as investments, contracts or other significant decisions) will be rendered inevitable.

13. Identify 2-3 possible **pathways** and probabilise, that is allocate probability to each of the pathways.

14. **Prioritise** probable and preferable **paths**.

15. Compare and close the gaps.

16. Identify flags (i.e. milestones, signals or indicators, including horizon dots/weak signals) and triggers (which make a certain path highly probable for some time to come) for each path. *Note:* path-jumping and path crossing may be possible.

17. Juxtapose probable scenarios and path development with strategic objectives and reconcile, i.e. make requisite adjustments in strategic decisions and planning.

18. Ideally (in the future) deploy transdisciplinary real-time sensor network for real-time monitoring of progression along possible scenario paths.

19. Adjust the preferable path based on sensor network input at industry-appropriate intervals.

At an overall level, and to inspire futures-consciousness, executives are encouraged to ask eight key questions for strategic foresight:

1. Which **obsolescent habits** have precipitated **current trend breaks**?

2. How do we discern the **noise-to-signal ratio**?

3. Does our generation have, and do we inspire, **futures projects**?

4. How do we overcome the risk of **akrasia** & develop humble courage?

5. What are we learning from our **skunkworks** through **Experimentation and Rapid Prototyping**?

6. Of what are we the **nimble and agile harbinger**, that is, the shining light of things to come?

7. Where are we the **vanguard or bellwether** across sectors, i.e. what are we signalling to future generations?

8. **What should we be designing as evidence of our leading anticipatory competence?**

Executives are typically over-scheduled. Their intellects are taxed to extreme levels. For those who take seriously their obligations for creating more preferable futures, their intellectual time must be distributed with consciousness. A rule of thumb has emerged for the intellectual time budgets of senior executives, known as 20-30-50. According to this heuristic, senior executives must dedicate 20% of their intellectual time on the past, in which they will contemplate the framework created as OPATCH, that is the consideration of Origins, Patterns, Attitudes, Traditions, Cultures and Habits. 30% of the intellectual time of the senior executive must be dedicated to the present, in which an ongoing trans-disciplinary scan is conducted and compared to tactical results. Finally, senior executives are encouraged to dedicate at least 50% of their intellectual time to a time yet to come. The main reason for this apparently disproportionate allocation to the future, is that senior executives hold such a significant proportion of the future in the power. The scope of impact of decisions by senior executives is potentially gargantuan, especially in large, globalised organisations. The future of talent, suppliers, investors, graduates, the society and the natural ecosystem are all impacted by the consequences of executive decision-making.

The current future is not the current or present; it is the evolved, intensified version and result of both explicit and tacit patterns of their momentum interaction and emergent properties. The wise executive is compelled to make decisions based on the likely evolution of possible futures, not simply an extrapolation of the patterns of the past, nor a sense of comfort with the status quo. Discerning executives must therefore consider not only the current future, but multiple futures with relative probability, including the decay, mutation or death of current trends and the birth, non-linear development and convergence of yet unborn and emerging realities.

10.3 **Futures Bias Barometer**

The future, in its multiple possible forms, presents tremendous opportunity. Indeed, one might argue that it is the only thing that ever does. It is often assumed that hard work and determination are sufficient for (future) success. As we discover the ever-increasing complexity of the present, largely expected to grow exponentially, the capacity of leaders to see the opportunities presented by the future - to sense where opportunity may be created, and to perceive the viability of options - is now becoming critical to the pursuit of organisational, societal and planetary success.

One way of interpreting this quantum capability is to argue that it is part of the cognitive suite of competencies essential for executive decision-making. The call for 'new thinking' by leaders and activists alike seems to resonate widely in principle, with limited consequential action. In broad terms, new thinking for executives may be facilitated by novelty in three areas:

i.   Thinking content – the bouquet of subject matter reflected upon
ii. Thinking level – thinking at higher strata, typically with broader consciousness and extended temporal frames
iii. Thinking methodology – variously structured forms of inquiry which produce novel insights through alternative modalities of interrogation.

This final approach to facilitating new thinking presents a cognitive suite which may include various thinking modalities. One such critical cognitive competence is strategic thinking, a full-enterprise contextual perspective elucidated by my work on the InCOME PRESCRIPTS 5i Framework. Another modality is systems thinking, facilitated by the lens of holons, that is interrelated, pregnant parts within multiple a-symmetrical containing systems. Others may include design thinking (governed by human centricity and creative reframing), analytical thinking (sub-optimisation through segmentation and linearisation), creative thinking (association from divergence of ideation) and effectual thinking (stochastic resource acquisition through risk-adjusted loss and gain perspectives). These competencies form cardinal axes of the intellectual domain of executives.

Yet another of these critical competencies is futures thinking. This modality is distinct from other forms of thinking mentioned above, in that it presents, at its very foundation, a concern not for past performance or present analysis, but for the nature and opportunities presented in a time yet to come. Perspectives on the study of the future range across a wide spectrum from those gazing into crystal balls, to statistical modellers who seek the perfect formula, to cynical defeatists who argue that future blindness is an inevitable characteristic of the linear perspective of time and that the future can only be unveiled as it occurs. The future, the nihilists argue, can only reveal itself. In practice, executives possess no such luxury. They therefore adopt an intersectional approach which merge strategic thinking and 'pure' futures through strategic foresight, in which they are compelled (through experience) to accept the non-deterministic nature of the future, while nevertheless explore options of higher likelihood through a probabilistic lens.

One of the ways in which competence in strategic foresight may be enhanced is through the identification and dissolution of cognitive bias. The notion of preference is inherent in the way in which reality is perceived, and executives are by no means immune. While it may be considered normal and natural, preference has been shaped by experience and exposure, often referred to as schema. Coming to terms with the executive schema, and recognising the bias it presents, is a powerful way in which such executives may overcome the limitations and blind spots in their decision-making. There are myriad other ways in which to study the future, but the attempt here is to create an index of the most prominent and frequent forms of bias to which executives may be vulnerable.

There is often a call for executives to combat bias by managing their emotions and to develop emotional intelligence. While consciousness is useful, this call *per se* is not sufficient. While equanimity is certainly a valuable pursuit, advisors in this field seldom help executives to identify their bias in order to overcome it. The opportunity now exists to offer clear support to senior executives (whose decisions will have far-reaching implications) with their cognitive development by making salient their specific areas of future blindness. Patently, there is enormous value for high-quality decision-making by raising awareness of bias in order to prevent such bias from skewing potential insights and commitments for institutional resource allocation.

While bias could be defined similar to the three forms of new thinking above (that is content, level and method), the focus here is mainly methodological, that is the manner in which an executive decision may be skewed.

An index of possible types of bias appears below. This index may serve as a means of initiating personal bias review and reducing future blindness in executive decision-making.

1. Psycho-dynamic bias, including:

    - **Transference** – conferring thoughts or feelings for one person onto another
    - **Projection** – conferring one's own motives and perceptions onto another
    - **Attribution** – assuming intent on the part of another without examining his or her true intentions

2. Status quo bias – assuming that the future will resemble the present

3. Confirmation bias – selecting from a range of data points only those which support one's assertion, and ignoring all other evidence

4. Personal optimism bias – the belief that risk will be lower for one's personal case than for the general population

5. Boundary bias – the belief that elements inside one's circle are safer than those outside

6. Similarity bias – the belief that elements which resemble oneself are somehow superior or inferior for that reason only

7. Paradigmatic bias, relating to foundational conceptions of the nature of the world. An expansive discourse appears in chapter 8 above. In terms of frequency, some of the most significant forms include:

    *   **Axiological bias** – preference for codes of ethics or aesthetics as foundation for decision-making

    *   **Ontological bias** – using narrow definitions of the nature and origin of entities and assuming others hold a similar view

    *   **Epistemological bias** – dubious grounds for the recognition of what one defines as knowledge, i.e. what we know

    *   **Doxastic bias** – a view that a certain belief has greater value than another, even in cases where neither belief proves greater benefit or less damage

8. Selection bias – manipulating the nature and quality of a sample by excluding relevant data and including a skewed sample to prove a thesis. This includes:

    i. **Hindsight bias** – selecting from one's own earlier predictions only those elements that prove to be true as the future emerges and claiming that one had therefore anticipated the future correctly from the start

9. Dominance bias – any singular dimension deemed as superior to all other data inputs

10. Bottom-line bias – the belief that multiple factors all amount to a singular, underlying fact

11. Novelty or recency bias – skewed validity based on the energy and level of experience of recency and newness. This includes:

    *   Personal novelty bias, i.e. the assertion that something is better or worse because it is new to the observer or agent

12. Structural bias – preference or deference for shape, form and process

13. Causal bias, including:

    *   Singular cause bias – assuming a relationship of causality between two dimensions in which one is the result of the other, without recognising other potential contributing factors

    *   Original cause bias – the perspective that the first contributing factor is the most significant

14. Proximity bias – the belief that what is closer has a different risk or opportunity profile simply because of its proximity

15. Control illusion – the belief that one's action has a determining impact on the outcome

16. Schematic bias – the belief that only experience in one's own schema or one's own total historic formation is relevant

17. Availability bias – noticing only what is accessible in the immediate environment

18. Positivism – the belief that only data received via the senses have validity. Also called vividness bias

19. Provenancial bias – the belief that data validity is determined by quality of its origin or history

20. Loss aversion – making decisions on the grounds of the avoidance of potential damage rather than potential gain. The opposite of upside bias

21. Upside bias – the opposite of loss aversion

22. Halo effect – ascribing a special beneficial quality to someone, which masks any potential faults

23. Fundamentalism bias – the belief that a singular belief should form the foundation for all other behaviour and belief

24. Recurrence bias – characterised by periodicity, the belief that current and future problems are simply a repeat of past problems, justifying re-use of previous solutions

25. Cure-based diagnosis – ascribing causality to a condition typically improved by an intervention when that intervention appeared to lead to amelioration, i.e. the cure explains the cause

26. Anchoring – the habit of 'sticking to our guns' despite new evidence to the contrary

27. Sunk-cost bias – evaluating future value (and the likelihood of continued investment) based on the scale of the investment that has already been made

28. Passion bias – evaluating the feasibility of a future venture based on the degree to which it aligns with a personal motivational driver

29. Personal interest bias – selecting a future course of action based on the benefit only to oneself or one's organisation, and ignoring longer term circular damage from those who will sustain one in future, such as customers

30. Randomness bias – the belief that all possible actions for the future are equal owing to the random nature of the future and the lack of certainty about the future.

Determining the possible nature of the future – whether as fecund or moribund – requires higher order cognitive processing. The ability to identify types of bias is one way in which executives may transition from mere awareness to deep insight into potential alternative cognitive processing for enhanced future consciousness. Recognising and overcoming cognitive bias is a powerful way of arriving at more accurate foresighting and embracing the richness of opportunity that the future holds.

10.4 **What will the humans do? The 10Ps Framework**

As if decision-making is not per se sufficiently complex, it is in addition, frequently made by humans. This may have seemed self-evident in a previous epoch, but in the current era characterised by a dramatic increase in artificial intelligence, robotics and the internet of things, the way humans make decisions deserves renewed attention, from both machines and humans. We may have imagined that, given the expanse of literature in the fields of Psychology, Sociology, Anthropology and business libraries filled with volumes on leading people, the species would have decoded its most likely decisions by now. But we continue to surprise ourselves with strange tales of our own choices, such as with Brexit, the rise of Trump, climate change fatigue and funny cat videos.

The field of Behavioural Economics, most notably through Kahneman and Tversky, has developed a sophisticated way of re-examining the assumptions of rationality of neoclassical economics. A number of observable paradoxes and inconsistencies in decision-making has led to a new appreciation of the human as influenced by many contextual factors in the process of making a decision.

Emotional Intelligence (made prominent largely by Goleman) and its pseudo-metric cousin, EQ, have had much attention as an important qualifier of decisions. But EQ alone is not sufficient for higher order, requisite quality cognition. Equanimity can only contribute to a favourable mental state in which decisions may be processed; it does not process the decision, much as a favourable terroir creates the opportunity for fine wine, but does not make the wine, or as windows allow for light into a building, but do not constitute a house in and of themselves.

In previous articles, I have explored cognitive competence through Leadership and the role of the intellectual, where the value of the intellect was expounded upon through eleven lenses on leadership. High quality cognition was further described in strategic terms with the InCOME Prescripts 5i Framework, which laid out an extensive ecology of concepts for strategic decision-making. Some examination of a systemic approach to thinking was discussed for its cognitively liberating qualities as well as an innovative methodology for learning in the era of complexity. In a recent article, an index of bias was established as a preventative mechanism for future blindness.

This article continues the pursuit of high-quality decision-making for the future (the only available temporal option) by investigating the somewhat mysterious nature of human decisions. In a style similar to the creation of previous frameworks and indices, it posits a bounded realm of indicators that aim to move the anticipation of human decisions from the expanse of the possible into the large-holed net of the probable, driven predominantly by what humans may regard as plausible and preferable, often ignoring levels of the probable. Naturally, all models and frameworks on the nature of the creature known as 'human' is, by definition, incomplete and ever-evolving, but it is suggested that the process by which humans choose is, by contrast to the largely deterministic processes of machines and most current-state artificial intelligence, typically probabilistic, and that such probability may be derived from those properties that make us truly human.

This is not a search for the essence of humanity, as systemic wisdom argues against the possible grasp of any fundamental essence or true nature of elements. It is, instead, a humble attempt at anticipating what others might decide based on a selection of indicators. Examining the presence of these indicators in the containing social system in which a sample of humans reside may suggest some of the most likely tendencies for decisions. In a self-deprecating manner that ridicules the attempt at decoding the human, this author has proposed the indicators all as starting with the letter 'P' for "probable. The 10P indicators, then, may include:

1. Pleasure and pleasantness, including the exhibition of laziness, and the aversion to pain

2. Profit, whether in the forms of:

    - Money
    - Time
    - Angst
    - Effort

3. Play, including gaming it (homo ludens)

4. Protection and Predictability, including habit & the need for certainty, balanced by probabalism

5. Poiesis, that is making, creating, organising and creative productivity. This includes autopoiesis, that is self-organisation and self-regeneration, as well as allopoiesis, that is organising and generating new elements outside its original dimensions.

6. Prominence and status

7. Power/autonomy and influence, including power over the self and others

8. Pairing and *apetitus societatis* (the need for the company of other humans)

9. Parity and equality

10. Philosophy and Purposefulness, including the search for meaning, pre-occupation, choice and the need for belief

Such a range of major indicators of probability by no means renders the human demystified, as the dominant species on the planet simply grows more mysterious with every unfolding insight. It is indeed true that some of the indicators above are, in certain contexts, even contradictory. Consider, for example, how the Brexit vote may be driven simultaneously by the needs for Protection, Power and Parity, as perceived by the voter.

To decode human decision-making into ten dimensions is patently over-simplistic. Simultaneously, to imagine that there is no difference between AI and HI (Human Intelligence), is also to generalise humans beyond a point of recognition. As an active decision-making agent, the reader of this article may evaluate a personal sense of which indicators above may feature prominently in the assessment of the validity of this article. But with the rise of robotics, artificial intelligence and the internet of things, in the view of at least one author, the human would be well advised to behave and make decisions in a way that only humans can. This may sustain the role of the human as a creative agent in a complex and dynamic evolution to alternative futures.

10.5 Bespectacled strategy – advanced spectatorship through 5 'spections'

Strategic decision-making requires the meaning integration of internal processes and external dynamics. Such decisions must transcend operational and even tactical levels of adjustment. For these purposes, sense-making of the competitive landscape of both the transactional (often called operating) as well as the contextual environments is a prerequisite.

One may refer to this process as strategic hermeneutics, which may be defined as the art and science of interpretive sense-making in order to enhance understanding of the strategic landscape and ecosystem for the purpose of taking reasonable decisions as the basis for competitive action.

In the era of 'wokeness', the quality of competitiveness in strategy has attracted the chagrin of the woke police, who argue for some utopian dispensation in which everyone collaborates. Naturally, a cohesive society characterised by mutual respect is highly desirable. But the reality on the field of play, for those with skin in the game, that is those willing to risk their own resources, can be brutal and remorseless. This reality is often overlooked by those activists who, with little direct risk to themselves, argue for enforced egalitarian distribution and cooperation. Such naïve idealists often ignore their own embedded normative reality. In addition, not everyone should win. Consider, for example, that carbon-intensive industries compete with those who seek a carbon neutral future, although a carbon negative pursuit is only sustainable path for the medium term). In this example, it is clear that the genuine philanthrope and eco-phile must support the development of strategic competitiveness by those who seek a more just planet and society. Researchers must seek to avoid their own bias, but I must confess here that this illustrates my own motivation for work as an advisor on strategic foresight: I am sick of the bad guys winning. Therefore, the good guys are in desperate need of higher levels of strategic competitiveness.

The above mentioned strategic hermeneutics may be understood through a range of lenses. The metaphor of the lens is significant in the world of strategic foresight, as it is perspective (literally *looking through*) which governs the largest swathes of decision-making of this kind.

To this end, executives may consider the virtuosity offered by the English language as a means of developing quantum-like appreciation of the landscape. This can be done in the forms of '*spection*' the language has developed.

Executives who seek such understanding may consider the 5 'spections":

1. **In-spection**, decisions on the target of investigation, ideally governed by a scientific, truth-seeking and structured form of inquiry, rather than by adversarial and ego-driven bias.
2. **Intro-spection**, a penetrating investigation of behavioural and mindset reality of the self and the institutional entity they represent.
3. **Retro-spection**, an investigation of the past, not for the purpose of protectionism, retentiveness, or naïve nostalgia, but for the pursuit of latent legacy, coupled with the discernment for identifying strategy-accelerating and retarding dimensions which may linger, ghost-like, in the minds of decision-makers. The OPATCH Framework articulated in the Futures method above, may offer further clarity.
4. **Exo-spection**, the deliberate casting of the gaze towards dynamics external to the traditional institutional boundary.

5. **Pro-spection**, the capacity for anticipation and the playful intellectual boldness for meandering around multiple possible futures, beyond the singular-future traditions of classical strategy.

One might argue that the future is all that remains. Simple descriptions and impressions will not offer the requisite level of decision-making for the 21st century executive. The quantum entanglement of the executive with the strategic opportunities presented by the future requires higher order intellectual inquiry.

10.6 Interrelations and research validity of the Mindset Index

The MI is an ipsative test that consists of 168 questions presented in item pairs, wherein participants are asked to select the statement that most applies to them. These 168 items are combined into 24 construct pairs.

Far beyond face validity, which has been confirmed by clients around the world, Mindset Index represents a robust scientific instrument upon which users may rely for a range of interpretive decision-making dimensions.

 Mindset Index subscribes to the highest standards of scientific robustness, consistent with best practice in the Social Sciences.

The nature of the assessment is ipsative, that is the sum of scale scores from each respondent adds to a constant value. It offers a wide range of forced-choice options, organised on forced choice between two assertions. Ipsative tests offer many benefits and provide a sophisticated methodology of assessment and scoring. It is thus assessed against the test-taker's own mental orientation based on personal responses within the controlled architecture of the assessment. Normative (inter-individual) assessment may occur at subsequent stages when one individual or group is compared with another. However, the experience of the test-taker in Mindset Index is purely ipsative. The test-taker is blind to any normative assessment which may arise after completion of the assessment.

Validity

If a test is reliable, it is providing a consistent measurement of a construct over time. However, this does not answer the question of: what construct(s) is the test assessing? Validity attempts to answer this question and provide insight into whether a test is measuring what it aims to measure.

There are several approaches to examining a test's validity. In this report, exploratory factor analyses (EFA's) were used to establish construct validity by reviewing the factor structure and uni-dimensionality of the constructs. The methodology for the EFA's was designed to accommodate the unique requirements of ipsative items, based on the research and syntax provided by Anna Brown, a specialist theorist in the domain of forced choice testing.

i. **Content Validity**

Mindset Index was created on empirical grounds, i.e. it was developed as the result of practical engagements with senior leaders in large organisations around the world. In order to comply with criteria for content validity, Mindset Index contains its claims to the constructs it identifies with the emerging construct of mindset. The assessment claims only to identify and measure responses on pre-defined dimensions of the mindset construct. In this way, content validity is assured through controlled assertions on a specified set of constructs.

ii. **Construct Validity**

Questions are offered blind to assessment users, and are linked to report only on specific dimensions of the Mindset Index, that is, every question is linked to a specific dimension. In this way, questions can only assess that which it claims to assess.

The degree of possibility for convergent construct validity is admittedly limited to the availability of mindset assessment instruments. Because of the original nature of Mindset Index, alternative assessment tools offer limited availability. For that reason, correlation between a significant number of questions per construct is used.

Inverse correlation emerged through the study of responses to assessments designed for constructs outside the domain of mindset, confirming the presence of high levels of divergent construct validity.

iii. **Internal Validity**

Related to requirements for construct validity above, Mindset Index asserts that responses to questions assess only specific dimensions within the assessment. The assessment is taken individually and conducted electronically. This avoids interference of external factors or variables that may influence assessment results. In this way, Mindset Index thus measures without interference or external bias. Non-interference is designed into the nature of the assessment and therefore offers high levels of confidence.

Because test-takers are blind to any connection between questions and constructs, they are not able to identify patterns. Questions are presented randomly, without any markers of the constructs which are assessed per question.

iv. **External Validity**

Assessments are conducted in natural settings, not in laboratories. Mindset Index makes no claims to generalisation of findings to populations which have not taken the test. It reports strictly on the responses of test-takers. The assessment does not suggest that findings can be transported to any outside populations. Inferences are made based only on the actual responses of test-takers. This also eliminates observer bias.

v. **Concurrent Validity**

Mindset Index does not claim to replace any existing assessment. It offers an innovative instrument for the assessment of the construct of mindset.

vi. **Predictive Validity**

Due to the ipsative nature of the assessment, predictive performance against criteria is applied only to decision-making. The governing principle is that mindset is a contributing factor to decision-making and subsequent behaviour. Claims of any causal relationship is controlled by equating the mindset dimension with that which will contribute to influencing decision-making and behaviour. Therefore, no logical leaps are made between assessment results and any other criterion.

It is possible to compare Mindset Index profiles with successful decision-making and behaviour, but such claims are not within the assessment itself.

vii. **Statistical Conclusion Validity**

Claims made by the reports produced are based on test-takers responses only. The assessment relates a minimum of seven (7) forced-choice questions per dimension assessed. In this manner, test-takers are invited to offer repeated responses to the same construct.

The assessment establishes discriminant validity by avoiding repetition of any single forced-choice question. In this way, indicators of one dimension are clearly and observably dissimilar from others in the assessment.

Reliability

Reliability can be defined as the extent to which changes in test outcomes are due to true score differences or to measurement error. There are two common methods used to measure reliability: internal consistency and test-retest reliability. Internal consistency is used to provide an introductory view of the reliability of the MI scales via Cronbach's alpha coefficient.

Item consistency measures the degree of interrelatedness of item responses per scale. If a test demonstrates internal consistency and if a scale's items are perfectly reliable (that is there is no random error in the scores), then participants are expected to respond in a consistent way across all the items that assess the same scale/construct.

Mindset Index subscribes equally to the highest levels of reliability. The ipsative design of the assessment is such that it is driven by the responses of test takers only. For that reason, assessment results offer high levels of consistency.

i. **Test-retest reliability**

    This dimension of reliability is controlled by the test methodology. Through forced-choice questions, test-takers are limited in their responses. Due to the social and dynamic nature of both the test subjects and the constructs assessed, it must be noted that mindset may indeed change over time, even under the same conditions. The large number of questions further reduces the risk of recall bias.

ii. **Interrater reliability**

    The role of the rater (administrator) is entirely removed through self-guided electronic assessment, for that reason, no interference is possible on the part of the administration process. The method of data collection is standardised, thus removing rater interference. Observer bias is thus rendered impossible.

iii. **Parallel Forms reliability**

    Due to the original nature of the assessment, there are no equivalent versions of testing. The use of a single test for mindset ensures the highest level of parallel forms reliability. All test items are based on the same theory of mindset, which further enhances this form of reliability.

iv. **Internal consistency**

    Internal consistency analyses were conducted to provide an introductory view of the reliability of the MI. However, it must be borne in mind that an ipsative format may distort traditional measures of reliability. Some researchers find that forced choice questionnaires over-estimate reliability, while others find they underestimate internal consistency when dealing with a large number of scales.[5]

In this study, internal consistency was conducted with the above in mind to provide a view of each scale, and to allow the comparison of scales to one another, as well as the comparison of items within scales.

All items used as indicators for the same construct are directly related to that construct. No question is repeated, either for the same or for another dimension. Each question is carefully formulated to relate only to the associated construct in the assessment.

Exploratory Factor Analyses (EFA's)

The factor structure of the MI was assessed per section, with seven analyses being run in total. Overall, the results showed strong factor structures for the MI constructs.

Inter-correlations within the MI

Correlations between the constructs of the MI were conducted to review how they function together and provide insight into convergent and discriminant validity. The results can be used to determine whether theoretically similar constructs demonstrate a relationship with one another, and whether theoretically dissimilar constructs show low or negative correlations with one another.

As with the internal consistency analyses above, these correlation results are statistically designed for continuous variables, and thus their veracity may be influenced in the face of forced-choice data. Despite this, correlations provide a straightforward way of determining the relationships between variables, especially for smaller sample sizes.

The assessment demonstrates significant variance in item responses. The latter will be further enhanced by collecting larger datasets, although questions that are heavily skewed towards one answer may be impacted by social desirability. It is best practice within ipsative tests to make all options equally "desirable" as far as possible. For this reason, questions are formulated in the most neutral language possible in relation to social desirability.

ENDNOTES

1   Goleman, D. 1996. Emotional intelligence. London: Bloomsbury.

2   Meadows, D.H., Meadows, D.L., Randers, J. & Behrens, W. 1972. *The Limits to Growth*. Washington, DC: Potomac Associates.

3   Bertolt Brecht Quotes. (n.d.). BrainyQuote.com. Retrieved September 30, 2024, from BrainyQuote.com Web site: https://www.brainyquote.com/quotes/bertolt_brecht_131165

4   Dweck, C. 2006. *Mindset: The new psychology of success*. New York: Random House Publishing Group

5   Brown, A., & Maydeu-Olivares, A. (2012). Fitting a Thurstonian IRT model to forced-choice data using Mplus. *Behavior Research Methods*, 44(4), 1135–1147. https://doi.org/10.3758/s13428-012-0217-x.

INDEX

W

X

www.ingramcontent.com/pod-product-compliance
Lightning Source LLC
Chambersburg PA
CBHW080539220326

41599CB00032B/6315